A new life…
A new look
at childbirth…
A new chance
to be a full and
joyful participant
in one of the

IMMACULATE
DECEPTION

"A book which should be read by any woman who is having or intends to have a baby, her husband, her obstetrician, her pediatrician; in fact, by anyone who has anything at all to do with the birthing process. It asks questions many mothers have wanted to ask for a long time."

—*Boston Globe*

"Destroys conventional wisdoms with every page. It makes a clear distinction between a medical system that is supportive when needed, and one that oppressively approaches each birth as if it were a medical problem."

—*Human Behavior*

"Demystifies and pleads for rehumanizing the entire birth and postpartum, for the sake of both mother and child, whose psychic and physical welfare Arms sees as inseparable."

—*New York Review of Books*

"With passionate commitment and a firm grasp of statistics on the high U.S. infant mortality rate, the author challenges American childbirth practices that rely on technology, drugs, and the mystique of the all-knowing doctor."

—American Library Association *Booklist*

A NEW LOOK AT WOMEN
AND CHILDBIRTH IN AMERICA

BETTER HOMES AND GARDENS ® BABY BOOK

CHILDBIRTH AT HOME by Marion Sousa

COMPLETE BOOK OF BREASTFEEDING
by Marvin Eiger, M.D. and Sally Olds

FEED ME! I'M YOURS! by Vicki Lansky

MOVING THROUGH PREGNANCY by Elisabeth Bing

NAME YOUR BABY by Laureina Rule

NINE MONTHS READING: A MEDICAL GUIDE
FOR PREGNANT WOMEN by Robert E. Hall, M.D.

PREGNANCY NOTEBOOK by Marcia Colman Morton

PREGNANCY: THE PSYCHOLOGICAL
EXPERIENCE by Arthur and Libby Colman

PREPARING FOR PARENTHOOD by Dr. Lee Salk

SIX PRACTICAL LESSONS FOR AN EASIER
CHILDBIRTH by Elisabeth Bing

IMMACULATE DECEPTION

A New Look at Women and Childbirth in America

SUZANNE ARMS

With a Foreword
by Frederick Leboyer

IMMACULATE DECEPTION

A Bantam Book / published by arrangement with
Houghton Mifflin Company

PRINTING HISTORY
Houghton Mifflin edition published May 1975
2nd printing ...... June 1975
Serialized in the
San Francisco Chronicle-Examiner April 1975
and in PREVENTION May 1975
Bantam edition / June 1977

Quotations on pages 66, 98–99, and 153–158 are abridged by per-
mission of William Morrow & Company, Inc., from Woman's
Doctor by Dr. William J. Sweeney III, copyright © 1973 by
William J. Sweeney III and Barbara Lang Stern.

Quotations by Margaret Mead on pages 11, 96–97, 126, and 178–
179 are reprinted by permission of Delacorte Press/Seymour
Lawrence from Pregnancy, Birth and the Newborn Baby, copy-
right © 1971 by the Boston Children's Medical Center.

ISBN 0-553-02257-1

Published simultaneously in the United States and Canada

PRINTED IN THE UNITED STATES OF AMERICA

0 9 8 7 6 5 4 3 2 1

FOR THE MIDWIVES

Foreword

It takes a lot of courage to write such a book as this. Especially in these days of secret, unexpressed fears, and in the face of medical claims of great achievement.

And courage always commands respect.

Yes, medical science, as it is now called, claims great achievements. And, no doubt, medical technology has made tremendous progress.

But, paradoxically, public health is getting worse and worse, no matter how many statistics try to deny it and prove the contrary.

To speak of only one area, prematurity and mentally retarded children have become prominent in our day. So much so that one may ask: what is the point of "medical science" after all?

Maybe medical research progresses best when public health deteriorates.

A healthy person never sees a doctor. He does not even know what it is to see a doctor. *Boasting* about all of our medical paraphernalia may only be a way of glossing over or ignoring the truth of the sad condition in which we find ourselves these days.

Possibly research and public health are helping each other. But not in the way we would like to think.

As for the sophisticated medical technology we have evolved, it certainly benefits many factories and the workers they employ.

Whether the health of the economy and health of the people progress together is another question. It may well be, as more and more people begin to suspect, that although they are closely connected, they "progress" in opposite directions.

Poor workers always complain about their poor tools.

Putting as much emphasis on instruments as is done in our day ought to be a cause of concern rather than a cause of satisfaction and pride.

It is a gross mistake to look upon medicine as merely a technique and upon medical people as technicians.

There are technical aspects in medicine, no doubt. But there is more to it.

A science?

No.

Medicine is an art.

Although it may be difficult to say what, actually, an art is, sensitive persons (and such are still to be found among doctors), any sensitive person, will know immediately whether it is a "piano technique" or a Rubenstein who is playing.

Possibly it may be more difficult to produce Rubensteins than well-trained technicians, engineers, or foremen.

Indeed, I am afraid there is no way of producing, manufacturing, or processing Rubensteins. They simply flower.

Yet we are intent on producing machines which are so easily duplicated. Whether they ultimately help health and happiness is quite another question.

Frederick Leboyer
Paris
March 1976

Acknowledgments

This book could not have been written without the constant support and help of Pat Holt, my editor at San Francisco Book Company, and Holly Brecherman, my close friend, to both of whom I am truly grateful.

Special thanks to Chong Lee for all the photographic printing, and to Werner Erhard.

And thank you all for your assistance: Gwen Rankin, Bernard Bradman, M.D., Jim Ames, Ann Barbee, William (Bill) S. Silverman, M.D., Elisabeth Bing, Jack Beeler, Eleanore and Loren Davis, Nick and Sheila Carey-Thomas, Barbara Charles, R.N., Delsia and Herschell Gabbard, Doris Haire, Judy Goldschmidt, R.N., Cornelius (Kees) Naaktgeboren, PhD., Rosemary Mann, R.N., Norma Lestiko, Ted Long, Lester Hazell, Arianne Hertzberger, Randi Jähne, Marshall Klaus, M.D., Y. Kloomp, M.D., Roy Lahr, Daphne Lera, G. J. Kloosterman, M.D., Marjorie Bayes, Margaret Hardy, N. Edward Boyce, M.D., Madeleine (Lynn) Shearer, Raven Lang, and Nancy Mills.

Birth is above all an intensely private experience. I could never have been so candid in revealing the full experience of childbirth were it not for the women who so generously granted me permission to share their privacy. To each of them I owe a special thank you.

The photographs in this book were all done in loving appreciation for every birth I witnessed, and with deep respect for all women giving birth.

Contents

	PREFACE	xiii
1	Your Sister Has A Baby Girl	1
2	Immaculate Deception	9
3	Your Sister Has A Baby Boy	29
4	Worse Than A Scandal	41
5	The New, Improved, Quick-and-Easy, All-American Hospital Birth	61
6	Birth's Machine Age	107
7	Reunion of Mother and Child	125
8	Pain and Childbirth: The Doctor's Fallacy	145
9	Fear: Woman's Curse	163
10	Natural Childbirth?	175
11	The Return of the Midwife	191
12	The Practicing Midwife: Nancy Mills	209
13	Home Birth	229
14	An Anonymous Midwife Speaks Out	249
15	Birth of a Movement: Raven Lang	259
16	The Midwife Goes to Trial: Norman Casserley	281
17	Granny, Come Home!	303
18	England and Denmark: Midwifery on the Brink	325
19	Holland: Caretaker of the Normal Birth	345
20	Your Sister Has Twins!	373
	BIBLIOGRAPHY	385
	INDEX	390

Preface

LIKE THOUSANDS OF WOMEN in America today, I had hoped and prepared for a "natural" birth. And like thousands of others, the birth of my child was a product not of my own efforts but of medical science and all the latest "improvements" that hospitals can provide. Strangers appeared and reappeared to examine me internally. While I focused my total attention on breathing, sedatives were administered without my knowledge or consent. A caudal was inserted incorrectly and later removed because it dripped blood. Labor stopped completely. Pitocin wafers were placed next to my gums in quantities that should have started labor in a horse but didn't restart mine. After twenty hours of labor and three shifts of hospital attendants, I was finally wheeled into delivery, completely exhausted, frightened, and ready for anything the doctor had to offer to get me out of the experience forever. A lengthy incision was made, then forceps were used. My placenta came out in pieces and my cervix tore, requiring internal stitching. I came out of delivery numb from the waist to the knees, dry and sour in the mouth, flat on my back, and strapped to a metal table four feet off the ground.

For three years I could not shake the feeling that I had failed; somehow it seemed as though I had lacked the faith, courage, and determination to give birth naturally without "help" from drugs or machines. In a sense this was true, for like many other women I had walked into the hospital unconsciously expecting that my baby would be delivered to me by the doctor and his staff. Thinking back now, it seems I was only a child at the birth of my own baby, dependent upon a greater authority to shield me from the intensity of the experience and my own fear of the unknown. But it wasn't until I finally got up the nerve to question my doctor about it that I realized an entire system of medical procedures and interferences had been established to treat normal birth as a risky, dangerous, painful, and *abnormal* process in which pregnant women have no choice other than to submit graciously.

Since then I have spent many hours listening to other women recall their own birth experiences. Most mothers are eager to share the smallest and most intimate details of their experience, and initially they describe their births as good and satisfying. But with rare exceptions, women who have given birth in hospitals become upset the longer they talk about it. They recount incident after incident of loneliness, fear, frustration, humiliation, loss, and a deep and guilt-ridden belief that they have missed the most profound experience of their lives. Not a few of them cry, and many admit they have never shared these feelings with anyone before.

Today scientists are beginning to report evidence that supports what many women have felt for generations: that where and under what conditions a woman gives birth greatly affects the course of her labor, the normalcy of her delivery, the health of her baby, and the lifelong relationship of mother and child. Women have always felt a need to find a "safe" place for birth, safe from harm and disturbance. The hospital, we have been assured, is that safe place. But we are beginning to wonder.

The pregnant woman in America today actually knows little more about her coming birth than the child in the street. She can probably recount many stories about other people's births, including at least one chilling tale of a friend who supposedly "wouldn't be alive today" if it had not been for a quick-thinking obstetrician who intervened to save the day. But information about what really goes on inside the hospital stops at the front door. In making this book I have tried to show what has happened to birth in American hospitals, what we have lost in our national push for progress, and what alternatives to current practice still exist. Childbirth is one of the most profound, personal experiences a woman can have. Yet our present system of uniform care does not allow her the freedom to choose her own way of birth and reclaim the experience as her own.

This is a book about childbirth in America. It is neither a medical textbook, nor a political treatise, nor a "whole birth catalog." Rather, it is a statement that grew out of my need to understand and explain my own birth experience. It is my contribution to anyone interested in the American way of birth.

SUZANNE ARMS

Mill Valley, California
November 1974

1
Your Sister
Has A Baby Girl

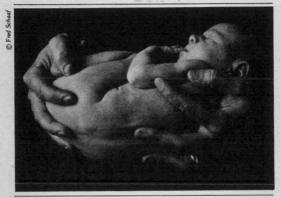

Your Sister
Has A Baby Girl

IMAGINE YOUR distant ancestor in her late teens, living in a small village on the edge of a forest. She is a member of a small group of hunters and food gatherers. The time is late summer, when days are warm but nights chilly. This young woman is ready to give birth. She lives in a small hut with several members of her blood family, younger brothers and her mother and her mother's brother. It is midafternoon and she has been cultivating the village crop of squash, working slowly in the sun, bare breasted, her full round belly making her somewhat awkward as she stoops over the ripe yellow plants. The older women in the village have been watching her these past few days, sensing that the infant is soon to arrive. The village is nearly empty of men, for they are on a long hunt which will take them several days away from the village. The women and children and old people remain behind, and there is much for them to do in preparation for the coming winter.

For several weeks the young woman has felt new sensations in her abdomen besides the swimming movement of her child. These new sensations are twinges in her groin and, while she notices them and marks them in her mind, she gives them little conscious thought. Several times today she stopped in the middle of work, brushed long hairs from her eyes, and mused over what her child will be like. This is her first child. She has watched her two youngest brothers being born and she recalls it well—the moist smells, the bloody fluid on the moss underneath her grunting, squatting mother.

There is a sharp, quick tugging inside her abdomen, down very low, and she is at once alert. It is followed by another some minutes later, and then a third. The sequence becomes a rhythmic pattern as the dying sun marks the end of the day's work outside. The young woman stops her digging and walks to her family's hut across the way. She calls to her brothers as she walks, and sends one of them to fetch water in the big earthenware jug that stands just inside their home. It is cool inside and the young woman wraps a thin skin around her shoulders and turns to the evening's work, the preparation of food for the family.

The sharp quick twinges grow longer and the young woman knows now that it is time. Often, while preparing the fire for dinner or cleaning and cutting the vegetables, she stops, places her hands on her jutting belly, and breathes deeply. She continues with the meal. Her mother and her old grandmother and her brothers gather just as the sun sets to share food on the hard dirt floor of the hut, around the fire pit. They swap stories of the day, and the mother and young woman talk about the hunt and their men who are away. Then the daughter speaks to her mother for the first time of the feelings inside her belly, which cause her to stop and breathe deeply each time they come. The two older women decide it is time to fetch the village birth attendant. One of the boys is sent off carrying a gift of bone implements. While he is gone the women busy themselves with cleaning up from the evening meal and preparing the children's beds—small skins covered with clean grasses and dried moss, which are taken from a large pile in the corner.

The mother is in a reminiscent mood and regales her daughter with stories of the past, births she has had, births she has seen. The young woman tends to the fire, piling on ever-larger pieces of wood to burn through the night. Her contractions are several minutes apart now and last long enough for the young woman to feel most comfortable squatting. With each contraction she drops into a hunched position, feet apart, buttocks on her heels, and lets her head fall back as she exhales heavily. In the intervals she is up and moving about the hut, bedding down the children and helping her grandmother, who is making new skins into clothing at the edge of the fire.

The midwife comes, a woman in middle life, her black hair beginning to gray. Carrying her birth tools in a small pouch over her arm, she greets the young woman with an appraising look and begins to tease her about the oddly pear-shaped body she now has. The mother and grandmother join in the good-natured fun, but stop in silence at every contraction in the young woman's belly. The midwife helps the young woman and her mother prepare a bed against one wall of the hut out of the draft. Chatting about the prospects for the hunt, they spread skins on the floor and top them with a mat of grasses. A newly softened skin is rolled and put to one side. This will be used to cover the baby.

The young woman's contractions are very close together now as she squats every several minutes to wait out the building wave inside her groin. Now the teasing and giggling and the telling of stories cease. As the old woman continues to work over the skins, the mother and midwife turn with quiet attention to the young woman on her mossy bed. Several times during the evening she has left the hut to urinate and then has continued about her work. Now, as the contractions become too strong for her to want to move around, she squats and does not get up, eyes closed during the minute that each lasts, breathing very slowly, very deeply. The two women breathe along with her, naturally following the pattern of her exhalations. The midwife puts an ear to the woman's belly and listens to the sounds within. Another contraction; the young woman throws off her skin wrap and begins to perspire, heated by the work of her body. Her mother brings her a warm beverage, tea made from raspberry leaves.

Soon there are no sounds except the approving grunts of the older women, the deep slow breathing of the younger, and the crackling of the fire. The young woman's belly rises into a tight mound and she stands up, uncomfortable, to pace around the hut. She asks for more tea. She squats again and her water breaks, soaking through the spongy moss and the grass mat. The midwife replaces these and takes the wet vegetation outside. She wipes the woman's forehead with her cool dry hand and smiles and grunts approvingly with each contraction. The young woman's eyes are large and round, avidly searching her attendant's face. She breathes a little easier now that the pressure within has been relieved a bit by the breaking of the water. The midwife places her hands on the woman's belly, pressing firmly and slowly, feeling for the outline of the child. In the expectation of the moment, the room is absolutely hushed. Even the old woman stops to watch.

At the next contraction the young woman does not

exhale her breath but catches it and begins to push as if to defecate. A bit of fluid and feces falls onto the moss during the long minute that she strains down. After that contraction the midwife cleans the bedding once more, replacing the soft dry moss and patting the woman's now relaxed face. The two older women gather closer and speak in low whispers, which the younger no longer hears. She is reclining against the wall, her eyes closed, hands loose at her side. The next contraction begins and she opens her eyes. She leans forward onto hands and knees and pushes once more, her face red and wet from the effort, pushing with full lungs. With each contraction the older women grunt in chorus, pushing too. The grunting ends in a long moan as the contraction ends and the young woman leans back again against the wall. The air is warm and smells of salty sweat. The young woman enters a faraway world between contractions. Her eyes closed softly, her face absolutely flaccid, her breathing now light, she dozes when her body is not working, in the stillness of the small hut.

Ten, maybe twelve more long contractions, and each one harder, pushing harder, harder still. The young woman squats again with her feet wide apart and half sits back on the mossy bed, exposing her vagina. The skin is bulging around the opening. Her anus is open, too, and with the next pushing contraction the women see a small dark circle of flesh and hair at the mouth of the vagina. It is the baby's head. Now the midwife squats before the young woman and places her hands on the bulging flesh between the legs, creating an open circle with her fingers. She presses with the next contraction, smoothing the taut skin, which parts to show even more of the baby's head. The young woman watches her midwife's face, in focus once more. She closes her eyes, only to push with the next hard contraction. There is barely time to catch her breath before the next, and with this one the head pops out from between the midwife's circling hands. At that moment the young woman has let out several breathy panting sounds and bent her head to see her child emerge below. The older woman does little now but gently massage the skin, which has not torn, and support the baby's head. With one hand and a crooked finger she pulls mucus from its open mouth.

A hot, sweet smell fills the hut, and during the next two

contractions the young woman barely works at all, letting her body slowly squeeze the infant out, one slippery shoulder at a time, after its head has rotated to the side. The tiny body jerks. It sputters, cries once, and begins to breathe on its own, its body still half immersed in its mother. Another moment of silent expectation and the midwife is holding the new baby in her hands. The young woman reaches between her legs to touch it too. She lays the baby on the clean moss, and the three women lean close to hear it breath and watch the thick twisted cord pulsate. Four hands are on the baby, gently wiping the fluid from its small body and from its eyes and mouth. It cries out several more times with a high squeaking voice, then lies with its head to the side, eyes open wide: a girl, a small wet purple-skinned baby girl. As she lies there quietly breathing, the young woman leans back to rest from her work, smiling. The cord soon stops its pulsations, and the midwife takes a length of strong sinew and a sharpened stone from her pouch. She ties and severs the cord and hands the baby to its mother to put to her breast, wet skin pressed against sweaty skin. She lays a clean freshly worked skin over the pair and helps the mother lie flat on the bed which the other woman has cleaned and changed once more.

There is a high mound of soggy moss and grass outside the hut now, a sign that the process is almost complete. As the new mother explores her infant with tentative fingers, the other two women wipe her body clean. The baby nuzzles its mother's breast and discovers the nipple. It first licks, then begins to suck, hard, and a visible contraction occurs in the woman's now smaller belly. Minutes later the young woman breathes one long push and the afterbirth slips out from between her open legs. The midwife wraps this large red mass of tissue in moss and sets it to one side to be buried in the field the next morning.

The young woman will bleed some more during the coming weeks, and dried moss will once again soak up this moisture and be replaced with new. The baby will be slung at her side in a pouch of skin filled with moss for it to wet on. The new mother will stop often in her work to feed her child from full breasts whenever it cries. Each time the infant sucks she will feel a quick twinge within her abdomen as her uterus contracts and her belly begins to flatten and grow firm once more.

Three days later when the men return from the hunt, successful, there is no sign of change in the village, except for the soft pouch the young mother wears as she stoops over her crops and tends the fire and prepares the evening meal.

2
Immaculate
Deception

Immaculate Deception

TODAY MANY WOMEN have the notion that childbirth was somehow easier for the primitive woman, and in some respects it was. Primitive woman was accustomed to long hours of physical labor, which not only prepared her for the strenuous effort of childbirth but also, during her pregnancy, moved her baby into an advantageous position for normal birth. She was sturdier, too, for having led a life unencumbered by restrictive layers of clothing or over-heated houses; and because primitive societies did not encourage crossbreeding with different cultures, her pelvic size was correctly proportioned to the size of her baby. Her diet was not affected by the processed or prepared foods that weaken the system of civilized woman, nor was she susceptible to the ravages of "civilized" disease: syphilis, tuberculosis, typhus, cholera, diabetes, and other ailments had yet to touch her body, and her pelvic bones had not yet been damaged by the effects of rickets and other diseases caused by long-term nutritional deficiency, which also appeared with civilized society.

None of this, however, made the physical effort of childbirth any "easier" for primitive woman; it simply allowed fewer complications to occur, and it made the normal process inherently less "dangerous" than we think of it today. Since most American women do *not* suffer from disease or pelvic disproportion, the physical disadvantages we do have—poor diet and lack of physical work—can usually be rectified by conscientious attention to nutrition and exercise during pregnancy. As doctors should regularly point out (but often fail to mention), lifestyles may change from nation to nation and century to century, but the physical process of childbirth is and always has been the same. It is today just as strenuous and just as awe-inspiring as it was in primitive times.

What, then, separates primitive woman from the American woman today? Basically it is attitude: primitive woman was accustomed to seeing all of life's processes—birth, death, reproduction—take place immediately around her. Childbirth was part of the natural order of things, a commonplace occurrence, and she dealt with it matter-of-factly, instinctively, and without fear. She did not expect what we call "pain in childbirth," as pain to her was associated with unnatural occurrences such as sickness or injury. So her midwife was reluctant to tamper with the process for fear of creating an unnatural situation which might cause pain, or bring death, to the birthing mother.

Woman's built-in knowledge of childbirth was something she could not articulate or explain; it was unquestioning, unselfconscious, and uncomplicated. But this was not the case for the men of her culture, who were separated from the process and could only observe what woman literally embodied. In an attempt to understand this unknown natural force, men developed notions and myths about childbirth that often bore little resemblance to the reality of woman's experience. As Margaret Mead notes in *Pregnancy, Birth and the Newborn Baby* (1972):

> In societies where men have never been allowed to witness childbirth, their fantasies about its terrible nature may be unbounded. Arapesh men give pantomimed accounts of childbirth in which women are conceived as writhing in screaming agony, whereas in actuality the women of the tribe give birth quietly and matter-of-factly, in difficult and uncomfortable circumstances, on the damp ground of a steep slope, in the dark, with no one to help except one other woman.... The contrast between men's nightmares and the actuality is striking.

Man's simultaneous wonder and fear of childbirth was a natural response to the simultaneous forces of creation and destruction he believed woman possessed. In many cultures her monthly appearance of menstrual blood was thought to be a "fatal poison" which could unleash destructive powers on her mate, family, or the entire community if she did not leave the area for a period of time or undergo a purifying ritual. So the blood of childbirth was thought to combine the threat of death with the presentation of new life, and woman became recognized as both benign goddess and mysterious power, both a life giver and life destroyer, to be feared and desired, loved and scorned.

Man's confusion—and his wonder—about woman increased with the beginning of civilization. As hunting societies gradually settled into agrarian communities, it was woman who first began to gather, then cultivate food from the earth. Men, who in many cultures did not understand the connection between sexual intercourse and childbirth, deduced that only woman could create life in her own body and in the body of the earth. Today we speak of "Mother Earth" or "Mother Nature," for it is not simply fertilization but the development of life itself that resides in all things female—earth, nature, and woman.

Many cultures believed the fetus was an independent being that was capable of speeding up or slowing down its own birth. Often the midwife would sing or chant in order to "coax" the baby out, but in some cultures (especially, it seems, where men had a hand in birth ritual) more aggressive tactics were used. In many groups the woman was placed in the middle of a gathering of friends and family who screamed at the top of their lungs, beat on drums, or danced violently around her to frighten the baby out of the womb. In some cultures she was thrown up and down to be shaken into labor, or hung from a tree while her midwife and other assistants pulled on a strap around her abdomen. Or she was laid upon the ground where her birth attendant actually walked or sat upon her belly. Among some tribes of American Indians, the laboring woman was placed in a clearing to face a man on horseback who

The doctor said to me, "Do you want to quit having these hard pains?" I said yes. I didn't want a spinal, but he sat me up. I was in a contraction

galloped toward her, turning aside at the last moment, in an attempt to scare the baby out of her body.

Sometimes it worked. Even hanging the mother upside down from a tree, which did happen in some cultures, might have moved the baby from what is called a breech position today to a more conducive position for normal childbirth. And each time it did seem to work, those who had conceived the idea became convinced of their power to influence and control nature. That the midwife would have waited for the natural process to move at its own pace, and that her quiet assistance would have been enough to see the process through to a safe conclusion were often forgotten in the face of such dramatic evidence that man's power to reason could shape and control nature.

These primitive methods for inducing labor were the first attempt by humankind to "improve" upon the natural process, although it was not until many centuries later that such interferences would reach a level of sophistication. They did, however, open the way for the early priest-physician to move in on normal childbirth at the first sign of complication. In primitive times this high official might have done nothing more than offer a prayerful chant to alleviate a woman's condition, but in more advanced societies his counterparts introduced new practices of sanitation and hygiene that were to counteract many of the problems of crowded, "civilized" conditions. As medical expertise about the complications in childbirth increased, physicians relegated the "lowly art" of normal birth care to the midwife, who by contrast had not changed her practice since the beginning of humankind.

---

and he yelled at me to put my elbows on my knee. And the next thing I knew they rushed me to delivery.
    —SANDY BELEW, *after her third birth*

Thus normal birth remained separate from sickness, disease, and disorder.

Many ancient physicians attempted to. pass on a basic knowledge of obstetrics to midwives, and it is recorded that even the "father of medicine," Hippocrates, and the world's first obstetrician, Soranus (a Greek who brought advanced medical techniques to Rome), set up training courses and distributed written works specifically for midwives. But these efforts were largely ignored, as the midwife was not interested in medicine, nor in treating complications of abnormal labor. Since she was required to call in the physician in all cases of abnormality, her major concern was only to improve the simple tools of her craft that she did use. It was the midwife, then, who devised the ancient birthing stool (a horseshoe shaped chair with an open seat through which the baby was delivered into the waiting hands of the midwife) as a means of assisting, not altering, the natural process.

Because midwifery was practiced solely by women, and because few other occupations were available for women, the midwife organized with other midwives and guarded her domain zealously. Her clannishness, her reluctance to educate herself under the guidance of physicians, and her grudging acceptance of rigid sanitary restrictions made the midwife appear ignorant and unclean to the men of her culture. At the same time, however, she was invaluable to women, not only as the sole attendant of normal birth but also as advisor in matters of sex, children, abortion, contraception, and herbal cures. Although among ancient societies the science of medicine reached its zenith with the Greeks, the midwife and birthing mother continued to share a secretive relationship that preserved the mystery and wonder of birth. And, since normal processes of the body were exalted to the level of godliness in the Greek and Roman civilizations, woman's instinctual knowledge of birth with all its creative/destructive power remained intact.

It was a peculiar combination of circumstances, then, beginning with the advent of Christianity, that initiated a two-thousand-year development of the modern deception most Americans believe today, that normal childbirth is *inherently* dangerous, risky, painful, and terrifying. For with the passage of one era to the next, and with the development of new laws, new morals, and a new religion, everything changed for woman in Western civilization. It came to be believed that Eve ate of the apple out of Original Sin, causing the banishment of humankind from Paradise. Man was consigned to a life of toil, but woman was to be punished forevermore by her own body. The Bible warned:

> I will greatly multiply thy sorrow and thy conception; in sorrow thou shalt bring forth children; and thy desire shall be to thy husband, and he shall rule over thee.
>
> —*Genesis* 3:16

> Therefore are my loins filled with pain; pangs have taken hold upon me, as the pangs of a woman that travaileth.
>
> —*Isaiah* 21:3–4

> They shall be in pain as a woman that travaileth.
>
> —*Isaiah* 13:8

> . . . and upon her head a crown of twelve stars: And she being with child cried, travailing in birth, and pained to be delivered.
>
> —*Revelation* 12:1–2

By placing a curse on woman's childbearing ability, early Christianity laid a solid foundation for Western civilization's attitude toward woman. From that time on, man saw his partner as less than equal, shamed, sinful, and debased, and the proof of her degraded position was childbirth. Now the creative/destructive nature of woman's built-in fertility was split into the opposing forces of good *or* evil. Life on earth was branded a "vale of tears," a wicked world of great pain and suffering. Woman, gateway to this world, could only be despised. Tertullian, one of the Church fathers, wrote to woman: "The sentence of God on this sex of yours lives in this age. You are the devil's gateway. You destroy God's image, man."

That woman was inherently evil could be seen by the monthly appearance of menstrual blood and by the pain, fear, and blood of birth. To be *good* she had to renounce her body entirely and follow the chaste and spiritual path of the Virgin Mary. Her choice was to lead a life of ascetic devotion as a nun, or a life of service to her husband, as St. Paul wrote in the First Epistle to Timothy:

> There is a difference between a wife and a virgin. The unmarried careth for the things of the Lord, that she may be holy both in body and in spirit: but she that is married careth for the things of the world, how she may please her husband.

As a wife she was humbled and as a mother she was shamed. Tertullian wrote of the "bitter, bitter pleasure of children," and asked, "Why should we be eager to bear children, whom, when we have them, we desire to send before us in glory. . . . desirous as we are ourselves to be taken out of this most wicked world and received into the Lord's presence."

The beginning of Christian civilization produced other changes that were to affect women in childbirth. Earlier forms of education, medicine, and science that had reached an advanced state with the Greeks and Romans were buried in monasteries and regarded as forms of heresy. Now man abandoned his power to reason and replaced it with religious faith. Disease was the work of the devil, and the power to cure it resided in God alone. Birthing mothers passively accepted their plight; midwives, forgetful of simple hygiene and practicing what was by then a truly degraded profession, carried unwashed birthing stools from house to house and spread innumerable infections among women. Both women and men lost much of their health in the crowded, unsanitary, putrifying cities of Europe. And birth became the harbinger of pain, sickness, and danger.

So woman lost her intuitive knowledge of childbirth and replaced it with fearful expectations of tortuous agony. How could a body so cursed, so inherently evil, possibly give birth in the matter-of-fact manner of primitive woman? How could a husband, seeing his wife screaming in pain, attempt to help her when they both believed it was God's will that she must suffer in childbirth? Only the midwife remained something of a constant figure throughout this violent upheaval in the patterns of childbirth, as her soothing presence and constant attention at least provided sympathetic support throughout woman's travail. But it was not long before the midwife's role changed drastically, too, especially when the barber-surgeon, acting in the name of God to save unborn souls, moved in on normal childbirth at the first sign of complication. Since it was heresy for even the barber-surgeon to expose his eyes to woman's private parts, he was required to tie a sheet around his neck and extend it to the woman's neck to obscure his view and leave his hands free to work. Since lengthy or difficult labor might indicate that the baby would die before delivery, he was required to insert a syringe filled with holy water up through the birth canal to baptize the fetus. If the infant was within reach, he (or, following his instructions, the midwife) pulled out whatever part could be grasped, usually a leg or an arm, and cut it off with a crude saw. Each part was doused with holy water until as many parts were pulled out and hacked off as possible, by which time, of course, both child and mother had probably died.

For the most part, however, normal birth remained with the midwives, primarily because the care of woman at birth was thought to be beneath men, and physicians who attended normal births were sharply criticized as potential heretics. Midwives retained their close and helpful relationship as advisors to women, and, in silent and secretive defiance of the Church's strictest doctrine, practiced abortion.

The confusion between witches and midwives was a simple one. Both were condemned by the Church for practicing "arts" involving sex and reproduction. Anyone who performed abortion or attempted by mysterious herbal concoctions to alleviate woman's pain in birth was easily branded "witch" and condemned to death at the stake.

Actually, the cult of witchcraft was an unholy or debased form of pagan fertility religions and celebration of the body. The witch was the black sister of the Virgin Mary, the other half of the female *persona*, the fertility goddess of primitive times now distorted to fit the neglected physical needs of Christianized woman. Through witchcraft woman attempted to regain the power of fertility she had lost. Witchcraft permitted woman to accept, even exalt, her body and her senses, and it was a powerful medicine for a repressed and shamed society.

In Christian man's attempt to exorcise the devil from his midst and pave his way to heaven, he found the witch, and by association, the midwife, an easy victim. The midwife's secret and intimate relationship to birthing woman often seemed to provide strength and courage for woman in her travail when she should have been suffering the pain of her God-given condition. And the supposed needs of witchcraft seemed to conform to the duties of the midwife, as William Blatty explains in the popular novel, *The Exorcist* (1971):

> "Well, I really don't know about ritual murder," said Karras. "I don't. But a midwife in Switzerland once confessed to the murder of thirty or forty babies for use at Black Mass. Oh, well, maybe she was tortured," he amended. "Who knows? But she certainly told a convincing story. She said she'd hide a long, thin needle up her sleeve, so that when she was delivering the baby, she'd slip out the needle and stick it through the crown of the baby's head, and then hide the needle again. No marks," he said, glancing at Kinderman. "The baby looked still born. You've heard of the prejudice European Catholics used to have against midwives? Well, that's how it started."

Fear of the midwife as witch existed outside continental Europe as well. In 1591 a Scottish midwife, Agnes Sampson, was burned as a witch on a hill in Edinburgh for merely attempting to relieve the pain of the woman she was attending in labor. The strange death of Ann Hutchin-

---

I actually had an American doctor come into my room and, when he found me nursing, said: "You know, Mrs. Rose, there's evidence in test animals that breast feeding causes breast cancer in

son, a colonial American midwife who was excommunicated and banished from her home in Massachusetts, also shows the confusion of midwife and witch. After resettling in Long Island, she was denounced for her outspoken views by the governor of the colony and was eventually scalped in an Indian raid. One version of this story, equally likely, states that she was tarred, feathered, and scalped by the men of her community who suspected her of witchcraft.

As the deception of the midwife as witch gradually took hold, so woman's place next to man, her wondrous position as life giver, and her responsibility in the process of childbirth gradually lost hold. Generation after generation and century after century, woman increasingly believed that childbirth was inherently dangerous, risky, painful, and terrifying, and that her body was to blame.

Had nothing else happened to childbirth, it is probable that modern woman would still bear the scars of this awesome and awful period of degradation, debasement, and shame. But, as if to implant the fear of childbirth in Western woman for all time, a final punishment for the curse upon her sex was yet to come.

The spread of pestilence and disease in European cities took such a heavy toll that the sick and starving could be seen dying in the street. As a means of saving souls (rather than treating the ill), the Church gathered the sick together in charity hospitals. Sufferers of spyhilis, gonorrhea, yellow fever, cholera, smallpox, malaria, tuberculosis, plague, leprosy, typhoid, diphtheria, dysentery, typhus, and other diseases were placed side by side in the same beds, as doctors, priests and nuns alike were unaware

---

the infant." So I looked at him and said: I had
a boy! And he said that makes no difference.
Can you imagine 24 hours after giving birth having
that kind of exchange with someone!
                                            —ANNETTE ROSE, *mother*

of the dangers of infection or the safeguards of sanitation. Howard W. Haggard, M.D., in *Devils, Drugs, and Doctors* (1929) quotes a description of a typical scene at one of these hospitals:

> In one bed of moderate width lay four, five, or six sick persons beside each other, the feet of one to the head of another; children beside grey-haired old men. . . . In the same bed lay individuals affected with infectious diseases beside others only slightly unwell; on the same couch, body against body, a woman groaned in the pangs of labor, a nursing infant writhed in convulsions, a typhus patient burned in the delirium of fever . . . and a victim of some disease of the skin tore with furious nails his infernally itching integument. . . . The whole building fairly swarmed with the most horrible vermin, and the air of a morning was so vile in the sick wards that the attendants did not venture to enter them without a sponge saturated with vinegar held before their faces. The bodies of the dead ordinarily lay twenty-four hours, and often longer, upon the deathbed before they were removed, and the sick were compelled to share the bed with the rigid corpse, which in this infernal atmosphere soon began to stink, and over which the green carrion-flies swarmed. . . .

So the first hospitals were not only centers of disease and disorder but disseminators of infection, and the effect on laboring woman was catastrophic. For many centuries woman lived with the fear that even if she survived the terrible agony of birth, a mysterious disease known as childbed fever might overtake her body a few days later, causing delirium, high fever, convulsions, and death. Occurrences of this sickness were at first comparatively infre-

I couldn't touch my baby for three days. He was in isolation in case there'd been an infection in utero. It was crazy! I had my baby and they took him away and I couldn't touch him. Then

quent, but as soon as women were herded into lying-in hospitals to give birth, the disease spread to epidemic proportions, sometimes killing entire wards of new mothers. Women were so terrified of the disease they would do almost anything to avoid entering a hospital for birth. But the poor often had no choice. "Physicians" of all kinds—students, barbers, butchers, and (in some areas) shepherds and hog gelders—worked on women in labor as part of their medical training. Often they would arrive with their hands still bloody from dissecting cadavers of diseased patients, and would then insert their hands far up into the birth canals of laboring women, infecting one and all with the germs that remained on their unwashed skin. So the "doctor" himself, sporting a bloodied apron as a badge of his "profession," became the carrier of the very disease he was supposed to cure, and childbed fever became the scourge of Europe for more than two centuries. If woman had anything left of the matter-of-fact sensibilities in birth of her primitive ancestor, she was now consumed with abject terror.

The cause and cure of childbed fever was not discovered until the nineteenth century by Ignaz Semmelweis, a Viennese physician who challenged the general belief that "the weather" had somehow contributed to the spread of the disease. Semmelweis observed that in his own hospital in Vienna, the mortality rate of birthing women in the First Division (a section run by doctors and medical students) was three times the mortality rate of the Second Division, which was run by midwives and nuns.. He noted no differences in the kinds of patients treated in either

---

we went home. As I was leaving, they put me in a wheelchair, plopped the baby in my lap, and pushed me out of the hospital.

— ANONYMOUS MOTHER, *age 28*

section, as birthing women were admitted on alternate days to each division. He did observe that women in the First Division were as frightened of the doctors as they were of childbirth, and he wrote later that these women "believed that the doctor's interference was always the precursor of death."

And they were right. It was not only the doctor's unwashed, germ-laden hands that carried the disease of childbed fever from cadaver to laboring woman, but also the aggressive practice of inserting his hands inside the birth canal, an interference in normal birth that midwives shunned. Under Semmelweis' authority all physicians were required to wash their hands in a solution of chloride of lime before examining a laboring woman, and after a year of this practice, not a single death from childbed fever occurred among mothers in the First Division.

But European doctors regarded Semmelweis' discovery with hostility, for they could not believe it was their own hands that had spread disease. Nor did they recognize that Semmelweis had uncovered an even more important fact: midwives, whose traditional role was to assist and not interfere with the birthing process, had historically attended pregnant woman with greater success than had physicians. So it was not until several years later that physicians did listen to Joseph Lister, whose techniques of antisepsis in surgery were new enough—and unthreatening enough—to bring about the gradual emergence of the modern hospital as we recognize today. More than half a century was to pass before childbed fever was brought under control, however, and even by 1929 over 40 per cent of maternal deaths in the United States were attributed to this disease.

Today the cure of childbed fever is considered a breakthrough discovery in the field of obstetrics, but like other breakthroughs in childbirth it only served to resolve a specific problem at a specific time. It did not affect the deep-rooted attitudes and problems relating to childbirth that had been developing since the advent of Christianity and which had linked birth with disease and disorder for at least eighteen centuries. So it was not long before birthing women began to believe that *only* a doctor and *only* a hospital could prevent such diseases from occurring.

Woman began to turn away from the midwife and bring her fears, her expectation of pain, and her distrust of her own body directly to the male physician. Gradually but willingly, then, she gave up her responsibility in the birth process to those who professed to know more about it than she did.

This step-by-step loss of responsibility was a side effect of every breakthrough in obstetrical science, including the invention of forceps in 1588. By this time, childbirth had become so wretched and tortuous for birthing women and labor had become so lengthy and difficult that even the patience and constant attention of the midwife was not enough to support woman through her travail. Although male midwives were at first considered heretics, then something of a joke among European societies (and something of a threat to midwives), men did enter the field of childbirth. Opportunists recognized a chance to "save" women from the curse of their bodies and possibly get rich in the process.

One such opportunist was Peter Chamberlen, who designed the first forceps but kept the secret of his invention within his family for three generations. A woman in difficult labor who could locate Chamberlen (and afford his fee) would never see the contraption he carried in a locked box to her bedside. Working under the sheet that extended from the woman's neck to his own, Chamberlen would open the hidden box and pull out the metal pieces, which would clank together in such a mysterious fashion that women held him in awe, believing he was employing a form of "iron hands." The Chamberlen brothers, sons, and nephews carried on the secret, attempted to organize and teach the midwives (who rebelled against them), flaunted their secret power of "saving" women from the throes of childbirth, and tried to sell the secret design of their instrument for what would be today a price of $7,500! Eventually the design of the invention leaked out, but by that time the wonder and mystery of forceps had become so legendary that doctors used the device on all but the speediest births, often harming rather than helping the process by their lack of training. Nevertheless, the awe and respect once granted the natural process was now given over to the doctor instead, and after centuries of neglect, birthing women were grateful for what seemed to be a new and advanced scientific technique. Although forceps delivery was excruciatingly painful (conducted then without anesthesia), it made the birth process faster and seemingly safer when performed by a physician.

Another "breakthrough" that transferred woman's authority in childbirth to the doctor had occurred a few years earlier, when Louis XIV replaced the birthing stool with a flat horizontal table. The king, it seemed, had a royal perversion. He liked to watch his various mistresses giving birth and took great sexual pleasure in hiding behind a nearby curtain. When the woman sat on the birthing stool he could see little, especially as she was dressed to her toes and her genitals were hidden from view by the extended sheet. So Louis called in a male physician who gently convinced the ladies of court that childbirth would be easier and simpler if they reclined on a high table. Of course the supine position was easier for *him*, as it gave him a closer view and better leverage in delivery, and it was better for Louis, who could see everything he wanted to see, but it was disastrous for woman, who no longer had the force of gravity working to her advantage and labored longer and harder in an effort to push the baby out. Gradually, however, all women of the court, and later their lesser counterparts throughout the country, copied the royal fashion of lying down at birth so that a male midwife or physician could deliver the baby and, in effect, take care of everything.

Then, in 1847, Sir James Young Simpson of Edinburgh discovered the anesthetic properties of chloroform, which was at first considered a boon to surgery but a sacrilege when used in childbirth. Ministers, priests, scientists, philosophers, and politicians all took to the podium to defend the Christian belief that woman's condition was to suffer in childbirth and that anything preventing this pain was against God. Simpson eventually won his fight by convincing Queen Victoria to take chloroform for the birth of her child in 1853. From that time on the drug was known as *Anesthesia á la Reine*, a fashionable, much sought-after relief from centuries of fear and pain. Victorian woman, even more ashamed of her body than her

European sister, received chloroform with immense gratitude, as she could now give birth, the ultimate elemental
experience, without having to deal with *any* of the ele-
ments—emotions, sensations, bodily secretions, smells,
blood. Floating into euphoria as she reclined on her back
on the doctor's table, woman released everything she had
—her power, her work, her responsibility, and her baby—
to the authority of the physcian, who willingly took it all.

There is no doubt that the history of childbirth can be
viewed as a gradual attempt by man to extricate the process
of birth from woman and call it his own. Indeed, some
anthropologists and radical feminists believe that man has
always been threatened by woman's exclusive power in
childbirth, and that by placing his strength and intelligence
against her docility and instinct he "won" an authoritarian
role in society.

It is true that from the very beginning it was man who
thought he could understand and control nature by using
his power to reason, and man who introduced the first
unnatural interferences to the birthing process. Dis-
interested in normal birth, man relegated the "lowly art"
of birth care to the midwife, then attempted to teach the
midwife about birth from his own distant observations. As
monk, priest, disciple, or physician, man translated his fear
of woman into punishment by placing a curse on her
body. It was man who moved in on normal birth to baptize
the baby and mother that he himself may have damaged;
man who spread disease, man who cured disease, man who
institutionalized birth in the hospital. Man placed woman
on her back in labor, then devised metal tools to pull her
baby out, then knocked her senseless with anesthesia. And
it was man who, throughout history, did it all in the name
of "saving" woman from her own body, from the curse of
her gender, from the "pain" of her travail, and from her
own ignorance. Today the male obstetrician with his kindly
paternalism comforts woman by advising her to leave
everything to him, to simply place herself in his hands
and abide by the procedures of his institution, the hospital.
And woman, that docile, ignorant, cursed, weak, and
dependent victim of deception, willingly agrees.

The purpose of viewing the history of childbirth in this
manner is not to assess blame but simply to recognize how

woman has been completely left out of the decisions and turning points in history that have affected her exclusive domain. And it confirms the fact that after centuries of ingrained fear, expectation of pain, and obeisance to male domination, she cannot easily come to childbirth a "changed woman" after a few classes in natural childbirth or a heavy dose of Women's Liberation. What she *can* do, long before labor ever begins, is to try to understand her real fears, where they come from and how they may affect her attitude about bearing children in even the most seemingly insignificant ways. She can inform herself as to the real nature of the childbirth process, what awaits her in the hospital, and whether her choices, rights, and decisions about birth are still within her own reach. If she has already had a child and feels vaguely dissatisfied, guilty, or sensitive about her role in the process, she can at least take some comfort in the knowledge that she is not alone and hasn't been for centuries. And finally, if she realizes that man may control the management of birth but is still separated from the process, she can reclaim her responsibility in birth and educate her mate and doctor as to its real experience.

Perhaps the most useful way of viewing the history of childbirth is to see it as a chronicle of interferences in the natural process. Civilization produced living conditions and attitudes that brought a wide variety of problems to birth, then doctors to deal with these problems, then still more doctors to deal with the problems the first doctors had caused. In the same way, new forms of hospitalization were needed to correct the errors earlier hospitals had brought to the process. Throughout it all, civilization changed, the role of doctor and midwife changed, and woman herself changed; but the process of normal birth remained as uncomplicated and inherently safe as it had been since the beginning of humankind.

Thus, if we believe today that childbirth is dangerous, risky, painful, and terrifying, it is only because as a race of people, we have made it so. If we turn to the doctor and the hospital as the only authorities on childbirth available, it is because we have turned away from the built-in authority of our own bodies. If we believe primitive woman had an easier time in childbirth, it is because we have made it complicated and difficult for ourselves. So many centuries have passed since woman approached birth with a matter-of-fact acceptance and without fear or expectation of pain that she has now become a total innocent—even more than man—of the very process which has always been exclusively and inherently her own.

3
Your Sister
Has A Baby Boy

Your Sister
Has A Baby Boy

IMAGINE HER on a blustery spring evening. She has just begun labor with the breaking of her waters all over the bedroom carpet. The doctor has been called. The young woman and her husband are making final preparations to leave for the hospital, twenty minutes away by car. Her bag stands packed by the door. She is in very early labor and has been moving around excitedly, fussing over each detail of leaving, suddenly reluctant to depart. It is late evening and cold outside the house. Her husband helps her get settled before starting the car. The contractions are only five minutes apart and mildly uncomfortable. With attention to her breathing and all her weeks of practice fresh in mind, the young woman moves on the hard seat with each tugging inside. Her eyes are closed. Between sensations she daydreams of her baby and looks back over her life with her husband, back to her childhood.

They drive up to a large hospital, mostly darkened for the night. Carrying her bag, the young man helps his wife out of the car. They hold hands as they walk, stopping for each new contraction, noticing that the pavement is wet from the day's storm, the air fresh. They enter the hospital, with which they feel familiar from an earlier daytime tour for expectant couples. It was active then, but now it is still and cool and feels emptied of all life. A receptionist asks if she can help and, seeing that the woman is in midcontraction, rings for the attendant to bring a wheelchair out front. Husband and wife are separated as she is pushed to the elevator and up to the third-floor delivery suite and he is directed to the business office, still open, where insurance forms must be completed and signed immediately. Twenty minutes later he searches upstairs for his wife, who is being readied for her labor.

The young woman is now standing in a small cubicle which contains a wash-stand and large metal hospital bed, its sides down. A nurse helps her undress and get into a short starched hospital gown slit at the back. Her personal things, clothes, and suitcase are stored underneath the bed to leave the floor clear. The woman, her insides knotting and unknotting every four minutes now, looks around her room. She is asked to climb onto the bed, then is given an enema by the nurse. Her pubic hair is shaved in several long strokes, and she is asked if she needs to use the bathroom just outside the labor room.

Another nurse with a pair of sterile gloves administers the first vaginal exam. The woman is told she is three centimeters dilated, which is recorded on her chart at the foot of the bed. She is still in early labor. One nurse leaves and returns immediately, pulling a six-foot metal stand and carrying a bottle of clear solution attached to a slender pink tube. She leaves once more and returns with a disposable sterile needle and prepares to hook up the intravenous apparatus on the back of the young woman's hand, after wiping it with alcohol solution and laying it flat on the bed, palm down. The hand is taped to an inflexible narrow board to keep the needle from falling out. An icy swelling feeling moves up her wrist, and the woman adjusts her body in the bed for comfort just as another contraction begins. The room silently empties, the door left slightly ajar.

A large clock is the only decoration on the wall opposite, and the woman watches the big hand closely, timing her contractions while concentrating on her breathing. In the next few minutes the husband enters and pulls up the single chair to the side of his wife's bed, which as he sits down is level with his chin. He takes her moist free hand and waits with her to begin the count for each contraction —timing, watching, speaking to her in a low voice. She gazes at an empty wall between contractions, only to return to the sensations deep within her huge stomach as new contractions begin, seemingly from nowhere.

Two nurses appear in the doorway, pushing a large squat machine with belts and straps and gauges. A small monitor like a television screen is attached, and the nurse asks the husband to move his chair aside as she rolls this new piece of furniture into place next to the free side of the bed. There is little space in which to move around now. A bed, an IV stand, one chair, a husband, two nurses, and a fetal heart monitor, all wedged into a seven-foot-by-eleven-foot windowless room. The nurse asks the young woman if she needs to use the bathroom again before they attach the monitor, which will stay with the woman throughout the rest of her labor, keeping a mechanical eye and ear on the contractions of her swollen uterus and the sounds of the fetus' heart inside.

The woman, after her next contraction, sits up in bed, slowly pulls her legs over the side, and edges clumsily toward the linoleum floor. Then, one hand behind her to pull the skimpy gown around her back, she shuffles her way toward the toilet on the other side of the room, the husband and nurse moving around each other as they follow two steps behind—half carrying, half pushing the tall metal IV stand with its swinging bottle of fluid, and half hauling, half pulling the huge bulk that is woman in labor. She eases her belly through the entrance to the toilet but cannot close the door because of the IV stand just outside. Her right hand, attached near the wrist to the slender tubing, sticks part way out the door. She has another contraction while there, and her breathing hastens. When she is ready to return to bed, the halting parade of husband, nurse, IV stand, and laboring woman resumes, a twelve-foot journey having been made into an elaborate production. Once in bed she turns on her side to a semi-curled position, her right arm jutting out flat to accommodate the IV as she breathes through the next few contractions, which are coming faster now, their waves lasting over a minute each. A second nurse returns and quickly injects a morphinelike substance into the woman's shoulder. Since she is in the middle of a strong contraction, the woman does not notice the shot. The nurse asks her to lie flat on her back for another vaginal exam. She is now four centimeters dilated, and this information is recorded on her chart. The other nurse directs the setting up of the fetal heart monitor and loops its wide belt around the woman's huge waist. The procedure takes the length of several contractions while the woman breathes with concentrated effort. Her husband, now perched diagonally across from the bed on the edge of the wash-basin, calls out the seconds to his wife over the backs of the nurses working to attach her to the monitor. It is done and their attention switches to the TV monitor with its rhythmic blips patterning the long strip of paper. The pattern is checked to see that it is normal before both nurses leave.

During the next few hours, as the woman's cervix thins and dilates to eight centimeters through stronger and longer and more frequent contractions, one or the other of the nurses returns every fifteen minutes to stand a moment before the screen. Each nurse has cautioned the husband against trying to massage his wife's now immobile belly, for that would disrupt the message to the screen and set up abnormal patterns on the paper. So he stands as near as he can get to the head of her bed and brings a cool washcloth once or twice to her forehead.

The woman is not focusing on anything but her body. She is unable to turn to a more comfortable position on the bed, which has had its metal side raised as a guard. Several times another nurse, part of a different team because the shifts have now changed, returns to perform a vaginal exam. Twice a resident on the floor comes in from the hall and chats briefly with the husband before asking him to leave so his wife can be checked. The woman is beginning to lose her sense of balance with her breathing and moves about restlessly, unable to find comfort in the grip of a strong contraction. The doctor is aware from her chart that she is planning to have a natural birth. He now senses she is in need of assistance and offers her medication. The woman is flustered. She turns to her husband and finds him gone. She asks the doctor what the medication will do, and he tells her that it will calm her. Not to worry, she can still have her natural birth. It will just help her relax. He leaves with her vague consent and returns immediately with a new nurse and an injection called a paracervical block. The young woman watches the long needle enter her vagina twice before a new contraction interrupts her attention. Minutes later the sensation inside her abdomen diminishes slightly. Her husband returns with a nod from the exiting doctor, who will come back several times more during the course of labor to render another double injection. Each time the husband will be asked to stand outside the door.

All the while the fetal heart monitor is an added presence in the quiet of the labor room, ticking and bleeping with each new squiggle on the paper. The woman's mouth is dry and cottony. She asks her husband for a drink of water. The nurse is questioned and refuses permission, saying that the glucose solution in the slender tube will give the woman all the fluids she needs. And besides, there's a new hospital rule against giving a woman in labor anything by mouth, lest she need to have a Caesarean and have to undergo general anesthesia. The nurse explains that "under general" the woman might vomit the fluid in her stomach, fluid that lies undigested after labor has begun. There is a danger that she may choke on the fluid, or aspirate, and bring it into her lungs with grave and possibly deadly results. So the woman lies in bed, going onto her eighth hour in this room, with nothing to do but wait. Nothing to think about but the contractions and her growing belief that it will never end.

A nurse changes the IV bottle and replaces it with a full one labeled glucose and Pitocin, a hormone to strengthen contractions. In the next two hours the young woman's body begins to change temperature. She feels hot, then cold, and wants another blanket, which her husband must go and find. The young man walks up and down the room to keep awake. The clock tells him it must be almost dawn outside. He listens to muffled moans from another room. His wife is quiet, still breathing carefully, too involved to talk.

She is entering the stage of transition and begins to tell her husband she's afraid of losing control of her breathing. She is restless between contractions and asks him to get the doctor. A nurse comes instead because the doctor is busy in one of the delivery rooms. She suggests that the woman have a spinal injection to give her relief from the severity of labor, which is indeed progressing rapidly now, as she notes from the woman's perspiring face and rapidly dilating cervix. Tired, frightened, and increasingly weary of her body, the woman strains to turn on the bed, impossible because of the straps and tubes attached to her. When the young man asks her what he can do to help, she blurts a curt reply. Nothing. Leave me alone. Forgetting the reality of the child still inside, she can now only focus on the tremendous sensation within, which she associates with pain. The husband's patient and firm directions to breathe, relax her shoulders, her hands, her feet, to pant and blow, now provide no structure solid enough to support his wife. She makes tight dry noises in her throat during the next contraction and announces she is drowning in pain.

At this point the door opens again and a nurse enters, saying that the anesthesiologist has arrived and will be in with an injection which will make everything "worlds better." The woman nods her head, sheds a few quiet tears. An examination given right in the middle of a contraction shows that she is now nine centimeters dilated. The nurse throws her gloves into the wastebasket and leaves. She returns with two assistants and a new male face, the anesthesiologist. He unstraps the woman from the heart monitor and asks her to sit up in the bed, a command difficult to follow since the woman has not sat or stood or moved for hours. She requires help from both nurses, and the machine is rolled back out of the room. Her head bent toward her flexed knees, the young woman exposes her naked back to the anesthesiologist's needle. A deep sigh, and she lies back down, face smooth from the sudden relief from all sensation except a tingling numbness below. A nurse asks the husband to follow her down the hall to change into delivery attire, a task forgotten in the earlier bustle of shifting nurses and staff.

New attendants, gowned and masked in preparation for delivery, enter the young woman's cubicle to listen to her uterus with a fetalscope, and to assist her in pushing out her baby. Because of the anesthesia, she no longer feels the urge to push. The nurse takes a new blood-pressure reading, gives another vaginal exam, and reports to the resident that the cervix is fully thinned and dilated and the baby's head engaged down into the pelvis. Pushing may begin at once.

She instructs the woman briefly how to breathe and push most effectively and tells her when to begin. A pillow is placed under her upper back and she is asked to keep her legs in the position used for vaginal exams, spread wide apart and flexed at the knees. Her hands are placed on her knees, her chin down on her chest. At the prompting of the nurse, she makes the first straining push and the husband returns to take a vacant spot next to his wife. He puts his arms around her shoulders for support and everyone grunts with her. Between contractions she lies back down and is propped up a minute later for a new one, which the nurse identifies by watching her belly grow small and hard.

The rumpled shift is pushed up around the young woman's breasts now as for the next half-hour she is cajoled and coaxed into doing the straining pushing for which she has no physical desire, due to the anesthetic in her spine. With every few contractions there is another blood-pressure reading, another listen in the fetalscope. The nurse asks the husband if he wants to hear his baby and shows him how to press the round end on the woman's belly. Meanwhile, the operating room has been quickly cleaned up from the last birth and another shift of doctors and nurses enters the room. They introduce themselves to the couple, then continue with the business of getting the woman to do as much pushing as she is capable of, while the delivery room is made ready for the new birth. The doctor scrubs up in an adjacent room.

Now the entire scene must change rooms. The woman is wheeled out on her labor bed, her husband following after a team of nurses who are simultaneously supporting, pushing, and pulling the mother, her IV stand, and her bed out of the cubicle, across the hall, and through the wide swinging doors of Delivery into a fluorescent-lighted, twenty-foot-by-twenty-foot room where she will be delivered. It is many degrees colder than the labor room, and the young woman shivers between contractions with the change in her body temperature and other effects of the anesthesia. She is helped onto the delivery table. Since the lower part of her body is numbed, dead weight, it takes three nurses to half push, half roll the woman's bulk up and over and into position. As soon as both bare legs have been strapped into padded metal stirrups, a scrub nurse begins to wash her down with yellow-staining antiseptic solution all around the opening of her vagina. A second nurse carefully drapes the woman's body from her breasts down with sterile green sheeting as the woman stares into the enormous round light tilted overhead. Her husband stands near her head now, unrecognizable in the elastic paper hat, mask over his nose and mouth, gowned to his ankles, and with paper shoes covering his own. He talks to his wife as they both wait for the doctor to enter and smooths the damp hair which has stuck to her neck.

Just as the draping and washing and strapping are completed, the woman is again urged to continue with her pushing on command. The doctor and the anesthesiologist enter. A forceps delivery has been planned, and the anesthesiologist is there to administer any additional anesthesia that may become necessary. The woman, now flat on her back, can barely see what is happening at the foot of her bed, where a nurse is helping the physician into his sterile outfit and gloves. He is a different doctor from the one who visited the young woman during labor, and he has arrived just in time for delivery. She has met him once before. He introduces himself to the expectant parents and immediately turns to the table of instruments at his side and then to the hole in the drapes between the womans' outstretched legs. He sits on a low metal stool and prepares to perform an episiotomy while giving instructions to the woman, telling her to push now—harder, harder, harder, as he assesses the need for medium or low forceps. Having sliced through layers of tissue at the bottom of her vagina to enlarge its opening, he turns to the delivery itself. This will be an uncomplicated birth, he decides, and takes the large metal spoons from the nurse at his side. He begins to deliver the baby.

There are now four attendants and one anesthesiologist in the delivery room handing instruments to the doctor, cleaning up around him, watching the blood pressure and respiration of the woman for any sign of stress to the mother or to the infant coming down the birth canal. Because of the lack of sensation during contractions, the woman pushes less effectively and must be warned ahead of each contraction and told how long to push. It takes the doctor long minutes to squeeze-pull the baby down the canal and through the large incision made in the perineum to accommodate the forceps. A shot of additional hormone is given through the IV in her hand to stimulate the contraction of the uterus and the expulsion of the placenta.

The baby's head is now appearing. The doctor hands the forceps to the nurse and guides the baby with gloved hands. He gives quick orders to the nurse at every step in order to have the necessary tools right there when he needs them. He makes an explanation to the intern on his right, showing obstetric details. The baby's head is out and the woman squints her eyes up at the light, catching a reflection of the action below. The nurse hands a small bulb syringe to the doctor, which he inserts into the baby's mouth and nostrils. A sound of gurgling. The baby chokes a bit and cries as he is brought out by one raised shoulder at a time. The slick knotty cord that was loosely wrapped around its body hangs in a limp loop, then goes taut as the doctor raises the child for one brief glimpse by mother and father. He quickly gives the cord one last squeeze before clamping it off twice with plastic clips, then takes the scissors and cuts it through. Then he places the baby on the edge of the table. A nurse holds and covers it as he makes a passing examination.

Another nurse picks up the blue-wet infant, covered with the fluid of the womb, wraps it hastily in sterile paper sheeting, and carries it across the room to a small heated table where it will be dried off, warmed under a heating unit, and examined more thoroughly. The pediatric resident is stationed there, called just in time to prepare for the arrival of a new infant. He checks the baby with the assistance of a nurse and a resident as the doctor sits low between the woman's legs to wait for the final contractions that will bring the expulsion of the placenta. The uterus has been stimulated sufficiently, and this third stage of labor takes just a few minutes before a large red mass slips out with a slight tug on the cord and the doctor picks it up. He examines it for any flaws or missing pieces before dropping it into the bucket at his feet, where the disposable sponges and pads to soak up blood and fluid have been dropped. He turns his back to the nurse and reaches behind him for the necessary implements to stitch the various layers of tissue in the perineum. This process takes longer than all the rest of his delivery, another twenty-five minutes. He chats with the intern.

The new mother watches the backs of the people working over her new baby, a boy, and in the light reflection above sees the doctor at her feet, head bent down. Her husband stares curiously at his son across the room, but chooses to stay with his wife. The doctor finishes the repair work and stands to congratulate the mother and father. Eyeing his work, he smiles, "Well, you won't be quite as good as new. But it'll work." He walks over to the pediatrician's table and chats for a moment, then exits to prepare for the next birth.

At the end of the clean-up process in the delivery room, the husband and wife are handed their newborn son, cleaned and footprinted and tagged, to hold for a few moments before it must be taken to the nursery at the other end of the obstetric wing to be watched for the next six to twenty four hours by a different team of doctors and nurses. Within an hour after the birth the husband and young mother are separated again. The husband goes down into the lobby to make phone calls before leaving for home; the mother is cleaned up, her draped sheeting changed for a clean hospital gown, and she is carried and rolled by all the nurses onto a guerney and pushed down the hall. In the recovery room she will be watched for another hour to see that her condition is stable with no extra bleeding. Then she is moved once more, to the elevator and up to her clean bed in the ward.

The mother is given a sedative in her room. The next morning she is awakened to an entirely new routine, that of the new mother. Her baby is brought to her after lunch and at regular intervals during the day in a plastic box on wheels, to be fed and held. Her son hardly wakes during the next days, and the young woman is assured he is just tired from his work of being born. The new mother has many empty hours in bed to fill with phone calls, reading, television, feeling her new pudgy soft body, and thinking back over the birth.

Four days after delivery the husband can take his family home. The baby is checked out by the hospital pediatrician, and the young woman changes her son into the gown and receiving blankets she packed so long ago. She looks at him anew without his white hospital wrappings. A nurse and attendant are called and arrive with a wheelchair. The procession—husband, nurse carrying the baby, wheelchair attendant, and mother—move to the elevator, down to the first floor, and along the corridor to the emergency exit where all babies leave the hospital. The automatic doors open onto a cool, bright day. The woman is helped out of the wheelchair and into her waiting car and is handed her son by the nurse. The husband places the suitcase on the seat in back and closes the door, gets in behind the wheel, and starts the engine.

4
Worse Than
A Scandal

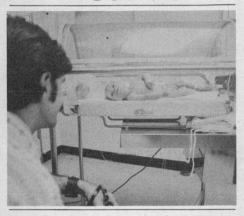

Worse Than
A Scandal

INFANT MORTALITY statistics have long been regarded as an accurate index of the safety of a nation's childbirth care. Although it is generally assumed that childbirth is safer in America than anywhere else in the world, a study of U.S. birth statistics reveals that the status of birth is quite different: for all our medical progress and technological advancement, the rate of infant mortality in the United States continues to be one of the worst among developed countries in the world today.

As Table I shows, in 1972 the rate of infant mortality was much higher in America than in fifteen other developed countries in the world, and the statistics will be similar when tabulated for subsequent years. This means that birth is safer in Denmark, East Germany, and Switzerland than in the United States. And it means that for every 1,000 babies born, approximately 5 more will die in the United States than in France, 6 more will die in the United States than in Japan, and 7 more will die in the United States than in Holland.

Significantly, American birth statistics are not rapidly

When I was five my mother told me babies grew in mothers' stomachs, but I was not to discuss this with anyone. All my friends talked about our births a lot—how horrible it was!
　　　　　　　—SANDY BROCKWAY, *mother of two*

TABLE I
INFANT MORTALITY RATES FOR
SELECTED COUNTRIES

Country	Rate per 1,000	
	1971	1972*
Sweden	11.1*	10.8
Netherlands	11.1	11.4
Finland	11.8*	11.3
Japan	12.4*	11.7
Norway	12.8*	11.3
Denmark	13.5*	
France	14.4*	13.3
Switzerland	14.4	13.0
New Zealand	16.6	
Australia	17.3	16.7
Canada	17.6	17.1
United Kingdom	17.9*	
East Germany	18.0	17.7
Ireland	18.0	17.7
Hong Kong	18.4	17.5
United States	19.2*	18.5

Information from the Statistical Office
of the United Nations provided by Doris Haire.
*Provisional.

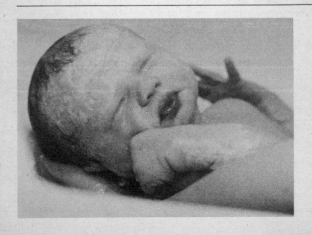

improving: in 1973, *Prevention* magazine concluded from World Health Organization statistics that "the rate of decline of infant mortality is faster in 20 other countries than it is in the United States." As early as 1968, Dr. George A. Silver, deputy assistant secretary for health and scientific affairs of the U.S. Department of Health, Education and Welfare, said that in comparison to other countries, "we estimate that between 45,000 and 50,000 babies die unnecessarily" in the United States "because of inadequate care." He added that "our infant mortality in this country is worse than a scandal; it is a crime."

Some doctors believe that statistics create a deception of their own, however, because many countries compile data by different measurements than ours. Of major concern to these doctors is the widespread lack of agreement over the ways in which nations report early fetal deaths for the computation of infant mortality. In the United States, all deaths of infants born alive after 20 weeks of gestation are reported, while in some European countries, only the deaths of infants born alive after 28 weeks are reported. Biostatistician Dr. Bernard Greenberg conducted a study of birth records over a four-year period (1954–59) in which he reworked the statistics in such a way as to prove that if European nations were to report deaths of infants born earlier than 28 weeks, their infant mortality statistics would increase by as much as 4.23 per cent. But Doris Haire, Copresident of the International Childbirth Education Association from 1970 to 1972, states that all of the countries listed in Table I "use the same U.N. standard for 'live birth' without regard for gestational age or birth weight, and most . . . collect their statistics on a uniform basis through their national health services." The United Nations defines "live birth" as "any product of conception, regardless of gestational age or weight, which shows signs of: heart beat, respiration, definite movement of voluntary muscles or pulsation of the umbilical cord." Since the first-year-of-life mortality rates in Table I were recorded for all infants born alive, this comparison shows that whether gestational age makes a difference or not, infant mortality statistics in the United States still rank among the worst among developed nations.

Haire also refers to two other studies which analyzed the slight variations that do exist between countries when such data is collected. Both showed that "when cross checked by other statistical data, the variations do not significantly alter the statistics."

It even turns out that discrepancies of gestational age criteria do *not* account for the recorded differences, as shown in a study published by the U.S. Public Health Service in 1967. In this report, data from the United States was limited to "fetal deaths of 28 weeks or more and a proportion of those with gestation not specified to facilitate comparisons." The list of countries, issued in 1964 (Table II) from the Statistical Office of the United Nations, confirms that whether statistics are computed by consistent data or not, the United States always maintains its low-ranking status among developed nations.

So much has been written in defense of infant mortality statistics in the United States, however, that it often sounds as though the American medical community is

What makes me angriest is women having things foisted off on them during labor. Instead of relying on words and feelings for support, the first line of defense for doctors becomes technological interference.
—MADELEINE SHEARER, *childbirth teacher*

TABLE II
INFANT MORTALITY RATES FOR
SELECTED COUNTRIES

(Rate per 1,000)

Country	1964
Sweden	14.2
Netherlands	14.8
Norway	16.4
Finland	17.0
Iceland	17.7
Denmark	18.7
Switzerland	19.0
New Zealand	19.1
Australia	19.1
England and Wales	19.9
Japan	20.4
Czechoslovakia (provisional)	21.2
Ukrainian SSR	22.0
France	23.3
China (Taiwan)	23.9
Scotland	24.0
Canada	24.7
United States of America	24.8

Information from the Statistical Office
of the United Nations, provided by
U.S. Public Health Service

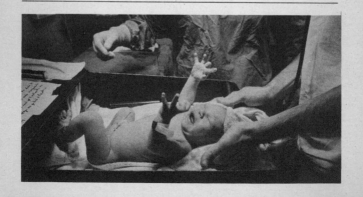

more intent upon sprucing up its statistics than dealing with the real problem at hand—the survival and health of newborn infants. Arguments can be made (and won) against doctors who insist that agencies that compile the data are at fault, or that it is the proportion of high-risk (especially low-birth-weight) infants that is at issue, or that the physiological makeup of women in different countries is more conducive to healthy birth than the makeup of women in the United States. Indeed, Dr. Greenberg even went so far as to emphasize that Scandinavian countries—whose statistics are historically the best in the world —produce fewer babies under the borderline weight of 2,500 grams than other countries. Thinking that genetic background might be a key to the defense of U.S. statistics, Greenberg conducted a study of counties in North Dakota and Minnesota that were heavily populated with Scandinavian "stock," as he called it. His results, as published by the Public Health Service in 1966, were as follows:

> The data showed that the counties with the highest percentage of Scandinavian stock had a lower proportion of births of 2,500 grams or less than did the counties with the lowest proportion of Scandinavian stock . . .

Well, there you have it. Americans have poor infant mortality rates not because of inaccurate data, not because of different guidelines, not because of gestational age, but because we're not all Swedes!

Actually, if Greenberg had been less concerned with

statistical manipulations and more interested in improving American health care for pregnant women and their babies, he would have noted that Scandinavian countries do differ from the United States in four very striking and very important ways; they depend upon licensed midwives to deliver normal births; they provide thorough pre- and postnatal care to every pregnant woman through national insurance; they consistently avoid elective medical interferences in normal births; and most important, Scandinavians as a culture practice unusually high standards of nutritional health and personal hygiene *wherever* they happen to live.

But apparently these differences are lost on many American doctors who continue to defend U.S. birth statistics. They would rather argue that the United States has a much more diversified population than the tiny and generally homogeneous populations of such countries as Holland or Sweden, and that a large proportion of our birthing population is particularly vulnerable to factors of poor health and low socioeconomic levels. The implication here is that women from poverty areas—because of lifelong nutritional deficiencies, crowded conditions, unsanitary environments, poor health care, and lack of education— are inherently less capable of delivering healthy children in normal births than healthier mothers in countries without such devastating poverty areas. Many doctors say that the poor by their very condition come to birth as high-risk patients; and it is the poor, they say, who are "ruining American birth statistics" today.

This is an extremely interesting argument because it

Too often in modern busy obstetric practice we doctors forget this meaningfulness of childbirth. In our anxiety and impatience, or in our sincere, but misguided efforts to relieve

raises the question of whether the medical community in the United States is truly responding to the needs of the *entire* birthing population. The issue is not whether low-income women are high-risk mothers (generally they are), the real issue is whether these same women, given adequate prenatal care, can reach a level of improved health that will allow them to give birth normally to healthy, well-nourished, full-term babies. (They can.) As has been proven time and time again, it is not the immutable defects of the poor that are "ruining American statistics," but our own lack of good prenatal care.

The most dramatic study to show the importance of prenatal care was conducted in 1968 by the Institute of Medicine of the National Academy of Sciences. Under the direction of David Kessner, professor of community medicine at Georgetown University, the study analyzed 142,017 births in New York City. Statistics were broken down to show the influence of prenatal care on mothers with social risks (poor education, large families, lack of financial support, unwed status); medical risks (high blood pressure, toxemia of pregnancy, diabetes); and low risks. Table III, compiled from data published in *Infant Death: An Analysis by Maternal Risk and Health Care*, by David M. Kessner, M.D. (1973), shows that infants of low-risk mothers who had received adequate prenatal care died at a rate of only 8.7 per thousand births: however, for low-risk mothers who received no prenatal care, deaths of newborn infants soared to 21.0. Similarly dramatic differences were noted with women who were considered to be both social and medical risks; the infant death rate for those who had received

*suffering (and childbirth is not without it),
we relieve a woman not only of this suffering
but also of her "birth right."*
—JOHN MILLER, M.D., Childbirth

TABLE III
RESULTS OF PRENATAL STUDY
OF 142,017 BIRTHS
IN NEW YORK CITY
(1968)

Prenatal Care	Social Risks	Medical Risks	Infant Deaths
Adequate	No	No	8.7 per 1,000
Adequate	Yes	No	12.3
Adequate	Yes	Yes	29.9
Poor	No	No	21.0
Poor	Yes	No	34.9
Poor	Yes	Yes	55.1

adequate prenatal care was 29.9; for those who had not, an incredible 55.1. According to an article in *Science News*, "if all the women in the New York City study had received adequate care, infant deaths could have been reduced by a third—from 21.9 per thousand to 14.7."

As described in *Maternal and Child Health Practices* (1973) by Dr. Helen M. Wallace, Dr. Edwin M. Gold, and Dr. Edward F. Lis, when prenatal and neonatal care was brought to low-income areas under Maternity and Infant Care Projects, dramatic reductions in infant mortality rates occurred. In Miami and Dade County, Florida, for example, the "rate for project infants. [most of them black] has been less than the rate for all Dade County white infants for three successive years." In Los Angeles, where the infant mortality rate of "public patients" at Los

Angeles County USC Medical Center was 37.7, the rate for infants born under the care of the Maternity and Infant Care program was 25.5. In Chicago, infants of mothers aged fifteen or younger died at an average of 36.8 per thousand, while infants of mothers of the same age whose care was provided by the Maternity and Infant Care Project died at a rate of only 19 per thousand.

Time and time again it has been proved that prenatal care is a key to lowering risks for poverty mothers and to paving the way for normal births and healthy children for all pregnant women. As early as 1962, the President's Panel on Mental Retardation reported that "large numbers of expectant mothers in the United States, particularly among the lower socioeconomic groups in both urban and rural areas, receive little or no prenatal care." According to Dr. Howard Jacobsen in the chapter entitled "Manpower in Maternity Care" of *Maternal and Child Health Practices*, the "devastating findings" of this panel came as a "profound shock." Yet five years later, the problem was just as bad, as President Lyndon B. Johnson stated in a speech to the U.S. Congress: "Even during these years of unparalleled prosperity, this year one million babies, one in every four, will be born to mothers who receive little or no obstetric care." According to Jacobsen, "this same dismal finding was reported in the Report of the Joint Commission on Mental Health of Children in 1970."

During the 1960s, large amounts of money for research studies and experimental projects were given out yearly to doctors and hospital staffs intent upon correcting the problem *at birth*, when all evidence pointed to the fact that in

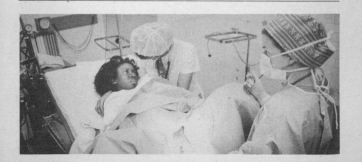

many cases the problem of infant mortality could be resolved months before labor even begins. Today the emphasis *is* on the fetal environment before birth, yet again this is more of a laboratory concern than a commitment to universal prenatal care. Doctors cannot dispute this, but many will argue that their obstetric skills are better utilized in the high-financed world of medical specialization and technology. This is the doctor's choice, of course, but it is too bad that more of them have not gone out into the community to tackle the problem of infant mortality where it really counts.

Why haven't they? For one thing, there is a massive shortage of obstetricians in America, and work in routine obstetrics (attending normal births) has become less and less popular in recent years. Today 15 per cent of all residency posts in obstetrics and gynecology stand vacant for lack of applicants. Rotation internship in every doctor's training now provides only six weeks of OB training, whereas it used to be twice that number. One-third of the residents on duty in our hospitals in the specialty of OB/GYN are graduates of foreign medical schools. And, while there has been a continuing decrease in the number of physicians entering general practice, there has been no increase in the number of obstetricians, so birth is left short on both ends.

Of the 335,000 doctors practicing in America today, only 19,000 are obstetricians, many of whom choose not to attend births at all as the hours are too demanding and the schedules too unreliable. Dr. Irvin E. Nichols, associate director of the American College of Obstetricians and

---

If there's one person who should not be around a laboring woman it's an obstetrician. I'm not talking about the ability to wield a mean forceps. I mean the ability to understand what a woman is going through in labor. They just don't. In four

Gynecologists, has said that men in his field give up doing births around the age of fifty, if not before. "The work is just too demanding," says Nichols, "so we relinquish it to the younger bulls." Naturally there are not too many "younger cows" to do this work, as only 3 per cent of all OB/GYNs today are women, and many of them also find routine obstetrics either too demanding or too boring. To quote one (male) obstetrician, "I cannot say there is anything challenging about delivering a normal baby to a normal mother. There is not. The challenge comes in the complication." And the complications come in specialization.

According to Dr. Louis Hellman, former special assistant to the president on population problems and coauthor of *Williams Obstetrics*, within ten years the shortage of physicians in America will be so acute that four out of every ten babies will be delivered without a physician of any kind in attendance. On the other hand, some doctors, such as Thomas Elmendorf, former president of the California Medical Association, question whether there truly *is* a shortage. "I think you get into academic discussions," he says. "There is a specialty maldistribution. You have distributional problems on lawyers, teachers, engineers, and garage mechanics. Everybody knows it's hard to get doctors sometimes. But if you look at OB/GYN as a specialty, you really have a pretty good ratio of obstetricians to the child-bearing female population."

It may not seem that way to the average woman in labor, whose doctor may arrive only five minutes before the delivery of her baby—or five minutes too late. Either way

years I've been taught by and worked under 20 obstetricians and observed 50 more. My feeling is they're good, condescending technicians. Most will admit it's a drag and a bore to deliver at normal births.

—RICH QUINT, M.D., *pediatrician*

he will probably miss the entire labor, unless he kindly pops his head into the labor room to offer medication. When at last the doctor arrives, his eye is always on the clock, since he must rush from one delivery to the next, from birth to gynecological surgery, from surgery to hospital rounds, and back to office hours.

Would the harried doctor's schedule be alleviated if there were *more* obstetricians to attend normal births? Probably not, says Alfred P. French, a psychiatrist at the University of California at Davis:

> Doctors, especially specialists, are "obsessionals"—they bend their whole lives trying to do two things at once: to get the intimacy they've got to have and at the same time protect themselves from it. The doctor's personality structure has got to be one of the most critical factors in the system. The health care delivery scene in America is molded around the physician's demanding personality structure.
>
> There's a raging debate about whether there is an artificially created physician shortage. I'm sure doctors are sincere when they deny it and say they do what they do only to protect patient care. For example, they keep numbers of graduates low to "protect" the quality of patient care, and they likewise oppose national health insurance, oppose expanding the role of paramedical personnel, and oppose any other issue which might change the system as it is now designed. It is always done in the name of protecting patient care, just as the politician feels safe if

he defends his actions on the basis of protecting the "national security."

It seems to me that we can explain much of the shape of the whole health care delivery system in America by seeing it as "designed" to let the physician be close to people while permitting him to control the distance and everything about the interaction. What wife or child, or patient, can criticize a man who rushes off to save a life? If he said he had to get some space from his family or his patients they'd hate him, think he was a schmuck. But if he's off to save suffering mankind or womankind, he's a hero and simultaneously safe from demands of too much closeness.

By being essential and in short supply, physicians have enormous bargaining power; and they use this to put the system together in the shape they want. All in the name of quality of patient care, of course. But I maintain the whole system is wrapped around the psychological needs of physicians like clay around a pretzel. So the massive resistance of physicians to any change in the system comes from a very deep place. There's nothing more terrifying to a personality of that type than to be unable to control the interpersonal distances in his life. There's nothing worse than free time, because somebody might get to him!

Of course observations like this tend to provoke angry response from doctors: "Somebody always throws up the remark that the profession is protecting itself. I consider that a lot of baloney," says Elmendorf. But is it? In the

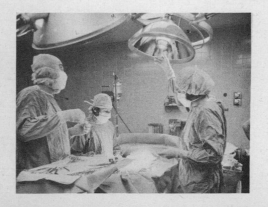

June 1, 1974, issue of the *American Journal of Obstetrics and Gynecology*, Dr. C. Ronald Christian was quoted as saying that obstetricians should spread "protective coloration" around the controversy of infant mortality statistics because of unreasonable attacks on the profession.

> We hear from every Fourth-of-July politician who speaks that we are No. 11, 12, or 14 in the world in infant deaths.... We are being attacked by the feminists in the self-help clinics who want to look at each other's cervix in the basement of a library and tell us, in fact, that they can do as good a job as we because, "look at our infant mortality rate." We are being infiltrated by the family physicians who now want to use any *entre* [sic] they can. In the tertiary-care hospital they say, "look, we do just as well as the trained obstetrician because look at your infant mortality rate."

According to most studies, 70 per cent of all birthing women in America, if given adequate prenatal care, could deliver their babies normally and without need of medical intervention at all. Another 20 per cent may have complications that require extra prenatal care and some special attention, but these mothers, too, could give birth normally, again, without need for medical interference. This means that at least 90 per cent of all birthing mothers can have normal, spontaneous births and have healthy babies. Many doctors, among them the noted author and natural childbirth advocate Dr. Robert Bradley, believe that 90 per cent is far too conservative an estimate for normal births, and that 93 to 96 percent is a much more realistic figure. Whatever the consensus, the rate of infant mortality in the United States, combined with a very real shortage of obstetricians and a nationwide lack of prenatal care, has made childbirth care in America a tragic embarrassment.

The real issue behind America's rate of infant mortality, then, is not the number of babies who die out of a thousand, but the ways in which the medical community is approaching this problem. While some doctors simply deny the statistics flat out, and others deal only with side issues, most will concede that if obstetricians as a professional elite are united in a single, ultimate goal, it is to "bring those mortality statistics down." As has been true with other problems facing the American people during the latter part of the century, our tendency as a culture is to turn to our advanced technological and scientific resources to find the answer. This in itself has created a movement toward increased use of medical interference in both high-risk and normal birth and has turned what was once a natural process into a complicated medical problem for which doctors, not mothers, are taking more and more responsibility.

Basic to the entire direction of American obstetrics today is an even more deep-rooted intention: to conquer all obstacles in the way of humanity's progress and development. It was combined technology and American know-how that discovered the polio vaccine; that built the Astrodome; that put men on the moon; that will cure cancer; and that someday may actually design a birth in which *all risk* of infant mortality has been removed. Whether a "guaranteed safe" birth is possible or not (it probably is not), this concept is basic to the entire authoritarian position of the obstetrical community in the United States today. The no-risk birth may seem a legitimate and obvious goal, but actually it has created a deception of its own for which women, not doctors, are already paying a high price.

Melinda Barbee:
One Mother's Birth

I NEVER DID BELIEVE a baby could come out of *my* vagina, and I guess I still don't. I assumed no choices about my birth; perhaps that's how I wanted it. I thought doctors must know what they're doing. After all, I'd never had a baby before.

The hospital bed in my little room was so high I climbed up on a stool. Stiff cold sheets, like porcelain. Actually, I loved being taken care of. I was only afraid they'd send me home, that they'd say it wasn't really labor. They did send Bob home. They told him it would be many hours, and to let me rest.

I lay there listening to women all around me scream. I wasn't in pain. As soon as the nurse left me alone I had my first real contraction and I screamed right through it. She came back and asked if I was in bad pain. I said, "I don't know because I don't know how bad it will get." She said, "We'll make you feel more comfortable" and gave me two pills.

I don't remember another thing until I woke being shaken by a nurse. She wanted to show me my baby being born. I could have cared less; I just wanted to sleep. I woke again, being wheeled out. They said I had a girl. She was fine, but a bit grey and in oxygen. I turned to Bob and said, "I did a good job, didn't I? I get a gold star."

When I took Linda home I began coming unglued. They gave me four pills every four hours, but I felt worse every day. I was hospitalized for three weeks and relatives had to take care of my baby. I remember wondering if she was really my baby.

Before my birth I thought only dummies do it without drugs. All I wanted was the end product, a baby. I feel very different now.

5
The New, Improved, Quick-and-Easy, All-American Hospital Birth

The New, Improved, Quick-and-Easy, All-American Hospital Birth

WHEN A PREGNANT WOMAN checks into the American hospital to give birth to her child, she may not be fully aware that she is automatically stepping into an institution that is solely designed for the treatment of disease and disorder. In the midst of deeply discomforting contractions, she may concentrate only on moving clumsily from lobby to labor bed, leaving her husband behind to take care of the paperwork while attendants bustle around her. From then on she is told not to worry, that she will be taken care of, that her doctor will be there shortly, that her husband can stay if he "follows the rules," and that birth will proceed as quickly and easily as possible if she will simply put herself "in our hands." It is easier for everyone if she does, because in the hospital the procedures, equipment, staff, and rules are all geared to treat her not as a birthing mother but as a full-fledged "patient."

The American medical community has invested a great deal of time and money in hard selling American women on the value of hospital births, and for generations we have bought it whole. We believe today that the thousand-some-odd dollars expended for a normal birth in the

---

When I think of pregnancy I think of being heavy, swollen, lying on a hospital table on my back, my feet in stirrups, my stomach full of stretch marks. People busying themselves around me. I think I'd rather adopt.
—SUSAN KROMELOW, *age* 28

hospital will buy the advertised package—a safer, easier, faster, more scientific, and more streamlined way to give birth than any other in the world. But since the hospital staff is working on its own system of reason and is isolated from the everyday events of the community outside, the pregnant woman soon finds herself in the midst of an autonomous world of authoritarian rule to which *all* patients must conform if they are to regain their health and return to society.

Once the birthing mother accepts this basic premise behind the hospital birth, everything that happens to her will fit into the particular logic of hospital procedure. Thus, what is legitimately criticized as obstetrical interference on the outside is promoted as "medical improvement" on the inside; what is historically considered the sole responsibility of birthing women on the outside is reduced to a matter of "doctor's orders" or "hospital policy" on the inside; and what are correctly defined as deceptions on the outside are generally acknowledged as "scientific fact" on the inside. If a woman is not completely secure in her role as birthing mother before she goes into the hospital, it is not long before she has docilely bowed her head to let "the experts" do her work for her. Whether she is to blame for this, or whether the medical community is to blame, or whether the American way of life is to blame are questions to be considered in another context; the point is that she is victimized by it and so is her unborn child, all the same.

It is time, then, for American women to examine the theory and practice of hospital birth long before labor ever

---

There isn't any one kind of birth. A uniformity is imposed on birth in this country.
—LESTER HAZELL, *anthropologist*

begins. We must question the medical community's insistence that laboring women give birth in the doctors' institution, the American hospital; and we must ask why healthy women are treated as sick "patients" simply because they have *entered* the hospital.

For generations, birthing women have been deceived and awed by the power of obstetrical science and its intention to correct nature according to human design. Certainly in cases of true disease and disorder the medical profession has provided miraculous care for millions; and for that small number of birthing women with complications that necessitate medical interference, the obstetrician's scientic skill is to be legitimately respected and preserved. Since birth itself is not a disease or disorder but a normal process of the healthy female body, obstetricians tell their patients they must step in anyway to *prevent* disease and disorder from damaging the natural process.

The unspoken assumption of obstetrics today is that what is predictable is certainly more safe than what is not. And the process of birth is not predictable enough. In an effort to control birth and make it predictable, obstetrical science has devised a routine series of interferences designed to "improve" upon the normal birth. The obstetrician thus patterns his practice in normal birth after his practice in abnormal birth, forcing the majority of women to undergo procedures that are unnecessary for all but a few women. This makes the birth process a more predictable operation for the doctor, even though any interference can create a greater risk to the woman than the original problem it was intended to solve. Whether inter-

---

It is very difficult for a person trained in technical know-how to do technically nothing during a normal birth.
—MICHAEL WHITT, M.D.

ferences are worth this risk is a question the physician feels only he is qualified to judge. In her reliance upon her doctor's authority, the pregnant woman is seldom aware that such decisions are being made over her prone body, and she is rarely informed of the potential dangers to herself and her baby of *each and every* alteration of the natural process.

What she does hear, if she is lucky, is that such "improvements" are made for her safety or her child's, and that preventive interferences are the doctor's way of turning sloppy old nature into a clean, safe science. He may explain that obstetrical science is simply a "just-in-case" game of playing the odds in her favor: just in case you hemorrhage, we'll give you simulated hormones before you expel the placenta; just in case your perineum tears, we'll make a nice clean incision before delivery; just in case labor tires you out, we'll give you an early sedative; just in case you need a general anesthesia (for an emergency Caesarean), we'll keep a vein open and stop you from eating and drinking throughout labor, even if it takes twenty-four hours; and just in case you totally lose control, we'll anesthetize you out of all sensation. Hearing this, the pregnant woman cannot help but believe that normal birth is loaded with unpredictable horrors that only her doctor can prevent.

The result is that birthing mothers have given up their responsibility in birth to obstetricians, who have then turned the *normal* into the abnormal for the sake of preventive procedures, which in turn have caused greater (but more predictable) risk, and this in turn has required even more preventive technology to interfere further with what

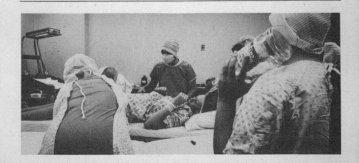

was once a natural and uncomplicated process requiring no interference at all.

All of this happens under the immaculate protection of the sterile hospital environment, the home of medical technology; and all of it has led American women to believe in one of the greatest deceptions of all, that hospital births are the quickest, safest, and easiest way yet available to bring babies into the world. Quite the contrary; today many American women find normal birth in the American hospital agonizingly slow, impersonal, inefficient, and risky to *both* mothers and child.

It would be fine if the interferences created by obstetrical medicine were as appropriate for the healthy mother as they are at times helpful to the high-risk mother. But the truth is that in at least 90 per cent of all births, these interferences are unnecessary, costly, and in many cases damaging to either mother or child, or both. A brief examination of the most prevalent "improvements" in American hospitals today will show why.

Induced Labor

If labor is late, or slow in getting under way, doctors often make the decision to induce. The practice of induced labor is so common today as to be routine in many American hospitals, since doctors are concerned that overdue labor may be harmful to the infant. And, too, for many years induction of labor has been performed for the convenience of mother, doctor, or hospital staff. In 1971 the prominent obstetrician Elizabeth B. Connell suggested an

---

My mother had three children and she's never seen a new born baby.

—Joan Weiser, age 32

advantage to inducing for nonmedical reasons. "Pick the time when the pregnancy is ripe," she said, "and have babies by appointment." Induction is still offered in many hospitals today as a reasonable solution to the drudgery of waiting for lazy nature to take its unpredictable course. "What a change from women screaming with pain," Dr. Connell continues, "to a well-controlled delivery with a calm and happy patient." This may be fine for the mother —it certainly is more efficient for the doctor—but for the infant, results of induced labor are often less than satisfactory, if not dangerous.

The simplest method of induction is to enter a woman's vagina with a blunt, sterile instrument and puncture the membranes that form her bag of waters. This in itself may stimulate labor if the body is willing, but once the membranes are open the doctor has created a direct pathway for infection to mother and baby. Many doctors believe that if delivery does not occur within twenty-four hours after labor has been induced, a Caesarean operation must be performed.

A second means of induction is to administer an artificial facsimile of oxytocin, a hormone that is naturally secreted by the pituitary gland for the purpose of managing contractions from the beginning of labor to the end of birth. When artificially inducing and stimulating labor, doctors most often use Pitocin (the pharmaceutical trademark for simulated oxytocin) or other oxytocics to speed up and increase the "efficiency" of the uterus. They must take special care to administer Pitocin in proper doses so as not to rupture the uterus and cause probable death to the

---

Talk about American birth . . . Let's talk about birth as shown on film and on television. There's always great pain and great danger. And usually, if you remember, the mother or child dies.
                                        —KENDRA DAY, *mother*

infant and extreme danger to the mother's life. My own obstetrician, commenting on the efficacy of Pitocin and other hormonal stimulants, has praised this interference highly: "You can take a flabby uterus which feels like a wad of cotton and make it contract down to one-third its normal size until it feels like a weight-lifter's bicep." He does admit, however, that the long-range effect of the drug is to slow the process down after the second stage of labor: "When labor has been artificially stimulated, the uterus gets lazy. It needs more help." Thus, more Pitocin is needed to correct a condition that the earlier dosage had created. And few women are informed that the use of Pitocin in labor increases the likelihood of postpartum hemorrhage.

Nevertheless, the basic assumption underlying the practice of induced labor is that man is merely giving nature a prod, and most doctors see nothing wrong with it. As the obstetrician William Sweeney states in his popular book, *Woman's Doctor* (1973), not only are inductions perfectly acceptable for nonmedical reasons, but also, "as long as inductions are managed properly they're just like normal labor."

One of the world's foremost authorities on the effects of induced labor is Dr. Roberto Caldeyro-Barcia, president of the International Federation of Gynecologists and Obstetricians, and director of the Latin American Center for Perinatology and Human Development of the World Health Organization. At the March 1974 conference of the American Foundation for Maternal and Child Health, Dr. Caldeyro-Barcia stated that it is "unnecesary" to use

---

Having the mirror up there was like watching TV.
It didn't seem like it was happening to me.
—ANONYMOUS MOTHER

oxytocics in as much as 90 per cent of the births where they are administered today, and he also questioned the practice of rupturing membranes to speed up labor. Explaining that under normal conditions nature has arranged for membranes to rupture late in labor, he said that he considers early ruptures, even when they happen spontaneously, to constitute an actual complication. He reasons that when the membranes break early, the mother's protective bag of waters can no longer cushion the infant's head from powerful contractions which press the walls of the birth canal against the fetal skull. Tracings from fetal heart monitors have shown that as each contraction increases this pressure, a marked decrease in blood to the baby (and oxygen to its brain) occurs in cases of early ruptures, but is rarely seen in cases where the mother's membranes are still intact.

Also, Dr. Caldeyro-Barcia explained, X rays from recent studies show that disalignment of the parietal bones of the baby's skull occur with twice the frequency in infants of induced labor than with infants who were not induced. In the former case, the baby's head is very elongated on the top and back, and a bump appears where the parietal bones are shoved out of alignment. Further, when membranes rupture early, the blood vessels under the infant's skin rupture with greater frequency than blood vessels of infants who have not been induced.

Deformation of the baby's head has occurred so frequently in America that women often think it is a natural result of the baby's long and traumatic journey down the

birth canal. There is a certain amount of natural "molding" that does occur in normal birth, but this is not the same as a definite disalignment of the baby's skull from early rupture of the membranes. Not only is this condition visually disturbing to the mother, but it can also cause damage to the infant brain, possible hemorrhage inside the brain, and signs of asphyxia and cerebral trauma.

To explain the difference between the impact of spontaneous rupture and induced rupture, Dr. Caldeyro-Barcia referred to a collaborative study he had recently supervised in twelve medical centers throughout Latin America. In this study, he said, it was found that spontaneous rupture occurred most frequently at the end of the first stage of labor or at the beginning of the second, pushing stage. The usual time for artificial rupture in hospitals, however, is at four to five centimeters dilation—early in the first stage—and this has significantly correlated with disalignment of the infant's parietal bones. When oxytocic drugs are used, the study showed, uterine contractions are so intensified that Dr. Caldeyro-Barcia concluded, *"When you give oxytocics, you produce too strong contractions."* These, too, can cause disalignment of the parietal bones. Finally, the study showed that the umbilical cord, normally protected when there is fluid surrounding it and when contractions are not too violent, becomes compressed when labor is artificially induced, and this can cause infant asphyxia. Dr. Caldeyro-Barcia concluded that in oxytocic-induced labors, even with all proper precautions—such as the lowest effective dosage given and proper monitoring of mothers—almost 75 per cent of the mother's uterine contractions were shown through fetal heart monitor tracings to result in a reduction of oxygen to the baby's brain.

A more subtle reaction to induced labor is an increase in lactic acid in the mother's blood, which in turn alters the acidity of the infant's blood. There is always the risk that too great or too sudden a change in the acid-base balance of human blood will contribute to acute illness, even death; in birth, such alteration of infant acidity has been linked to brain damage and requires further interference to prevent this outcome.

For mothers, especially those who attempt a natural childbirth, induced labor so often alters the process from its natural rhythm that the mother cannot maintain control. She believes her body has gone haywire, and becomes frantic in her effort to keep up with contractions that continuously catch her off guard.

It should be emphasized that in all cases of induced labor—and this is true with other interferences as well—it is not the mother, nor the doctor, but *the baby* whose delicate system must correct the effects of such interference as soon as extrauterine life begins. Since many of the infant's vital organs are only beginning to function at the time of birth, and since recovery from the natural trauma of birth requires immense energy all by itself, such artificial effects as change in acid balance, respiratory sluggishness, or disalignment of parietal bones—no matter how slight—are extraordinary burdens to place on such a physiologically innocent beginner of independent life.

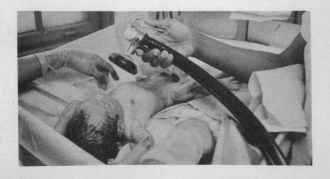

When it is remembered that induced labor is often unnecessary in the first place, the fact that American obstetricians and hospitals have made this practice a routine
procedure seems particularly brutal in light of the consequences to the baby.

Fetal Heart Monitor

In recent years, many hospitals have introduced a new
technological device into the birth process called the fetal
heart monitor, an imposing, boxlike machine with long,
heavy, armlike straps that encircle the woman's abdomen
and record internal vibrations. Although the fetal heart
monitor was originally designed for the detection of
complications in abnormal births, scientific studies have convinced many doctors that monitoring is an effective preventive procedure for normal births as well. Few women
in normal labor question the use of such a formidable piece
of technology when it is wheeled into the labor room. If
they think to ask at all, their doctors may tell them that
"just in case" something goes wrong during the long
hours of labor, the monitor will alert the hospital staff at
the earliest possible moment. What prospective mother
would reject such new and impressive scientific protection
for her baby?

The process is simple. The strap around the upper part
of the woman's abdomen contains a tocodynamometer, or
pressure gauge, which records uterine contractions; the
strap around the lower part of the abdomen holds an ultra-

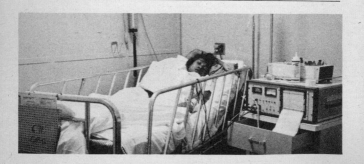

sonic transducer, which records the fetal heart rate. Both straps are connected to a breadbox-sized machine on the top of a cabinet that translates this information onto a long roll of paper or strip chart by a series of wiggly lines that resemble seismographic or brain wave patterns. The mother must be checked frequently—or at least the machine is checked—by an attendant or doctor with specialized knowledge in the interpretation of monitor tracings.

The machine is so sensitive, however, that it may pick up vibrations from the mother's intestines and circulatory system, and these sounds may interfere with tracings of the fetal heartbeat. So many doctors prefer to use *internal* monitoring. Here a plastic catheter is passed up through the partly opened cervix and the attached spiral electrode is literally screwed into the scalp of the fetus. (The membranes must be ruptured.) For many mothers, external monitoring may be used in early labor and then switched to internal monitoring later in labor to produce more accurate results. With external monitoring, the fetal heartbeat is best transmitted if the laboring mother lies flat on her back and remains virtually immobile for many hours. Often she is also hooked up to a constant intravenous flow of artificial hormones and a continuous blood-pressure monitor as well. Attendants who touch her may disturb the tracings on the chart, and the father must sit where he can find space, since the universally tiny labor cubicles are cramped even further by a machine that dominates the labor scene.

The internal monitoring system, when properly managed by highly skilled doctors, nurses, and technicians, has

Society in general makes every possible effort to prevent the pregnant woman from accepting pregnancy and labor as a natural physiologic function. The same amount of attention to eating would make most of us have nervous indigestion.
—F. W. DERSHIMER, M.D. Pregnancy, Birth and the Newborn Baby

been proven to be extremely useful in abnormal cases where fetal distress is suspected, even though risks of infection to mother and child are high. According to physical therapist Madeleine H. Shearer, former editor of *Childbirth Education* and present editor of *Birth and the Family Journal*, studies of *external* monitoring in normal birth have shown that the monitors give "an entirely false suggestion of precision," and that monitored data is "inadequate" as much as 43 to 66 per cent of the time. Furthermore, the data itself, even when accurate, may be misleading and open to varied interpretation: "Mixed signs frequently crop up together on a tracing and they change rapidly. In all the literature on fetal monitoring, one cannot find exact data on when to terminate labor in the presence of abnormal FHR [fetal heart rate] patterns." Indeed, one doctor has said that although he is aware of the built-in inaccuracies of the fetal monitor data, even a 25 per cent chance of accuracy is reason enough for him to terminate labor and perform an immediate Caesarean.

The fact that the popularity of fetal heart monitors continues to increase in larger hospitals throughout the country may be due to a study in the mid-1960s of over 28,000 women which found that lower infant mortality statistics resulted for high-risk women who had been monitored than for low-risk women who had not. This study—along with another that showed a lower Caesarean rate for monitored mothers—has been quoted many times by doctors who insist that the fetal heart monitor, although imperfect, is potentially the greatest boon to the detection of fetal anoxia (loss of oxygen) yet devised. But Shearer

I've never known a woman who was medicated for birth who said she'd had a positive experience.
—HELEN NAIL, *California lay midwife*

suggests that the very presence of a fetal heart monitor in the labor room requires such increased surveillance of the birthing mother that the *added care in itself* may be the reason for such excellent results. Mixed signs, variable patterns, illegible tracings—all of these should alert the attending staff, not to terminate labor immediately but to administer a series of tests from fetal blood samples to verify the monitor's data. In large hospitals where the more accurate internal monitoring systems have been perfected since the beginning, oscilloscopes have been placed in a central room where an attendant can maintain a constant check on fetal heart tracings for each monitored mother at one time.

So the question is whether these studies proved what doctors, in their fervor to lower U.S. mortality statistics, would like to think they did: it may be that the *use* of the monitor in hospitals with highly skilled attendants can be linked with lower infant mortality rates and lower Caesarean rates; but whether the monitor itself is responsible for lower mortality rates because of the accuracy of its data is highly doubtful. If, as Shearer suggests, use of fetal heart monitors requires better care, and this in turn increases the safeguards for the baby, why not simply provide more care and dispense with such complicated machinery in normal labor?

Nevertheless, the fetal heart monitor—specifically, the less accurate external system of monitoring—is being adopted by many community and teaching hospitals whose staffs have little or no specialized training in the interpretation of monitor tracings. Since a doctor uneducated

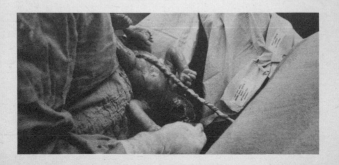

in the complexities of the monitor can be deceived by such data and conclude that labor must be terminated, it is no wonder that the rate of Caesareans is rising in hospitals throughout the country where monitors have only recently been introduced (see Chapter 6). Although it is true that the rate of Caesareans is going *down* in a few hospitals where the monitor has been used for some time, this can be attributed more to the skill of the attending staff in interpreting the monitor tracings than to the accuracy of the monitor per se. One day, perhaps, both the internal and external monitoring systems will be so perfected—and doctors, technicians, and staff will be so thoroughly skilled in reading the data accurately—that the device will be used without a large degree of risk to either normal or high-risk birth. But this will take some years. In the meantime, how is a birthing mother to know which hospital, which doctor, which nurse, and which attending staff are fully grounded in the proper management of the monitor when the machine is wheeled into the labor room?

Even if we were assured that use of the monitor is completely safe, this lengthy and difficult procedure seems an awfully high price to pay for an extra bit of insurance that is unnecesary in normal birth in the first place. Not only is the birthing mother suddenly dependent upon machines and experts around her more than her own body, but also, safe or not, the external monitor does have a secondary effect, and it is risky: the long-term immobility of a mother lying flat on her back can cause "supine hypotension," a condition that lowers her blood pressure and in turn restricts the amount of blood flowing to the baby. This will

---

I lay on the table and looked up and I could see the doctors in the reflection of the light overhead. I didn't want to watch, but I couldn't take my eyes off. I had to know what was going on.
—ANONYMOUS MOTHER

show up on accurate tracings of the fetal heart monitor as an alarming FHR pattern, thus proving once again that the very interference used to "help" the natural process only provides further complications that hinder the process as well.

Shearer does mention that a study on patient acceptance of the monitor showed that 92 per cent of the women interviewed were pleased with the "care and attention given them during monitoring." If the mother herself is no longer worthy of attention, at least her uterus is! Women apparently will accept what little they are offered in the way of attention, and are grateful for the least assistance in labor. Such is the attitude of any person who feels dependent on outside help and is unable to control her own birth process. However, Professor G. J. Kloosterman, chief of obstetrics and gynecology at Amsterdam University teaching hospital in Holland, put the machines away after several months of use when he discovered that actually less and less attention was being paid to the woman herself. He cautioned that monitors were not to be brought into labor rooms unless clear medical evidence required them, and he advised his doctor colleagues that the best way to judge whether such a need existed would be to ask themselves if they would use the monitor on their own wives under the same conditions. Few felt obliged to use the monitor in normal births any longer.

One of the early pioneers of the fetal heart monitor is Dr. Caldeyro-Barcia, who with Dr. Edward H. Hon, professor of obstetrics and gynecology at the University of

Pregnancy is a fundamental event which must be fully experienced if it is to be a source of inner renewal and inner celebration.
—ARTHUR AND LIBBY COLEMAN, The Psychology of Pregnancy

Southern California School of Medicine, has perfected the interpretation of fetal heart tracings in his studies on the impact of drugs and the supine position in labor. At a world medical congress held in Paris in 1972, Dr. Caldeyro-Barcia was asked if he thought all laboring women should be monitored and if there should be a worldwide organization formed to provide funds to assist birthing mothers in obtaining this aid. He answered that in his opinion more lives could be saved by spending this money to buy food for the world's pregnant women than to monitor them. Yet today more and more hospitals are equipping every labor room with its own monitor and attaching monitors routinely to laboring women.

Drugs

For many years, the placenta was believed to be an organ of such miraculous power that it could provide nourishment to the child, transfer various antibodies in utero, and shield the unborn child from all harm. Even today, despite doctors' pronouncements of the "screening ability" of the placenta, there is still a great deal that remains a medical mystery: we do not yet know in complete detail how the placenta permits the unborn to receive nourishment within minutes of its mother's eating; how it trades life-supporting oxygen for waste produced by the infant; how it keeps out most threatening bacteria while bringing in antibodies that will give the baby immunity to a host of diseases. The placenta has been thought to screen everything that enters the infant's growing body. Yet the

---

In favorable cases, under the influence of the drug triad, the patient falls into a deep quiet sleep between pains . . . When the patient awakes, the obstetrician is rewarded by hearing her ask, "Doctor, when am I going to have my baby?"

truth is that it is nothing more nor less than a "bloody sieve" which cannot stop the flow of unwanted chemicals that may damage the infant's organs, directly deform the infant's body, or indirectly cut down the supply of oxygen to the infant's brain.

In March 1974, Dr. Sanford Cohen, associate professor of pharmacology and pediatrics at New York University School of Medicine, spoke at the conference of The American Foundation for Maternal and Child Health, and stated in his most careful language:

> There is nothing magical offered by the protection of the placental membranes. Most of us have been taught that the placenta acts as a protective barrier for the fetus. I think it is true almost across the board that drugs given to the mother in significant dosages to produce results will cause significant concentrations of these drugs in the fetus.

In *Maternal and Child Health Practices*, Dr. Jeffrey B. Gould and Dr. Louis Gluck provide a drug-by-drug accounting of the many medications used during pregnancy and labor, a sampling of which follows:

> Antithyroid medications readily cross the placenta and affect the fetal thyroid-pituitary axis.
>
> Barbiturates cross the placenta in all stages of gestation.
>
> All narcotics used in labor readily cross the placenta and may produce clinical depression in the newborn.
>
> All (inhalation anesthetics) . . . readily cross the placenta and can depress the newborn.
>
> Regional anesthetics readily cross the placenta. . . .

The quickest way I know to prove that the child is already born is to have her feel her own abdomen. A newly restored waistline soon convinces even the most skeptical.
> —ALAN GUTTMACHER, Having a Baby

Thiazide diuretics readily cross the placenta. . . .

Coumarin anti-coagulants cross the placenta. . . .

And so forth and so on. Perhaps the best summation of drugs and their easy journey across the placenta has been stated by Dr. Yvonne Brackbill, professor of obstetrics, gynecology, and pediatrics for psychology at Georgetown University School of Medicine. She says firmly that "the placental barrier is not a barrier at all; almost anything smaller than a golf ball will cross it."

This means that all drugs taken during pregnancy and labor—including over-the-counter drugs such as aspirin and cold tablets—will reach the baby. M.L. Houston, in "Ecology of the Womb," an article in the Winter 1973–74 issue of *Expecting* magazine, has further noted that "The three most socially acceptable drugs in America—caffeine, nicotine and alcohol—are all under suspicion as being harmful to the fetus."

So much for the reassuring words of physicians who pat their patients on the hand and repeat soothingly, "*This* drug will not reach your baby." Such a statement can no longer be truthfully made. Drugs do get to the baby. That is the message of the 1970s.

It should be emphasized that drugs are administered in normal labor to speed up, slow down, or otherwise manipulate the process for the convenience of the doctor and the hospital staff; or they are administered to make the normal birth process more comfortable for the birthing woman. They are very rarely given "for the sake of the baby," yet doctors most often use this excuse in convincing their patients to accept drugs. Nor is it often explained that it is not the doctor, nor the mother, but *the baby* who is most adversely affected when drugs cross the placenta or when they lower the mother's blood-gas exchange to the fetus. Doctors Louis R. Orkin and Gertie F. Marx, specialists in anesthetics at the Department of Anesthesiology at Albert Einstein College of Medicine, sum up the problem succinctly at the conclusion of *Physiology of Obstetric Anesthesia* (1969):

> The fetus lives in a delicate balance, and at a relatively low level of survivability, in an environment over which he has little control, and in which he can make only minor adjustments. He is adversely affected by any reduction in blood-gas exchange and transport, by alterations in acid-base balance, and by the actions of most drugs. Unfavorable changes in his environment may be augmented by the influence of drugs given for any multitude of reasons. When such drugs cross the placenta, the fetus is physiologically and metabolically unprepared to cope with their pharmacological effects.

Doctors Jeffrey B. Gould and Louis Gluck, in the chapter of *Maternal and Child Health Practices* entitled "Perinatal Pharmacology," write that "In utero, drugs that reach the fetus are cleared by the placenta. Following birth, the neonate must depend upon his own ability to chemically inactivate these drugs." However, many of the systems with which its mother is equipped to handle the drugs are only partially developed in the baby. "The pathways

All my life as long as I can remember I have asked why. I want to know. And I can't remember anything about my baby's birth.
                                        —LAURA ROSSITER, *mother*

for oxidative detoxification," among others, they state, "are immature even in the term newborn."

Generally, there are two types of drugs administered to the birthing mother: analgesics, given during labor; and anesthetics, given during dilation and actual delivery. Regarding analgesics, the late Dr. Alan F. Gutmacher wrote as early as 1962 in his popular *Pregnancy and Birth*:

> As a group the analgesics are nervous depressants, depressing not only the sensation of pain but other nervous mechanisms, including respiration. The mother's breathing center, located in the brain, is relatively resistant to their depressing effects, but not so the respiratory center of the newborn, which is highly susceptible so such inhibitory influences.

Even when drugs indirectly affect the fetus by lowering the mother's blood pressure and reducing the amount of blood flowing to the baby, a condition called hypoxia may result, which is defined in *Maternal and Child Health Practices* as "a state in which a relative or comparative lack of oxygen exists." With the development of an hypoxic state, the authors state:

> ... the fetus may evidence progressive effects such as tachycardia ([heart rate] above 160/min.), hyperactivity, defecation with meconium staining of the amniotic fluid, respiratory efforts with aspiration of amniotic fluid along with meconium and other amniotic debris, peripheral vasodilatation, decreased blood ph [acidity], cyanosis bradycardia (below 100/min.), flaccidity, shock, cardiac irregularity, cardiac arrest, and finally death. If delivery occurs

---

MRS. A'S BIRTH CHART

Time	Dilation	Drug/Procedure
1:00 a.m.	3 centimeters dilation	Nisentil
3:00 a.m.		Nisentil
5:00 a.m.		Nisentil
9:30 a.m.		Paracervical Block and Buccal Pitocin
10:00 a.m.		Buccal Pitocin
11:50 a.m.		Nisentil
12:45 p.m.	4 +	Paracervical Block and Caudal
3:00 p.m.		
3:20 p.m.	7 centimeters dilation	Catheterized
4:00 p.m.		Catheterized
6:00 p.m.	6 centimeters dilation	

before death from hypoxia, the newborn may exhibit varying degrees of cardiac irregularity and bradycardia, flaccidity, apnea or gasping respirations, cyanosis, absent reflexes, meconium staining and acidosis.

In utero, then, locked in its chamber of amniotic fluid and struggling against a reduction of vital oxygen, the fetus may prematurely defecate its first stool (meconium) and, in severe cases, may attempt to breathe too early, inhaling both the amniotic fluid and the meconium into its lungs. Meanwhile, its heart rate has soared ahead (tachycardia) in an attempt to get more blood from the mother, and this, in severe cases, may end in failure of the circulatory system before delivery. Doctors may say that it is unfair to measure the effects of drugs on the basis of the most severe and damaging risks, yet they are hard-pressed to explain why meconium staining of the amniotic fluid has become an increasing problem in hospital delivery rooms throughout the nation. Moreover, how many mothers are told *any* of the risks involved when they are coaxed into taking one drug or another?

Like Dr. Guttmacher, Dr. Brackbill states that while adult humans have an amazing ability to withstand crisis and to bounce back from trauma, babies do not. She emphasizes that the human baby is born neurologically incomplete and is, therefore, "particularly vulnerable to stressful stimuli. Significant environmental effects change the way in which a baby's brain develops and the rate at which it develops." Since the growth of the human brain lasts for at least the first eighteen months of life after

6:25 p.m.		Buccal Pitocin
6:45 p.m.		Buccal Pitocin
7:00 p.m.	6 + centimeters dilation	
7:20 p.m.		Nisentil
8:15 p.m.		Paracervical
9:15 p.m.	Fully dilated, + 2	
9:30 p.m.	station head	
10:50 p.m.		IV Pitocin
11:05 p.m.		Spinal (Saddle Block)
11:25 p.m.	Delivery	Mid-Forceps
11:37 p.m.	Placenta delivered	Cervical Laceration; manual uterine exploration; Pitocin

birth, there can be no doubt that trauma during that time, as well as in utero, affects the brain, and may affect it permanently. Dr. Brackbill feels that analgesic and anesthetic agents given in labor and delivery do fall under the category of environmental effects that are traumatic. These drugs, as well as others that cross the placenta screen, are known to concentrate in the brain and liver of the newborn.

It must be concluded that whether drugs indirectly affect the baby by lowering the mother's blood-gas exchange, or whether they have a direct effect by concentrating in the baby's organs, they do carry risk of brain damage when they are administered at any time during pregnancy, labor, and delivery. As Doris Haire of the ICEA states:

> It is not unlikely that unnecessary alterations in the normal fetal environment may play a role in the incidence of neurological impairment and infant mortality in the United States.

When challenged to defend the use of drugs during labor and delivery, doctors will often refer to the existence of "good Apgar ratings" as evidence of the baby's general health directly after birth. Introduced to the medical community in the mid-1950s by Dr. Virginia Apgar, an anesthesiologist, the Apgar score is used as a general measurement of post-delivery health: the baby's heart rate, respiration, muscle tone, color, and reflexes are scored within a range of 0 to 2 points at one minute after birth and again at five minutes after birth. In America, a score of 10

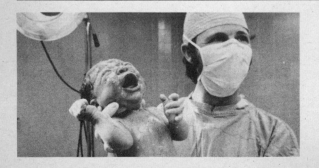

points (i.e., 2 points for each of the five signs checked) indicates perfect health; a score of 7 to 9 is considered normal; scores of 5 to 6 indicate some distress; and scores of 4 or below are considered poor and indicate a need for immediate treatment. In Holland, where Apgar ratings of 9 to 10 occur far more frequently than in the United States, doctors look hard at scores below 9 as clear warning that the baby may be in some kind of trouble.

Apgar ratings do show some effect of drugs on the baby even when all other evidence seems to indicate perfect health. Dr. Charles E. Flowers, chairman of the Department of Obstetrics and Gynecology at Baylor University College of Medicine, writes in *Obstetric Analgesia and Anesthesia* (1967) that even if effects of analgesics are not always "clinically evident," differences in oxygen saturation at birth are apparent when a series of infants is studied. "Such a series will also contain a larger number of infants with Apgar scores below 7 than infants delivered of mothers who had no obstetric complications and received no analgesia."

So the Apgar score does give doctors an indication of newborn health, but in America it has become so universally accepted that many doctors are now relying on it as a means of defending their hospital procedures—leaving the pediatrician or specialist in neonatology and perinatology to deal with whatever long-lasting complications may later appear. Dr. Apgar herself considers it only a general measurement, however, and many of her colleagues have expressed increasing concern over its limitations. As Doctors Gould and Gluck have stated:

Although the Apgar score is important for the quantitation of acute depression, studies of infant behavior show the necessity of extending our view of the depressant effects of drugs beyond the first five minutes of life. Studies of sucking and visual attentions during the first four days of life have demonstrated response depression induced by analgesia.

One of the most popular analgesic drugs administered today—and one whose effects on the baby often do not show up in Apgar scores—is Demerol, a pharmaceutical trademark for the narcotic compound meperidine. In the February 1, 1974, issue of the *American Journal of Obstetrics and Gynecology* Dr. Brackbill stated that in Great Britain, "estimated frequency of usage is 80 to 90 per cent of all deliveries," and estimates of usage and administration of Demerol in the United States have frequently been just as high.

To study the effect of meperidine on newborn infants, and to assess the long-range effectiveness of the Apgar score, Dr. Brackbill tested one group of 25 infants whose mothers had been given meperidine and a supplementary group of 19 infants whose mothers had been given a variety of drugs. Although Apgar ratings of the two groups did not differ on either the one-minute or five-minute score, other tests, such as the Neonatal Behavioral Assessment Scale and a test of the "habituation rate of the orienting reflex," revealed dramatic differences. "Infants of mothers who had not been premedicated with meperidine habituated twice as fast as infants whose mothers had

Although the recent Collaborative Perinatal Study of 55,000 children from before birth to the age of ten has cost the taxpayers over $110 million, it did not even have a sufficient control

been premedicated," Brackbill found. She also discovered that "infants whose mothers received no meperidine performed more capably and efficiently on many Neonatal Behavioral Assessment Scale items than did infants of premedicated mothers." Brackbill concluded that the study provided "clear-cut evidence that meperidine produces outstanding neonatal differences in ability to process information." And to her, the inference was clear that "a major obstetric danger may now be medication itself."

Dr. T. Berry Brazelton, writing in *Redbook* in February 1971, also expressed concern about what childbirth drugs can do to the newborn infant. Dr. Brazelton described what he found to be a common syndrome in newborn nurseries around the country where babies had been sent in with decent Apgar ratings to be bathed and given clean clothes:

> But all too often, as the nursery nurse made one of her frequent checks, she found the new infant blue, cold, breathing shallowly and difficult to rouse. When she tried to awaken him, he choked up mucus, coughed half-heartedly and made very little effort to rid himself of it. Since new infants are equipped with magnificently effective gag response that makes it nearly impossible for them to choke, this lethargy was even more striking. . . .

Dr. Brazelton went on to say that although doctors and nurses are accustomed to this condition, it causes him some alarm.

And so should the short- and long-range effects on

---

group of normal, unmedicated mothers and babies to compare.
> —Doris Haire, *speaking at 1974 conference,*
> *"Obstetrical Management*
> *and Infant Outcome"*

88

infants from all drugs cause pregnant women some
alarm. The paracervical block, for example, is promoted
by many doctors as a minor regional anesthetic that will
merely "take the edge off" the pain of contractions without
detracting from the experience of labor or the health of the
baby. Laboring women are told that the drug lasts only
forty minutes, but they are not informed that the drug
is often readministered several times during dilation, and
that its effect on the baby may be lifelong. One study,
presented at the International Symposium on the Effect
of Prolonged Drug Usage on Fetal Development at Beit-
Berl, Israel, in September of 1971, revealed the dangerous
effects of the paracervical block on newborn infants. The
results, published in *Drugs and Fetal Development* (1972)
showed that "paracervical block causes severe changes in
the fetal heart rate in 35 per cent of cases, changes which
are often followed by prolonged acidosis of the fetus with
a significant number of depressed neonates." And for those
doctors who tell their patients that paracervical blocks have
no effect on the long-range development of the infant, the
study concluded that "fetal depression, even if apparently
reversible, might later affect the motor and intellectual
development of the child."

Indeed, even the Apgar score will show effects of the
paracervical block, as indicated by Doris Haire in *The
Cultural Warping of Childbirth* (1972). Referring to one
study of the effect of this anesthesia, she states that "the
incidence of infant depression and Apgar scores of 6 or less
was almost three times greater among those infants whose

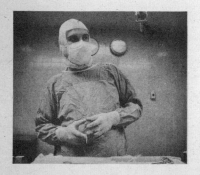

mothers had received paracervical block than among the controls."

The safest birth for the infant continues to be one where *no* medication of any sort is used. Dr. Charles Richard Gilbert, a leading obstetrician and gynecologist, and author of *Childbirth* (1967), writes that "the perfect analgesic or anesthetic has not been discovered. All have drawbacks." Dr. Geoffrey Chamberlain, the English obstetrician who received the Foundation of the American Association of Obstetricians and Gynecologists award for his research with premature babies, wrote in *The Safety of the Unborn Child* (1969), "No drug can be completely cleared of a low incidence or association with abnormalities in the unborn. We do not know the cause of most malformations, and, until we do, every alteration in the mother's body must be suspect." And M. L. Houston repeats this warning in his article in *Expecting* magazine: "All drugs are to be considered guilty until proven innocent."

How many times must it be said? *Drugs get to the baby. Drugs adversely affect the baby. Drugs may permanently damage the baby.* Any doctor who tells his patient that any drug used for any reason—including tranquilizers, sedatives, caudals, epidurals, saddle blocks, paracervical blocks, spinals, generals, or whatever—will not affect the baby is telling her an untruth: no drug has been proven *not* to affect the baby, and therefore, as Chamberlain says, "No drug can be said to be absolutely blame free." Why risk it? Why not turn the "just-in-case" game back to the doctor and say, "No, just in case *this* drug has

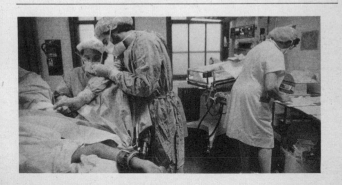

an effect on my baby that you don't know about yet, I won't take it."

It is a rare woman who receives no drugs at all during labor in America—fewer than one mother in ten is "allowed" to refuse medication of any kind. This is also true today in England, where the midwife and doctor give inhalation analgesia routinely at home and in the hospital. But it is not the case in Holland, where no drugs, including oxytocics to prevent hemorrhaging after the delivery of the placenta, are given routinely for the normal birth. Nor are they requested by mothers, since Dutch women have not been led to expect either undue pain in labor or the unnecessary, costly, and risky drugs that are supposedly designed to alleviate "the pains of labor."

Sumner Yaffe, chairman of the Committee on Drugs for the American Academy of Pediatrics, states that "the insistent demand of the public to take drugs for every ailment has contributed to drug misuse and abuse." He notes that although drug consumption in pregnancy is a world-wide problem, the United States has a further affliction: "Our society clearly differs from most other societies because of its striking use of analgesics and anesthetics during labor."

Today many American women believe they are protected by the regulatory powers of the Food and Drug Administration, but in reality these minimal protections are deceptive. Before the original FDA act was passed in 1906, torrents of untested cure-alls and miracle drugs flooded the market, leaving consumers on their own to decide which drug was safe and which was not. Even with the establishment of the

---

A man is an onlooker at birth. How can a man, then, ever jump that line and know what birth is like?

—KENDRA DAY, *mother*

FDA under Teddy Roosevelt, however, drug manufacturers found many ways to get around the act, and unsafe drugs continued to be sold to unwary consumers. With the passage of the Food, Drug and Cosmetic Act of 1938, manufacturers were required to present convincing evidence of safety to the FDA before new drugs would be approved for sale. From then on, new warnings were printed on labels, excessively dangerous drugs were banned, and penalties for violations were more severely enforced. But as Dr. Philip R. Lee and the pharmacologist Milton Silverman state in their book, *Pills, Profits and Politics* (1974), the 1938 act "did *not* require the drug maker to produce convincing evidence of efficacy," and it was this loophole through which many unsafe drugs were approved.

It is important to note that tests of the sedative Thalidomide had not resulted in damage to the fetuses of mice or other test animals except for the rabbit, leading the manufacturer to believe that results were inconclusive and that Thalidomide should be approved for safety when used by the pregnant human female. Sale of this drug was never permitted in America, not because procedural protections built into the FDA caught its dangerous side effects in time, but rather because of the last-minute suspicions of one administrator, who single-handedly withheld approval on the basis of a personal hunch. If there is any lesson to be learned from the Thalidomide tragedy of the early 1960s, it is that safety of drugs is often measured as much by what is *not* known as by what is known about their efficacy and side effects. Thus, M. L. Houston's warning for pregnant women should be repeated over and

over again, often to the drug-wielding doctor whose good
intentions may not be all that well informed: "All drugs
are to be considered guilty until proven innocent."

It was on the heels of the Thalidomide scare that the
far more stringent Kefauver-Harris amendment was passed
in 1962. Lee and Silverman note that among its provisions
this law "demanded every prescription drug advertisement
carry appropriate information on hazards and contraindications," and it further required that "no new drug can be
approved until its safety in pregnancy can be adequately
tested." There is, however, a major loophole in *this* law as
well, through which most drugs used in pregnancy, labor,
and delivery have escaped: any drug approved and placed
on the market before 1962 is exempt from retesting
according to the requirements of the Kefauver-Harris
amendment. Yaffe notes that unfortunately as much as
98 per cent of all drugs used in pregnancy, labor, and
delivery were approved before 1962. Further, in June 1974
the American Medical Association voted to "exert all
efforts" to amend or repeal the Kefauver Act. The reason,
as reported in the *San Francisco Chronicle*, was "largely,
they said, because the law allows the Federal Food and
Drug Administration to interfere bureaucratically with the
development and marketing of needed new drugs."

But perhaps that is not the main reason at all. As Lee
and Silverman point out, referring to statistics of 1967,
"the AMA's income from advertising—largely though not
exclusively for drugs—reached a new high of nearly $14
million, representing about 43 per cent of the total AMA

income." Today advertising specifically earmarked for drugs in AMA journals is billed at about $9 million a year, which accounts for 27.7 per cent of the AMA's total income. Since at least one-quarter of the AMA's annual budget is dependent upon the drug industry, it is no wonder that such a powerful doctors' association should continue its all-out support for more and more and more drugs. Lee and Silverman quote the commissioner of the Food and Drug Administration, who summed up the absurdity of this situation perfectly in 1963 when he stated, "In absolute terms, approximately three-quarters of a billion dollars is spent every year by some sixty drug companies in order to reach, persuade, cajole, pamper, outwit, and sell one of America's smallest markets—the 180,000 physicians."

And pamper and cajole they do. Advertisements in doctors' journals are so ludicrously high-powered and so often make the doctor into a hero if he uses this drug or that machine that it is astonishing to realize that intelligent people are actually persuaded to prescribe drugs by brand name, especially drugs for pregnant women. Here is little Cerise, age six, whose mommy would have had *such* a difficult time if her doctor hadn't administered Beauticaine, that special drug for special patients. Or what about little Teddy, whose heart had shown signs of fetal distress until the doctor rushed in with a dose of Speedo-caine and saved the baby from brain damage.

Advertisements, however, may only be the tip of the iceberg: doctors and pharmacists are besieged weekly by circulars and drug salesmen pushing the latest product,

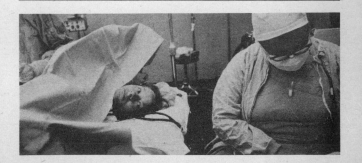

offering free samples ("Try it, *she'll* like it!") and other cracker-jack goodies such as I found on my obstetrician's desk recently. This was a three-inch cast-iron metal sculpture of a fetus in utero, which weighed several pounds and which served as a beautiful paperweight. This expensive little giveaway had been presented by the salesman of a drug company whose name, of course, the doctor might have quickly forgotten, had it not been emblazoned on the side of the ornament.

Put them all together, the AMA with its vested interests, the FDA with its weak regulatory powers, the strong lobbyist drug industry, and the ever-approachable doctors, and we are right back where we started. Today the "miracle drug" is not a miracle in that it will cure everything at once, but certainly it is a miracle in that it will give the doctor complete control and make his patients worshipful of his medical expertise.

Where is the American woman in all of this? Knocked out, flat on her back, tied down, and ever innocent of the political, economic, medical, and ethical questions that are being decided about drugs over her prone body. Yet even if she were fully informed of all aspects of drugs in pregnancy and labor, would she (would any of us?) ever feel she knew enough to challenge her doctor's expertise if he wanted to administer "just a small dose" of one drug or another?

The point is that *no one* knows enough to risk such irreparable damage on a newborn child, so the responsibility for such decisions must fall on those who conceived the baby in the first place, the parents. It does not take a

---

What a nice warm feeling a mother gets when she receives a free wallet-size portrait of her newborn from us in your hospital's name. . . . Patient relations are so important these days, and

special education in obstetrical science to realize why *all* drugs are risky and that *no* drug is necessary in the normal birth. Again, why risk it?

Forceps and the Vacuum Extractor

Drugs not only calm the woman and dull her nerves; they also dull the natural process in such a way as to slow labor down, sometimes stopping it entirely. Doctors may rush to the rescue with large doses of oxytocics to speed up the process once again, or they may simply "open her up" with a lengthy incision and move in with forceps to haul the baby out. Drugs also require a forceps delivery if they deaden sensations that normally cause the mother to push her baby down the birth canal, unless she can take her cues from surrounding attendants who watch her uterus contract and direct her to push.

Forceps are large, crossed metal spoons usually with holes in the centers to grasp the baby's head. High forceps refers to application of the forceps when the baby's head is not yet engaged—i.e., has not dropped into the mother's pelvis. Most authorities agree that high forceps deliveries should *never* be performed, because of extreme risk to both mother and baby. But it is generally believed that the risks of elective mid and low forceps deliveries are so minimal that they can be performed routinely. "The vast majority of forceps operations performed in this country today are elective low forceps," states the textbook *Williams Obstetrics.* "One reason is that all methods of analgesia interfere to a certain

---

96

extent with the mother's voluntary expulsive efforts, in which circumstances low forceps delivery becomes the most reasonable procedure." Forceps are often required, not elected, if the baby's head has not rotated fully, but here again "low midforceps . . . has become extremely popular with the advent and increasing use of conduction anesthesia, which so often leads to incomplete rotations of the fetal head" (*Obstetric Forceps*, 1968).

Medical indications include maternal exhaustion, premature separation of the placenta, prolapsed cord, excessive pressure on the fetal head, and changes in the fetal cardiac rhythm. Such complications certainly justify careful use of forceps, but often the *degree* of complication is so slight that interference with forceps becomes a matter of elective choice on the part of the individual doctor. Since most doctors believe more fully in their scientific expertise and technological skill than in the natural process of birth, and since the obstetrician's job in birth is often to prevent problems from occurring, the doctor is more likely to reach for forceps than wait for the process to correct itself in good time. It is no wonder, then, that today about one-third of all births in America are performed with forceps. This differs significantly from other countries, however, as stated in *Pregnancy, Birth and the Newborn Baby* (1972): "The routine use of forceps in uncomplicated cases has been one of the chief differences in the delivery of babies in this country, compared with European practice. In many European clinics forceps even now are used infrequently and only for the most difficult deliveries."

No primitive society leaves the mother alone, nor does any leave her alone among strangers. It remains for modern civilization in the isolation

On the other hand, in recent years some European countries have adopted use of the vacuum extractor, which is generally considered a safer and more easily managed means of pulling the baby out than forceps. This instrument is applied to the baby's head by means of a suction cup which literally sucks the baby's body down the birth canal. Although the use of the vacuum extractor has become somewhat more popular in the United States in recent years, some American doctors regard it as little more than a kind of obstetrical plumber's friend, to be used only in cases where forceps might cause excessive tearing of the woman's tissues or severe pressure on the baby's head. Indeed, the sight of a baby delivered by the vacuum extractor is visually horrifying: in order to grip the scalp tightly, the extractor must pull part of the baby's head into the cup, leaving a lump the size of a tennis ball protruding from its scalp immediately after birth. This lump usually disappears within a few days and cases of scalp necrosis, fractured skulls, intracranial damage, and the like are exceedingly rare. Follow-up studies of vacuum extracted infants two years after birth have shown that use of the instrument per se does not lead to motor or behavioral impairment unless it has been improperly applied. Again, in this and all other cases of medical interference, the success of the procedure is dependent upon the care and expertise of the attending doctor, who must weigh all the medical evidence correctly before he makes a decision to alter the natural process. The birthing mother is seldom informed of the risks of elective forceps and is left completely out of the decision-making.

---

*of cities and suburbs, to leave a woman
approaching childbirth all alone.*
—MARGARET MEAD, Pregnancy, Birth
and the Newborn Baby

Episiotomy

An episiotomy is the incision made in a woman's perineal tissue—tissue that normally stretches at the opening of the vagina to allow the baby's head to be born. Such an interference has become so routine in American hospitals that many women believe no birth could take place without tremendous, jagged tears ripping open their perineal tissues were it not for the episiotomy. Doctors often tell birthing mothers that American women need episiotomies because their bodies do not react with the same resiliency as the bodies of primitive women, and that a straight surgical cut is always preferable to a ragged tear. Neither argument is true: the same processes that naturally enlarged primitive women's perineal tissues are still at work in the modern body, and they still function just as well. As the late Nicholson Eastman, M.D., former professor of obstetrics and obstetrician-in-chief at Johns Hopkins Hospital, wrote in *Expectant Motherhood* (1970):

> The degree to which the vagina is distended as the baby is born is a source of dismay to many expectant mothers, who fancy that deep tears must be inevitable. It is true that the vagina of the nonpregnant woman could not be stretched to any such extent. Throughout pregnancy, however, the vagina undergoes progressive changes in the way of increased succulence and distensibility and toward the end may be easily stretched to many times its former capacity. Accordingly, tears which do occur are superficial and are readily repaired by a few stitches.

Nor is the episiotomy quite that easy to perform or to

In order to prevent tearing, your doctor may decide to make a small cut with scissors so that the opening will be wide enough for the baby's

endure. The operation requires local anesthesia, unless the doctor waits until the last minute when the pressure of the baby's head has deadened sensation to the tissue. Since most physicians prefer to be early rather than late in performing surgery, however, episiotomies are generally performed before full crowning of the head occurs, so that the doctor will have plenty of space and time to work. He will need this time, because it takes a great deal of effort to get a pair of scissors through healthy tissue, which bleeds profusely. Nerves and muscles are also severed in the process, and this can result in numbness to the area for months and years. The doctor may spend up to as much as an hour after birth sewing up the incision, which often tears right down (or will be cut open again) during the woman's next birth.

But the immediate effect of episiotomy is that bow-legged, tender shuffling and squeamish sideways sitting which so many people associate with motherhood. In *Woman's Doctor*, William Sweeney questions the entire procedure as a gross injustice to the laboring woman (although he too apparently succumbs to its practice on occasion):

> I'm always amazed to see the blasé attitudes that people have toward episiotomies. Even the nurses are the same way. But put the same length incision on a man's abdomen and it's a major abdominal procedure. He's not turned loose to go . . . to work taking care of a child. He's sent home in ten days. . . . After all, an episiotomy is two inches long on the outside but it's another two inches long on the inside—it goes up into the vagina, and

---

head to pass through. Such a neat incision can then be stitched up easily and will heal more quickly than a jagged tear.
—CARLO VALENTI, M.D., Mother To Be

muscles and all sorts of things are cut. And not only is it a four-inch incision, which is bad enough, but you've got to *sit* on it.... No wonder we see new mothers walking around the halls dragging their legs.

Confronted with a birthing mother who adamantly refuses an episiotomy, many doctors will argue that actually, such an incision is performed "more for the sake of the baby" than for the convenience of the mother. As is explained in *Williams Obstetrics*, doctors believe the episiotomy "spares the baby's head the necessity of serving as a battering ram against perineal obstruction. If prolonged, the pounding of the infant's head against the perineum may cause brain injury." This may be true if the doctor has already speeded up the birth process to such an extent that the baby is practically careening down the birth canal before the perineal tissue has fully stretched. And it is certainly true if the doctor has neither the time nor the patience to massage and gently restrain the perineal tissues around the baby's head, giving them time to adjust and stretch as the infant moves through the opening.

Doctors have a further (and more insidious) argument to convince their patients of the value of an episiotomy, if none of the above are found to be acceptable. They state that after birth husbands will be unable to enjoy intercourse with their wives if an episiotomy has not been performed, because the vagina will be permanently enlarged and misshapen. This argument is often reinforced with stories of women who did not have episiotomies and whose pelvic floors collapsed or whose reproductive organs actually

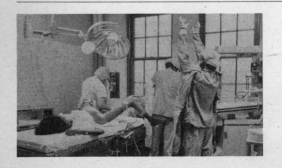

"fell out" after several births, thus requiring elaborate and expensive "face lifts" of the entire area. Naturally, no woman in her right mind would want birth to ruin her lovemaking permanently, yet despite doctors' admonitions that tissue stretched to the size of a baby's head can never tighten up to accommodate a mere penis, quite the reverse is true. The very muscles that bring the walls of the vagina close together during lovemaking to "grip" the penis also function after birth to tone up perineal tissues and return the vaginal canal to its former size. As Dr. Robert Bradley, author of *Husband-Coached Childbirth* (1965), has suggested, women who perform simple exercises with these muscles as a preparation for birth are often delighted to find that their sensitivity to and grip of the penis after birth are actually improved. Furthermore, there is *no evidence* that prolapse of organs or collapse of the pelvic floor can occur just because an episiotomy is not performed at birth.

In spite of American doctors' insistence that episiotomies contribute to the quick-and-easy birth, doctors in Holland and Denmark continue to avoid the routine use of this interference unless clear medical evidence indicates that it is necessary. Today's rate of episiotomies averages about 15 per cent of all births in England, and 8 per cent in Holland; it is estimated that the rate of episiotomies in the U.S. has increased to over 70 per cent in many of our hospitals. With this rise, there has been an increase in what is called the "fourth-degree median," which means that the incision accidentally went so deep that it cut through the mother's anal sphincter muscle.

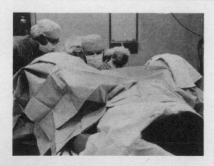

Supine Position

One factor aiding the doctor's glowing testimonial for episiotomies is the very position in which he places the birthing mother during labor and delivery. Lying flat on her back with head and shoulders on the same plane as her hipbones—a position that must certainly make birth one of the most boring and lonely times in the mother's life—the laboring woman becomes sluggish, inactive, and immobile, and so do the processes inside her body. As mentioned earlier, a condition called supine hypotension may result and lower the mother's blood pressure, which in turn lowers the amount of blood going to the unborn child. The problem is further intensified if the mother has taken any drugs at all during labor, as explained by Dr. Flowers in "Pain Relief in Labor and Delivery," a chapter from *Controversy in Obstetrics and Gynecology* (1969): "The heavy uterus may cause pressure on the great vessels when the patient is anesthetized in the supine position; this may result in a reduction in cardiac return, a fall in blood pressure, and a decrease in oxygenation to the central nervous system of the fetus and the mother."

Dr. Caldeyro-Barcia also suggests that with or without drugs or the occurrence of supine hypotension the flat-on-your-back position of giving birth is inherently harmful for *every* woman and child. "Except for being hanged by the feet," he states, "the supine position is the worst conceivable position for labor and delivery." Not only does compression of the uterus upon the inferior vena cava

---

$50,000. That's what the average hospital costs on a per-room basis to build and equip today.
—ANONYMOUS M.D., Confessions of a
Gynecologist

work against the birth process, but also "during labor contractions the abdominal aorta and illiac arteries may be completely occluded—pinched between the spine and the uterus—cutting off the supply of blood to the uterus and thus the supply of oxygen to the fetus."

Lithotomy—the medical name for the supine position— is further obstructive of the birth process in that it works against natural forces of gravity that are helping the baby to find its way down the birth canal. Moreover, with her legs splayed far apart and strapped onto the metal stirrups of the delivery table, the mother cannot help but create tension in her perineal tissues by stretching them unnaturally to either side. Rather than remain loose and resilient to accommodate the baby's head, these tissues become tight and inflexible, giving the doctor every reason to perform his treasured episiotomy.

It is no wonder, then, that American women associate birth with pelvic examinations, for the position of both has been designed for the convenience of the doctor, not the mother. Except for operative procedures, the lithotomy position is discouraged in most other countries, where women are allowed to move around during labor until they find the most comfortable position for giving birth. They may lie on their sides, balance on hands and knees, squat, or sit with their backs propped up, and of course there are no stirrups, straps, or cuffs to hold them in position.

Today some hospitals in the United States permit trained women to have their hands free to grab their knees and push, and to be supported at a forty-five-degree angle by pillows. Even such a small concession is helpful to mother and child, who can take advantage of the force of gravity in this way, rather than work against it in the lithotomy position. But it is not enough: the added pressure on the woman's perineum throughout the second stage of labor may combine with the effects of drugs and lithotomy during early labor to convince the doctor an episiotomy is needed, for which he must place the woman back in stirrups and the lithotomy position once again.

Doris Haire summed up the problems of supine position succinctly in 1972 by stating that the flat-on-your-back position of American childbirth tends to:

1. adversely affect the mother's blood pressure, cardiac return and pulmonary ventilation.
2. decrease the normal intensity of the contractions.
3. inhibit the mother's voluntary efforts to push her baby out spontaneously.
4. increase the need for forceps and increase the traction necessary for a forceps extraction.
5. inhibit the spontaneous expulsion of the placenta which in turn increases the need for cord traction, expression or manual removal of the placenta—procedures which significantly increase the incidence of fetomaternal hemorrhage.
6. increase the need for episiotomy because of the increased tension on the pelvic floor and the stretching of the perineal tissue. The normal separation of the feet for natural expulsion is about 15 to 16 inches, or 38 to 41 centimeters, which is far less separation than is allowed by the average American delivery table stirrups.

So this is childbirth in the American hospital today. Quick and easy? No, slow and agonizing, full of risk, expensive, lonely, demoralizing if not demeaning, and heading in a direction that may someday eradicate the need for woman's body (except her uterus) altogether.

Helene Galler:
A Mother's Reflection
on Her Birth

IT's TAKEN ME a long time to admit that my birth was a pretty awful experience. My pregnancy was fine and I trained for natural childbirth, but all the time not really believing I was going to have a baby. I took my doctors on referral from a friend, since we'd just moved to Washington. One was Chief of Obstetrics at the hospital there.

Labor wasn't at all the way I'd expected, drinking tea and watching TV in the early stages. I entered the labor room alone, while Rob registered downstairs. I did my breathing. Soon a doctor came in whom I'd seen twice before. "There's no way you can control contractions with breathing," he told me. He offered me a choice of a spinal or an epidural. He was so enthusiastic about giving me a shot. If he'd only been more positive about other alternatives. I guess I'd known all along *I* would need drugs. A few seconds after the needle went in I was out. I remember nothing.

I came to being wheeled past the nursery, everything foggy. I slept for two days, waking only to go back to sleep again. The nurses came and went and implied I shouldn't be sleeping so much. I felt guilty. I don't even remember Adam in those days.

As soon as we got home I became depressed. I thought Adam was cute; but I must admit there were no maternal feelings. I was too overwhelmed with anxiety to really care about him.

I've never expressed the rage I feel toward everyone about my birth—my mother, my husband, my doctor, my friends, who never mentioned what it would be like. Myself. I didn't know how to take care of myself. I didn't know what to ask for. I gave all responsibility away and gave up.

6
Birth's
Machine Age

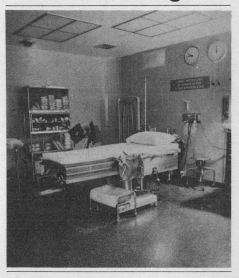

Birth's
Machine Age

THE BEST ALTERNATIVES to medical intervention in normal birth are simple patience and constant care. These forms of assistance in the natural process have proven successful since the beginning of humankind. In the American hospital, however, doctors, nurses, and attending staff have no time for such individual attention. How could they? In the hospital maternity ward, women in labor must be treated as a group if they are all to receive the uniform care that the hospital is committed to provide. They must be checked in, examined, shaved, given enemas, hooked up to intravenous equipment, and reexamined by rotating shifts of nurses and attendants. Everyone is too busy to "waste time" sitting out the long hours of labor with a birthing mother. Nor can a nurse or attendant make an exception to hospital policy or overturn a doctor's orders if a woman requests anything out of the ordinary (such as food or drink). The patient's own obstetrician may arrive only a few minutes before actual delivery begins, and until then she must trust the nurse or staff physician, neither of whom she has ever met before, to respect her particular needs and desires during birth. It is not long before she realizes that hospital procedure prohibits anyone from giving her the personal care she needs.

Conformity to hospital procedure is in itself a contribut-

We obstetricians are so clever with our tools and gadgets that we have rewritten the obstetrical drama in such a way as to make us the stars

ing factor to the increased use of medical intervention in normal birth. When the staff ignores each woman's individual needs, the hospital environment may seem so foreign and disabling that her resulting anxiety alone may adversely affect labor.

Although the woman is not the target of hospital routine and intervention, she is, most assuredly, the victim. When the delivery room is in active use, for example, she may be artificially stimulated for the simple purpose of moving her body to the delivery room as fast as possible so that other births will not be kept waiting. She is shifted from room to room, and rolled from bed to bed; she is examined internally by several attendants she does not know, and poked, stabbed, strapped down, and checked out by several more.

Of course not every doctor nor every hospital is so technologically dependent as to subject all normal births to all interferences. The point is that generally one interference leads to another in a kind of obstetrical merry-go-round that not only increases risk to the baby, but also strips the birthing mother of control of her own birth. Long before labor begins, therefore, it seems logical for a pregnant woman to seek out a doctor and hospital in her area that will provide the best environment for her. But if she attempts to gather hard facts on which to base her choice, she will discover that hospital records are rarely if ever disclosed to the public, and that information about the routine procedures of medical interferences are in essence none of her business! Such disclosures are of major concern to organizations like the International Childbirth

---

instead of women. We even accept the
congratulations of husbands and then wonder
why women are resentful of men.
    —JOHN SELDON MILLER, M.D., Childbirth

Education Association, which depend upon shared information from a variety of sources to assess the status of birth in America today, in order to inform the public. As Doris Haire of the ICEA states:

> There is no federal law which requires a hospital to maintain accurate and legible medical records. In most states there is no law requiring a hospital to retain records they do keep beyond a short length of time. We have no national agency that keeps statistics beyond mortality. Hospitals in my own state of New Jersey are not required to make public their incidence of resuscitation of the newborn.

Some hospital personnel, however, do feel this information should be shared, and they unofficially make it available. The figures in Table I, for example, were smuggled out of a large urban teaching hospital and may shed some light on the hidden world of hospital records. Especially noteworthy here is that episiotomies were performed on three out of every four mothers; at least one out of four were "assisted" by forceps delivery; almost half of all birthing mothers were given oxytocics. These percentages indicate that birthing women in this hospital were affected by technologically oriented procedures that may have overwhelmed their own efforts to give birth naturally and without interference. And the figures for this hospital are actually lower than for most private and community hospitals.

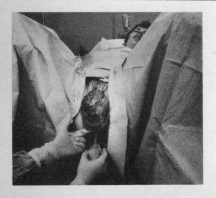

TABLE 1 1973

	Deliveries	Episiotomies	Forceps	Spontaneous Labor	Stimulated Labor	Induced Labor	C-Section
January	197	153	68	62	84	34	17
February	183	141	63	57	74	30	22
March	197	161	60	69	92	21	15
April	177	137	57	97	57	18	23
May	219	152	71	72	101	18	28
June	180	133	60	78	62	14	26
July	189	151	56	60	90	19	20
August	165	142	54	39	90	20	8
September	192	145	47	62	90	22	18
October	222	154	45	52	110	31	29
November	195	144	48	83	84	28	17
December	197	154	48	44	98	29	26
	2,313	1,773	629	775	1,032	284	249
Average:	192.75	147.75	52.42	64.58	86	23.67	20.75
		77%	27%	34%	45%	12%	11%

An obstetrical nurse with ten years' experience in a major hospital (1,200 beds) in St. Louis, Missouri, states that *all* of the patients at her hospital undergo fetal monitoring during labor, even "natural childbirth mothers," who are common at the institution. Seventy to 80 per cent of all its mothers receive at least one paracervical block. Demerol is practically routine in the first stage of labor. "Natural childbirth mothers" usually receive at least one injection (50 mg.) of Demerol, plus one paracervical block. At least 90 per cent of all mothers receive episiotomies, and the low-forceps rate for first-time mothers is at least 60 per cent!

Obviously, birth's machine age is upon us. This technological merry-go-round is not about to slow down and stop just because each interference in normal birth is questioned by mothers. Doctors quickly point out that with the advancement of technology, and with the increased skills of obstetricians and hospital attendants in using that technology, these risks are being reduced every year. They can prove statistically that in hospitals where medical technology has been properly (although unnecessarily) administered in normal birth, the rates of infant mortality and infant damage have gone down.

It will take many years before the risks of medical interference in normal birth are reduced to the extent that *all* hospitals, *all* doctors, and *all* technicians can be trusted to use this technology wisely and well. In the meantime, since hospitals are not willing to release information on their practices to the public, and since many doctors themselves are not fully skilled in the use of the newest tech-

---

Modern science has removed the medieval horrors of childbirth. The difficult labor need no longer end in tragedy. But in the technological advance, the uncomplicated labor has been neglected.
      —JODI FREDIANI, Birth Book

nology, how can a pregnant woman know which doctor and which hospital are best for her?

Even more important, is technologically controlled safety what we really want? Is it worth the effort to create a machine-age birth if it means that even our bodies are turned into machines? If the technological merry-go-round is not about to slow down, then where is it heading? Toward a more sophisticated package of combined interference? Or toward what may be "the safest birth in the world," the ultimate medical intervention, the standard Caesarean birth?

Traditionally, the medical reasons for performing a Caesarean operation have been few and specific: cephalopelvic disproportion (fetal head too large for the opening of the pelvic bones); organic problems of the mother (such as diabetes and toxemia); placenta previa (the placenta descends before the fetus); elderly first mothers (usually over 35 years); malpresentation (such as a difficult breech); prolapse of the umbilical cord. Today, uterine inertia (slowing of contractions until they are ineffective), prolonged labor, and fetal distress and previous C-sections are also reasons for doctors to elect to perform Caesareans.

Basically, the operation consists of an incision through the abdominal wall and through the wall of the uterus, where the fetus is removed manually. Twenty years ago this operation was considered dangerous to mother and infant, and doctors were advised to avoid the procedure unless medical evidence indicated that mothers could not be delivered safely any other way. These mothers comprised

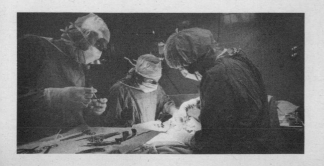

only 2 to 4 per cent of the birthing population and, in terms of *medically required* Caesarean births, that percentage is still accurate today.

During 1951–63, the Obstetrical Statistical Cooperative reported a Caesarean rate of 4.7 per cent out of 404,227 births. In the late 1950s, rates for Caesareans from major medical institutions in the country showed a range of 4.7 to 7.8 per cent. Already, then, some doctors were beginning to regard the C-section as an elective method of their own choosing rather than a mandatory procedure based on medical evidence.

Today statistics have shown that the rates of perinatal mortality of infants delivered by Caesarean have gone down, and many doctors have come to regard the operation as "safe" for mother *and* baby. *Williams Obstetrics* even goes so far as to declare, "In modern obstetric practice there are virtually no contraindications to Caesarean section, provided the proper operation is selected." The authors also suggest that although in the past fetal distress per se did not provide enough medical evidence to warrant the performance of Caesarean, today "there is an increasing tendency to resort to abdominal delivery in the face of fetal distress manifested by a slow or irregular fetal heart rate and the passage of meconium." While the Caesarean rate has risen steadily in the United States over the past fifteen to twenty years as its techniques have improved, it is only in the last few years that it has begun to soar.

Up-to-date statistics are difficult to obtain from major hospitals across the country, but the most conservative estimates of the average rate of Caesareans in the United

---

The business of having a baby now in an ordinary hospital is an expensive and frequently impersonal experience.
—GEORGE CUNNINGHAM, M.D., *Chief of Bureau of Maternal and Child Health, California*

States today range from 10 to 15 per cent, far above the "advisable" rate twenty years ago, and far higher than the rate in Holland today of 2 to 4 per cent. As Table I shows, the rate of Caesareans in one large metropolitan hospital during 1973 was up to 11 per cent. Author and natural childbirth authority Elisabeth Bing believes the national rate is even higher: "I would guess, from speaking to nurses and doctors all over the country—Ohio, Florida, North Carolina, West Virginia, New York, New England —that it is 12 to 20 per cent of all deliveries in many parts of the country." In numerous community hospitals in California, where the fetal heart monitor has recently been introduced, the Caesarean rate has risen to 20–25 per cent in 1975. According to a nurse on the obstetrical team of a large teaching hospital in New York City, the rate of C-sections for one month in 1974 was an unbelievable 50 per cent.

Could we be heading toward an era of the *routine* Caesarean birth? Why not? If the medical community establishes that surgical removal of the fetus is safer than other methods of birth, doctors may come to regard the Caesarean as the newest and best device available to "bring those U.S. mortality statistics down." The Caesarean places the natural process totally within the specialist's domain and relieves the birthing woman of any effort, indeed any responsibility, in her own birth. With an elective C-section there is no need for doctor and patient to "quibble" about the value of induction, oxytocics, monitors, drugs, forceps, or episiotomies. The mother herself, after enduring the trauma and pain of recovery follow-

In each of my last classes, two out of every ten mothers have ended up with a Caesarean.
      —BETTY CAHILL, *childbirth teacher*

ing major abdominal surgery, may find the Caesarean so quick and easy that she will tell her friends it was as simple as having tonsils or an appendix removed. As will be discussed in the next chapter, mother and child pay a price for this ultimate intervention that may far outweigh the value of Caesarean in the long run, but from the doctor's viewpoint, if it takes a Caesarean to insure *safety*, what else is there to worry about?

A second and perhaps more insidious reason for this shift to Caesarean is the mounting evidence that fetal distress may result in brain damage in the baby. This condition may take many diverse forms and may be categorized in many different ways, but under any name it has become a major problem in America during recent years. At the American Medical Association convention in June 1974, neurologists estimated that as much as 5 to 10 per cent of *all* children "show some signs of abnormal brain activity." According to Dr. Newell Kephart, director of the Achievement Center for children at Purdue University, learning and behavior problems resulting from minor and undetected brain injury have been discovered in as many as 15 to 20 per cent of *all* school-age children. The National March of Dimes estimates that each year a quarter of a million babies will suffer from birth defects, many of which affect the infant's brain. The National Association for Retarded Children states that six million children and adults in the U.S. are mentally retarded, and that a hundred thousand more will suffer from this condition each year. According to Herman K. Goldberg, M.D., and Gilbert B. Schiffman, "it is estimated that 20 to 40 per cent

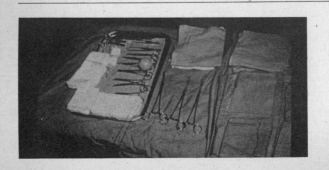

of our school population is handicapped by reading problems," many of which may be related to neurological impairment at birth.

Some of these brain-related problems fall under the category of "minimal brain dysfunction," a generic term used to cover a multitude of behavioral and learning difficulties that are seldom evident before children reach school age. Those who suffer from such a condition are often "hyperkinetic"—restless, noisy, overactive, and excitable children who simply cannot calm down and whose attention span is extremely short. As Carol Jean H. Goulder, a nurse and school psychologist, describes it:

> We are not talking about dull, normal, or retarded children when we speak of minimal brain dysfunction, and it doesn't necessarily mean "minimal" if you live with it or work with it. These children are not below normal intelligence, nor are they emotionally disturbed. They are average or above average in intelligence with some central nervous system damage or dysfunction. And the children who have it grow up to be adults who *still* have it.

So far the only treatment available for minimal brain dysfunction is an amphetaminelike drug, which in children has a reverse effect and depresses rather than stimulates activity. This drug may calm children down, but it also dulls their learning capacity.

Statistics on minimal brain dysfunction are difficult to isolate, because the problem has become so widespread that often children who are simply spoiled or unruly—or in robust good health—are labeled by their distraught

---

If you just want to have a rest and vacation when you have a baby, why not try the hotel industry. They're better equipped and cheaper for the purpose than a hospital.
—LESTER HAZELL, *author and mother*

teachers, doctors, and parents as "hyperkinetic." However, conservative estimates of the condition now indicate that minimal brain dysfunction is evident in about one out of every twenty school-age children in the United States today.

So it is a very real medical and social problem to obstetricians who are faced with the *possibility* of oxygen deprivation and brain damage resulting from signs of fetal distress. According to Elisabeth Bing, "it is my feeling that doctors are so worried about minimal brain dysfunction in children that they are performing Caesarean sections more frequently as a method of choice, in order to protect the baby from a prolonged or difficult labor and delivery."

Here again the medical tendency is to correct the problem *at birth*, while other evidence indicates that the solution may be found long before labor ever begins. Instead of examining the entire pregnancy, beginning with American dietary habits, prenatal care, and consumption of over-the-counter drugs, alcohol, and cigarettes; and instead of investigating drugs and other interferences in labor, many doctors are looking instead at the woman's body. They are beginning to express open doubt that modern woman is actually capable of delivering a healthy child without their help.

In the past, doctors pointed to unpredictable irregularities of the birth process that will cause brain damage; today they are saying that the natural process, *even when normal*, may be responsible for infant brain damage. During the lengthy first and second stages of labor, they say, the baby's head may receive a great deal of "battering," either from

---

It would be great to have maternity homes, with big soft chairs and double beds in every room. A woman could come in early in her labor and fix

uterine contractions themselves or by the "tight squeeze" of the mother's perineum (unless an early episiotomy has been performed). "The longer the fetus must endure such pressure," one doctor has said, "the greater are its risks to the brain." And in his reasoning the best protection for the baby's brain is to get the infant out of its mother's body as fast as possible.

It *seems* logical, then, for some doctors to conclude that medical science can do better for the unborn child by performing an early Caesarean—and the earlier the better, they say, because mothers recover more slowly from surgery if they have been allowed to exhaust themselves in labor. But an early Caesarean presupposes that the doctor's decision will be made on the basis of unconfirmed evidence so that surgery can be performed when the laboring woman is only three or four centimeters dilated. Thus a Caesarean may be scheduled if the physician merely *suspects* that a woman will have a long (what *he* determines is long) or difficult (*his* estimate of difficult) labor and delivery. As mentioned earlier, one doctor, while acknowledging the many disadvantages of the fetal heart monitor, has nevertheless stated that even a 25 per cent chance of accuracy from tracings indicating distress is enough for him to perform an immediate Caesarean. Many woman are prepared well ahead of time to expect a C-section by doctors anxious to avert possible trouble in labor or delivery. They are thus even less prepared to handle the normal sensations of a lengthy labor than the average woman, and may literally shout to have a Caesarean early in the first stage of labor.

In hospitals where technology has been carefully (even

the room up for herself. I love fixing the room where my baby is going to be born.
—KENDRA DAY, *mother, after two home births*

though unnecessarily) applied in normal birth, statistics have shown that rates of Caesarean have gone down. Such hospitals are expensive and difficult to find, however; the majority of American women today give birth in community or teaching hospitals where Caesarean rates are definitely on the increase and where risks from technological interferences in normal birth are still very much in evidence. Many doctors hold up technologically perfect hospitals as models for the future—havens of safety for pregnant women who are seeking the most sophisticated scientific care and the least personal responsibility.

Thus, the "ideal" of a risk-free birth is the underlying concept in the practice of obstetrics in American today. Madeleine Shearer speaks for many of her colleagues—and for many pregnant women—when she states her concern over the way American birth is directed:

> The question is whether doctors can really promise every woman a living baby every time. Today in the United States, physicians are attempting to do what every society around the world has traditionally viewed as the power belonging solely to God—to promise that *all* babies will survive birth in health. It's only an implied promise so far. But when you talk to your doctor and he tells you about the wonderful medical advances that have been made and you're confronted by the infallible coat of armor he wears, that is exactly what he is promising you. The other side of the coin is that the same doctor will tell you all the dire complications which will arise if you do not do exactly what he says.

So part of the doctor's heroic infallibility is rooted in

Once you step on the merry-go-round of machines and western medicine, it's tough to step off.
—RICH QUINT, M.D., *pediatrician*

the premise that our technology can save us from all risks of the natural process of birth. Well, suppose it can: suppose for a moment that all American hospitals can somehow perfect all technological interference to the extent that all pregnant women could be provided with a risk-free birth, either by means of routine Caesarean or by a combination of medical interventions in vaginal birth. What would be the consequences to the average pregnant woman?

In the first place, she would be so caught up in the technological merry-go-round that the success of her birth would be totally dependent upon the experts and machines around her, and not at all upon her own body and her own will. Secondly, such use of statistics and technology would further obliterate her own individuality so that even the slightest differences in the progress of her birth (and all normal births have variations) would be considered abnormal and would lead to further interference. She would be told, not advised, that if labor is late she will be induced; that if she appears uneasy, drugs are required; that if labor is too long, a Caesarean will be performed; that episiotomies are standard procedure (they almost are already); that forceps will probably be used; that oxytocics will be given throughout the process; and that she will not see her baby for as much as twenty-four hours after birth.

In this "ideal" context, woman would give up her responsibility so totally that she would become a willing prisoner to hospital technology for the sake of insuring absolute safety for her baby and herself. If that is what we want—if total, medically defined and technologically controlled safety is more important to us than any other factor in birth—then we may be assured that obstetrical science will give us this "ideal" at some time in the future.

For many women, of course, such an "ideal" is an absurd and illogical solution, especially since birth needs *no* outside interference for 90 per cent of all women. Yet an examination of the present hospital birth procedure reveals that in terms of decision making, control, and overall management of birth, woman is not very far from being a "willing prisoner" already. How often does she know about her doctor's ability to assist without interference in a normal (not emergency) birth? How many doctors take the time to advise her of the risks of induction, monitoring, analgesics, or anesthetics? How often is she asked if oxytocics can be used to speed up her labor? How many hospitals allow her to get out of bed during labor, to take food and drink, to forego stirrups and handcuffs during delivery so that she can manage delivery by herself? And how many institutions or physicians ask her whether she wishes to be separated from her infant for up to twenty-four hours after birth?

Some doctors will admit in all candor that actually there is no reason why the birthing woman should be consulted about the use of medical interferences in her birth. How could a woman, they ask, know more about

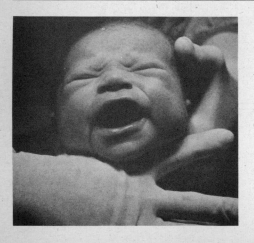

oxytocics or forceps than her doctor? Why would a mother want to challenge a doctor's expertise when he obviously has her safety and the safety of her child in mind? As Elisabeth Bing puts it:

> The mother who goes to the hospital to have her baby is in an impossible situation, really. If a doctor says he's doing something for the safety of her baby, there is nothing she can say. Once she is told a procedure is for her baby, she can offer no argument. If you were in a hospital and your obstetrician said, "Look, we are a little worried about your baby. We want to put you on a fetal heart monitor," what would you say? I don't think a mother really has a choice.

Obviously, no matter what the medical profession tells her, each woman does have choices, values, and rights. Since she is responsible not only for the outcome of the birth but the future life of her baby, she alone must make the decisions which affect not only the health but the relationship she has with her child.

7
Reunion of Mother and Child

Reunion of
Mother and Child

ALMOST FROM BIRTH we seem to put distance between us. We do not approve of babies' sleeping with their mothers, and even breast-fed babies are likely to be accorded a very limited patch of bare maternal skin. Our babies develop the senses of sight and hearing very early, but learn much less about touch and smell and the rhythm of their own hearts and breathing as this relates to the heartbeat and breathing of others. We have even invented an artificial soother, in the form of a steady sound tuned to the maternal heartbeat, to quiet little orphans or babies in hospitals who have no mother's heartbeat to attend to. Here again we have advanced a long way in making the world a safer place for babies; their own beds with their own sheets are easier to keep scrupulously clean; in their own beds they are in no danger of being overlaid by a mother lying in a too deep sleep; in a high crib or playpen no dog or older child can get at them. Hung high in the kitchen doorway, they don't get under the refrigerator or close to the stove. Where a mother is all alone, sometimes with two or three quite small children, these aids are invaluable; she could not possibly do without them. But inasmuch as they substitute sound and sight for touch the child is subjected to a different kind of loneliness. He comes to fret at the walls of the playpen that fence him in, as he would not have fretted in his mother's arms.

—MARGARET MEAD, *Pregnancy, Birth and the Newborn Baby* (1972)

It was six days after birth before I saw my child, because of difficulties he had. And it's taken three years to build our relationship.
—HELEN SWALLOW, *mother*

The bond between a mother and her child begins long before the contractions of labor start. Even before birth the mother's protective instincts appear. At any sign of danger her arms move to encircle her belly and shield it from harm. As her pregnancy draws to a conclusion she finds it difficult to remember herself when she was not pregnant and impossible to imagine what it will be like to be separated from the child inside her. She, her child, and the process of nature are at one. And the strength of this early attachment to her child does not even depend upon having seen or touched or heard it. While nature insures the attachment between a mother and child, an attachment which will satisfy deep emotional needs in the mother and insure the survival of the infant, there are critical points in the course of this developing relationship at which the bond can be either strengthened or damaged.

The baby, floating in its sea of amniotic fluid during the first months of pregnancy, begins to develop growing sensitivity to its warm, watery, intrauterine environment. It is believed that the fetus can hear sounds and feel vibrations through the fluid surrounding it, and that it can hear and react to touch—either by the mother's hand, absently rubbing the top of her swollen belly during the last month of pregnancy, or by the movement of the amniotic fluid when she walks, laughs, sits down, or sleeps. When the bag of waters breaks and the walls of the uterus begin to expel the infant rhythmically from its nine-month home, a natural trauma begins. The baby is propelled through a sequence of intensely uncomfortable changes in its environment: squeezing, pounding, pulsating, turbulent movements, every one a shock to its system. Physically and neurologically immature, the infant is brought into the world totally naked and stripped of comfort. It is in this sensitive state that the newborn baby begins independent life with its first breath. The shock of birth leaves it ripe for its first human contact, wide open to a new world of experiences.

Long before man ever attempted to improve upon the birth process, nature provided the pattern for the mother-child bond upon which the infant's survival depends. Placed directly upon its mother's belly while still connected to her placenta (by the unsevered umbilical cord), the baby finds the nipple and begins its first suckling activity. The mere licking of the mother's nipple triggers the nerves in her breast to alert the uterus that the baby is out and safe. In immediate response, the uterus clamps down to begin to expel the placenta. Meanwhile, the suckling action of the baby stimulates its breathing and heat productivity. Most important, the newborn finds peace and calm in direct contact with its mother's warm body. This moment of security is the first it has known since the onset of labor.

The natural position a new mother assumes when she holds, cuddles, and nurses her infant is a universal symbol for warmth, protection, and motherly love. Mother and child present an almost religious presence as they repeat the circular position of their first contact. The baby suckles; its free hand plays with its mother's lips, as she fondles its foot and her other arm cradles and supports her child. In this wordless interaction the direct contact of their eyes creates an aura of privacy and intimacy around them.

A friend of mine had rooming-in with her baby. And every night she was in the hospital she'd draw the curtain around her bed and take that baby into bed to sleep with her.

—ANONYMOUS MOTHER

All of this physical intimacy has a very definite bearing on the long-range relationship of mother and child, as it reinforces their deepening bond. But what happens to this process of bonding when medical science interferes with birth for the sole purpose of insuring safety and thereby alters the environment for bonding?

When labor is artificially induced, the protective cushion of the bag of waters is suddenly destroyed, and the baby feels itself pounded by the contracting action of the uterine walls. If labor has been induced early, this pounding may last several hours before the baby begins to move down the birth canal. If a fetal heart monitor is introduced internally, a metal screw is inserted into the baby's head. Drugs may slow down the blood-gas exchange from the mother *and* slow down the birth process so that the baby will be subjected to even more pounding. Oxytocics may suddenly speed the contractions up and increase their impact upon the baby. The metal spoons of forceps close around the infant's head, or the vacuum cup sucks the head hard and it is then tugged out of the birth canal. If an episiotomy has been performed, the baby may be unceremoniously pulled out into the world. Finally, instead of feeling warm skin against its own as it is placed directly at its mother's breast, the baby is placed in an artificial warmer and left to cope with independent life in strange surroundings, alone and apart from human touch with the one person who knows its needs best, its mother.

The newborn infant must be tagged, footprinted, and *shown* to the mother so that she will have no doubt the child is hers. Because the hospital is undeniably the center of many kinds of disease, and because newborns are extremely vulnerable to infection from innumerable sources, the baby must then be whisked off to its own bed in the nursery, there to listen to the cries of other babies in the harsh fluorescent lighting and wait for the time the hospital staff decides it should be brought to its mother.

The cold temperature (65–68°) of the delivery room itself provides the initial reason for immediate removal of the newborn infant, whose system is shocked by air temperature many degrees below its own, to an artificial warmer where heat lamps will shield it from the cold. As Tibor Heim, a pediatrician from Hungary, states in *Clinical Obstetrics and Gynecology* (September 1971): "Even if the baby's body seems to be adequately dressed and blanketed, the thermal impulses of inhaled cool air and cold radiating surfaces of the surroundings can simultaneously exert a considerable metabolic demand on the newborn." This means that in most hospitals the mother cannot hold her baby directly after birth. Nor will breastfeeding, doctors feel, stimulate the baby's heat and respiratory productivity enough to overcome the intense cold. However, according to Celeste R. Nagel Phillips, a registered nurse who has recently conducted a study on immediate separation of mother and newborn:

> More and more mothers are requesting to hold their infants or nurse their infants on the delivery table. Also, more and more new mothers are requesting rooming-in and are reluctant to leave their babies in a metal crib away from their sides for extended periods of time, beginning with birth itself. . . . This new breed of mothers

---

When the infant is first presented to the mother, she is asked to check the information on the identification band. The sex of the infant is shown to the mother. Subsequently, each time the infant is brought to the mother, the nurse

will no longer accept the answer from a nurse that her actions are "hospital policy" or "doctor's orders". . . . However, the nurses' responsibility for maintaining the infant's body heat has not changed.

Whether this "new breed" of mothers is aware of it or not, the situation they have created is a beautiful example of weighing quality and safety as equal factors. For some women, the importance of establishing immediate contact with their young, and of providing immediate nurture, is more important than possible risk to the baby from the cold delivery room. Furthermore, when they insist that the baby be laid nude on the mother's bare belly or breast and both of them covered with a warm blanket, before the umbilical cord has been severed, they feel they are minimizing the risks to safety (because skin-to-skin contact is the best way to protect the baby from heat loss) while maximizing the advantages of quality. Meanwhile, however, the doctor and hospital staff—who feel *they* are there primarily to insure safety—believe the mother is indulging in an emotional whim that may endanger the health of her child. For them, the mother's body is a second-rate substitute for the modern electric infant warmer and it is in the machine that they place their trust.

Until recently there have been few studies on the bond that exists between human infant and mother at birth. For many years, however, studies of animals have revealed the nature of this bonding phenomenon, and it is worthwhile for the pregnant woman to look first at the animal world and see if there might be parallels there that will pertain in a real way to her own experience.

---

speaks the mother's name and the sex of the infant and waits for the mother to confirm the identification of the infant.
—STANDARDS AND RECOMMENDATIONS FOR
HOSPITAL CARE OF NEWBORN INFANTS,
American Academy of Pediatrics

In his research on comparative obstetrics, Dutch zoologist Cornelius Naaktgeboren has found that among mammals the process of licking the newborn helps to stimulate the infant's breathing and also teaches the mother to recognize and accept her relationship to her young.

> Not only does [she] clean the young animal and stimulate respiration, but [the licking] forms an integral part of the very important mother-offspring relationship to follow: the [mother] learns to recognize [her] young from the scent of amniotic fluid. Only shortly before or shortly after giving birth does an animal feel the desire to lick a newly born offspring.

In this way nature assures that the infant will not be abandoned by its mother. Naaktgeboren notes, however, that if an interference were to occur during this licking process—if a lamb were to be taken from its mother just after birth, for example—the entire mother-infant relationship would be lost.

> Once the lamb is dry, it will never be licked by a ewe. Even its own mother would reject it if it were dried by a towel and brought to her a few hours after birth.

Marshall Klaus and John Kennell, professors of pediatrics at Case Western Reserve University School of Medicine, and perhaps the most prominent authorities on mother and child bonding, note also that this special period of recognition occurs immediately after birth.

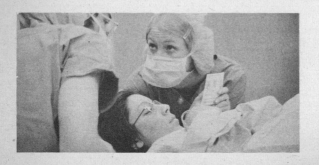

Goats establish stable and specific mother-infant bonds in the first five minutes after birth. If the kid is in contact with the mother during this short period it will be recognized, accepted, fed and protected. But if the kid is removed during the initial five-minute period and returned to the mother later, she will often reject it by butting and kicking, and will refuse to nurture or protect it.

California midwife Raven Lang notes in *Birth Book* (1972) that baby geese form a close attachment to their mother immediately upon hatching, which causes them to follow and stay close to her. If the eggs are hatched in an artificial incubator, however, the goslings "will follow the first large moving object that they see. They begin to relate to this object as their mother. So complete is this process, that if, after a few days, the goslings are given a choice between their real mother and the moving object to which they were imprinted, their choice is always the moving object."

Lang states that the process can be just as definitive if it orginates from auditory influences alone. A turkey hen who hears the sounds of her young chicks as the eggs hatch becomes imprinted to the sound alone, she says. "The introduction of a stuffed raccoon (a natural enemy) to the vicinity of the nest will move the hen to fight it. However, if a tape of the chick sounds is hidden within the body of the fake raccoon, the hen will spread her wings and accept the raccoon as one of her own."

How do these studies of animals pertain to human birth? For Raven Lang an event occurred at the birth of her own child that emphasized the importance of early and un-

broken bonding between mother and child. Undrugged at birth, and straining to catch a glimpse of her baby's head as it appeared between her legs, she heard its first cry—a cry she remembers "as clearly this minute as then." In line with hospital procedure, the baby was immediately separated from its mother and taken to the nursery, and Raven was wheeled to the maternity ward.

Each time the babies were brought to their mothers [the nurses] would bring the babies first to the mothers who were at the far end of the maternity ward. I was in the room closest to the nursery, and so I received my baby last. Each time I saw him he was sleeping or quietly looking around. Later when the nursing shift changed I heard the nursery door open and a crying baby being brought out to the mother. My uterus clamped down as it had when I heard my newborn's first cry. My breasts tingled and there was a definite gush of blood from my uterus which came from the contraction caused by the sound of the crying baby. When I realized that this was the first baby being brought out I thought it must be a baby belonging to someone else and would be going down to the other end of the ward, but with another sound of that cry my uterus again clamped down and I felt complete bewilderment and a sense of demand for my baby. Within an instant he was being brought into me by a different nurse. My body had known this child to be mine. . . .

Had I been drugged and or unconscious, the information that I received at the time of birth would certainly not have registered as acutely or at all, and as a result I would have had less instinctual knowledge of my baby. I feel that when a woman first sees and hears her child at the moment of birth—which is another kind of con-

I tried to nurse at home and my son took one look at me and screamed the next two days. He'd gotten used to rubber nipples and formula in the hospital. A public health nurse suggested putting

sciousness—that she is bound to her baby already in a capacity beyond what I think we are willing to admit. I feel this is part of our suvival.

This "other kind of consciousness" exists in a way that is not intellectually acknowledged by either mother or obstetrician, and therefore cannot be evaluated against scientific data about such objective matters as medical risk, safety, and health. Nevertheless, it exists all the same, and the patterns of behavior it produces during the process of bonding have been shown to have lasting effects on the *quality* of the mother-child relationship.

It is only in recent years that these effects have been studied in an effort to measure them in human birth through the work of Marshall Klaus. Perhaps his most dramatic findings occurred in 1970, when Klaus and his associates filmed the first contact of two groups of mothers with their newborns. One group of twelve mothers had their healthy, full-term infants undressed in bed beside them. Nine mothers of premature babies had their first real contacts through incubator walls. Mothers were filmed unobtrusively from a distance and were given privacy during the contacts in an attempt to discover if patterns exist in the ways mothers explore their newborns.

Klaus observed obvious differences in the way mothers in each group touched and handled their infants. Mothers of full-term babies showed an orderly and predictable pattern of contact. They began by softly touching the baby's arms and legs with the soft pads of their fingertips. After four to eight minutes they began to massage the

a little honey on a rubber nipple and placing it over my nipple. I did and he went for it immediately. From then on nursing went fine.
—ANONYMOUS MOTHER

baby's torso and head, using the palm of one hand in a smooth, circular motion. These mothers also positioned themselves *en face*—that is, face to face, with their eyes meeting their infants' eyes fully on the same vertical planes. All mothers in this group showed a great fascination with their babies' eyes. Mothers of incubator babies, however, showed greatly altered behavior. Time-lapsed films showed that these mothers' movements appeared jerky and awkward, and they seemed to poke at their babies' arms and legs in a random and confused fashion.

Klaus believes that nude skin-to-skin contact and *en face* eye contact foster the healthy development of maternal attachment. He states that even at this early stage babies are able to focus on coordinated movement (a fact that mothers have for years been told does not exist), and that *in the first hour of life* a newborn baby will follow objects in ways that it cannot do as easily for many days. Because of this, he suggests that mother, baby, and father be left completely alone immediately after birth, and that the drops of silver nitrate routinely administered to the newborn's eyes at birth to prevent gonorrhea blindness be delayed until the mother and child have established eye contact and bonding has begun. "The attachment of infant to mother is exquisitely important," Klaus says. "An infant's survival is strongly related to the strength of this attachment."

Klaus also believes that this special attachment is

In the hospital the nurses would bring me gauze pads and say, "This is sterile water. Before you nurse your son, please see that you clean your nipples." As if I would contaminate him.

—ANONYMOUS MOTHER

similar to close relationships between adults, and that most people form such intimate bonds with only a few persons during their entire lives.

In another study, to test the long-range effect of this attachment period immediately after birth, Klaus observed 28 mothers of similar backgrounds, all of whom had delivered healthy babies. The 14 mothers in the control group underwent traditional hospital procedures for initial mother-baby contact: each was allowed a brief glimpse of her baby on the delivery table, contact after six to twelve hours, and half-hour visits every four hours for bottle feedings. With the second group Klaus extended the period of contact by a total of only sixteen hours, beginning from the moment the baby was born until the end of the third day. These mothers were allowed a full hour's contact within the first three hours after delivery, and an extra five hours every afternoon. None of the women were instructed by nurses or attendants in the care of their babies; all were left in privacy to follow their own maternal instincts.

One month later, Klaus and his associates examined all twenty-eight babies, interviewed the mothers, and filmed them during feedings. He noted that "the extended-contact mothers were more reluctant to leave their infants with someone else, usually stood and watched during the exam, showed greater soothing behavior and engaged in significantly more eye-to-eye contact and fondling." Klaus con-

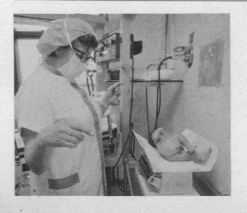

cluded that "a special attachment period in the human mother" exists that is "similar to that described in animals."

To find out if these differences had lasting effect, a year later Klaus and his team of researchers observed the mothers in a followup study. None of the researchers knew about the previous study's results, thus reducing the chance of preconceived findings. Again, the same striking contrasts were noted.

> The extended-contact mothers were more preoccupied with their babies. During the physical examination, extended-contact mothers spent more time at the tableside assisting and soothing their infants when they cried and were more likely to kiss their babies.

These same differences were noted as much as three years after the birth.

Klaus noted that it was especially "surprising" that given "the multitude of factors that influence maternal behavior" (such as the mother's genetic and cultural background, her relationship with her husband and family, the planning and the course of her pregnancy, and her own mothering as an infant), *just sixteen extra hours* in the first three days should have such visible and lasting effects.

New studies are now being conducted at Case Western Reserve and at Stanford Medical Center to evaluate the effects of early separation of mothers and their premature infants. The early-contact group of mothers can place

---

It's hard for first mothers. You are feeling your way and not all that confident. So it's hard to evaluate all the opinions of all those confident-speaking professionals and think for yourself.
        —KENDRA DAY, *mother of two*

their hands in the isolettes and give their babies simple care within the first five days after birth and thereafter throughout hospitalization. A second group of mothers have only visual contact with their babies through a glass-enclosed nursery, and are unable to touch, smell, or hear their babies for the first twenty days. In a third group, handling is delayed for thirty to forty days. A control group of mothers from similar backgrounds with full-term infants is also being observed. All of these mothers and children will be followed for 22–42 months to see if altered maternal attachment produces differences in the children's development. Preliminary results already show that months after discharge from the hospital, late-contact mothers hold their babies awkwardly, cuddle and change their position less often, and are not as skillful in feeding as early-contact mothers. Although all of the 100 mothers had stated their intention to keep their babies, some infants of the late-contact mothers have been given up for adoption.

Klaus and his associates feel that the "battered child syndrome" may be one ultimate effect of early separation of mother and child.

> The battered child syndrome provides the most dramatic evidence of a disorder of mothering. . . . Although multiple factors contribute to this problem (such as the mother's own rearing) early separation may be a factor. The formation of close affectional ties may remain permanently incomplete if extended separation occurs.

Marshall Klaus is a pioneer in the study of early mother-baby separation, and like Kaaktgeboren he sees patterns among all mammals:

> The knowledge that there is a sensitive period shortly after birth during which brief periods of partial or complete separation may drastically distort a mother animal's feeding and care of her infant would lead a caretaker or naturalist to be extremely cautious about any intervention in the period after birth.

> Observations in humans suggest that affectional bonds are forming before delivery, but that they are fragile and may easily be altered in the first days of life.

Mothers have always felt an overwhelming instinct to hold, nurture, and protect their babies immediately and continuously after birth. But dazed by the consequences of medical interference, and faced with admonitions from doctors and efficient hospital procedures, the birthing woman releases her baby to the care of experts who seem to know what is best for her child. Indeed, it is difficult for a woman to insist on her choice when she is totally immobile, "opened up" for the world to see, and struggling

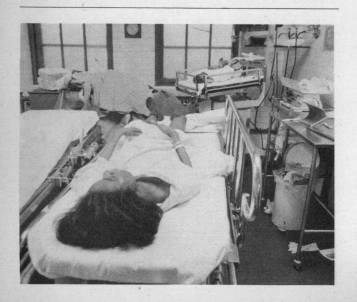

to regain a measure of dignity after the long hospital ordeal.

The delivery table is no place for woman to fight for her rights. But aligned with her mate, sympathetic doctors, and others of the "new breed" of mothers, she has the power to move mountains of technological equipment and procedures to preserve her absolute role as mother in the birth process, if she only knew it.

Doctors say their interferences do not physically harm the baby but are, in fact, designed to help the baby by insuring its safety through preventive procedures. Every year medical science moves another step forward in quantifying data, perfecting technology, and teaching new skills to obstetricians, nurses, and technicians to remove all risk from the birth process. And every year the bond between mother and child is more and more endangered. Such gross alterations of the fetal and maternal environments must be reexamined continually in light of their traumatic consequences, not only to the laboring woman and to the unborn child, but also to the relationship between them.

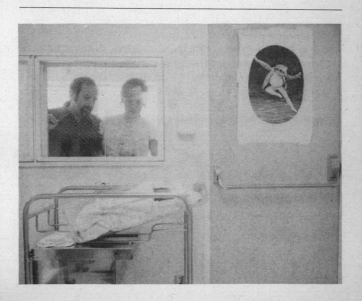

A Doctor Talks
about Birth and Death

Excerpts from a talk with William A. Silverman, M.D., former professor of Pediatrics at Columbia University College of Physicians and Surgeons, and Director of its premature nursery for over 20 years. During this time Dr. Silverman was involved with the development of technical methods for present-day intensive care of newborn infants.

IT IS MY BELIEF that we are limiting more and more of our experience by taking the problems of birth and death and dealing with them exclusively in institutions. How unusual death is now in our experience. In previous times death was a common occurrence. It was very visible when it happened at home, and so it was not strange in any way. When people actually buried their dead, death wasn't so mysterious. The minute death became "professionalized" and took place in institutions, when professionals took the dead body and prepared and buried it, our whole connection with death was modified tremendously. Our fear has been heightened because death is now so foreign. It is not surprising that because death is so feared, we have developed elaborate medical life-support systems which are effective in postponing death. We, the professionals, are taking more and more of the experience away from those who are actually involved, namely the relatives and the community. They have been excluded. And, as you exclude them from the experience, they then shift more of the responsibility for all decisions over to the physician. Physicians want to make the decisions anyway because they feel they've got more knowledge. And, sadly, there's a punitive streak that often colors the situation. It's the paternalistic, authoritarian attitude: If you don't do as I say, then take the consequences and be damned!

Much of this is true of childbirth too. When birth occurs in the hospital it is mysterious and feared. In many

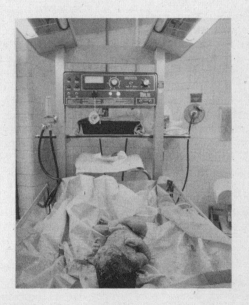

ways there is a "toilet" assumption at work: if you flush away messy unpleasantness or risk, you don't have to deal with it. But eventually you do pay the consequences. Technical advances in childbirth have been spectacular, but when all is said and done, it is the mother and father who have to live the rest of their lives with the results of decisions of technical experts. The whole system has had the effect of making sure we don't have to deal with life as it is. And life, after all, *is* messy. And it *is* risky.

There's no way of having a labor and delivery that are absolutely without risk. So the question is really how to define what the various risks are, to estimate the order of magnitude of different risks, and to compare these with an individual standard of benefit. Now the majority view today is that numbers are what really count: mortality statistics, damage statistics. These can be enumerated. The question is how to measure the numerical value of something like the effect of separation of mother and child, or the experiencing of all of birth (or death, for that matter); and these are not insignificant items. I think the price that has been paid for attempting to avoid all risk is a dehumanized birth.

The point is that we do not need blanket rules. In our plural society there are different value systems, and the standards of risk vs benefit in birth and death are not the same for everyone; this must be accepted. If, for example, some people want home birth, then part of the funds available for health care should be directed to providing services to them. With both birth and death we face the question of how far we are willing to go from the natural process just to protect us from risk. The agonizing experience of having to make difficult decisions is part of life. The whole quality of life today is interfered with because we attempt to avoid experiencing parts of life, and to lay down blanket rules about what is and what is not an acceptable risk.

8
Pain and Childbirth: The Doctor's Fallacy

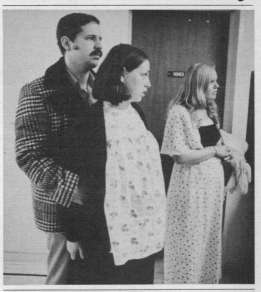

Pain and Childbirth:
The Doctor's Fallacy

THE POSSIBILITY of infant damage resulting from the use of anesthetics in childbirth is only one argument against drugs. A second is the enormous importance of a fully conscious mother and her complete participation in the entire birth process. Doctors tend to minimize this by stating that modern woman cannot endure pain in childbirth because she is not accustomed to hard work, her body is not strong enough, her pelvic cavity is not large enough, and her system is more dependent upon pain killers and tranquilizers today than ever before. Yet for all his kindly intentions, the American obstetrician who advocates drugs does much more than anesthetize a birthing woman to pain. He desensitizes her to the entire experience of childbirth, which is to her (not to him) one of the primary experiences in life. It is no wonder that psychiatrists have found that psychological problems in many women can be traced directly to their birth experiences. Women remember every detail of the birthing process, even when the experience has only been one of drugs and stupor. Women recall, even forty or fifty years afterward, the feeling of being drugged and of waking up to greet a strange child. The accompanying sense of loss, failure, or detachment may remain suppressed for a lifetime, never articulated but always *there* somehow, even if a

---

Even when I was a very little girl I remember hearing how much pain I'd given my mother during birth. Grandma joked that she never

woman recalls, "They gave me a caudal and I was glad. There's no sense going through all that pain. Besides, the doctor did a beautiful job."

What is pain? Webster's Third International Dictionary devotes an entire twelve-inch column to its definition. The word derives from the Latin *poena,* meaning penalty or punishment. It is significant that all the definitions mention emotional stress leading to avoidance behavior as a characteristic of pain:

> Physical or mental lack of well-being . . . ranges from mild discomfort or dull distress to acute, often unbearable agony . . . leading to avoiding reactions. . . . Usually produces a reaction of wanting to avoid, escape or destroy the causative factor and its effects. . . . The consequence of being injured or hurt physically or mentally or of some derangement of or lack of equilibrium in the physical or mental functions (as through disease). . . .

In other words, pain derives from an unwell state and is closely associated with disease and malfunction. The third definition in Webster's is specifically of the pain of childbirth:

> The protracted series of involuntary contractions of the uterus musculature that constitute the major factor in labor and are so often accompanied by considerable pain (e.g., her pains had begun).

Physiologically, the contractions of labor that produce the sensations we call pain are not unnatural, nor are they a sign of disease or ill health. They originate in the normal

---

wanted to see me because I'd caused my mother so much pain. I figure it must be terribly painful to have a baby for her to say such things.
—ANONYMOUS WOMAN

functioning of the uterus, which is merely hard at work expelling the infant from its nine-month home. Uterine contractions arise from the rhythmic shortening of the muscles that loop over the uterus and are attached to either side of the cervix. With each contraction, the cervix is pulled open, and with each release in between, a rich network of blood vessels pumps oxygenated blood into the fetus' system.

As early as the nineteenth century, the English philosopher William Dewees posited that excruciating pain in labor was unnatural and a product of civilization's emphasis on pathology. Nobody listened; the loud opposition of the multitudes who fervently believed that woman was suffering her just due for the sin of being woman effectively drowned him out. The multitudes, after all, had the Bible to speak for them:

> They shall be in pain as a woman that travaileth.
>
> ISAIAH 13:8
>
> And there appeared a great wonder in heaven; a woman clothed with the sun, and the moon under her feet, and upon her head a crown of twelve stars. And she being with child cried, travailing in birth, and pained to be delivered.
>
> REVELATIONS 12:1–2

In recent years scholars have disputed translations of the sixteenth-century Hebrew scriptures that continually refer to the Hebrew word "Etzev," originally translated as pain. They claim that the translation is inaccurate and probably resulted from the prevailing medieval association

---

At one point in my pains I remembered in the Bible where it said, "In sorrow she shall bring forth children." I know what that means. I said Thank you, Jesus, when it was over! Never, never

of birth with disease, danger, and death. If the translation is inaccurate, then the description of childbirth in the modern Bible is also an error of translation. A more accurate description would be labor, toil, or hard work.

If centuries of civilized development in language and culture have taught woman that pain exists in childbirth, she is hardly capable of refuting this knowledge alone, especially in the midst of the most strenuous, crisis-oriented period of her life. Certainly the doctor who advocates use of pain-killing drugs is acting out of sympathy, not condemnation, when he explains how far removed woman is from her ancestral sister who did not give much thought to pain. For he is not only criticizing womankind, but all of humankind for its overrefined lifestyles and its inability to deal with the harsher realities of natural functions. (It is ironic that he is guilty of the same failure he criticizes; natural childbirth is a phenomenon most doctors cannot or will not deal with, because if the mother breaks down—and he knows she will—the doctor's job is that much tougher. His own over-refined lifestyle in professional medicine presupposes that "the patient" remain at least partially unconscious so that the doctor can perform the specialty for which he was trained.)

But to condemn the entire human race for developing a heightened consciousness is only to increase the emphasis on pain. A more positive approach was taken by the late philosopher Alan Watts, who believed that refinement of the mind does not necessarily produce a weaker society, but a more sensitized one, and the result is an increased awareness of pain as well as pleasure.

---

do I want to do that again! My husband said, "Well, it's your fault. You gave the apple to Adam."

—EUNICE MITCHELL, *mother*

150

Unquestionably the sensitive human brain adds immeasurably to the richness of life. Yet for this we pay dearly, because the increase in over-all sensitivity makes us peculiarly vulnerable. . . . Sensitivity requires a high degree of softness and fragility—eyeballs, eardrums, taste buds, and nerve ends culminating in the highly delicate organism of the brain. These are not only soft and fragile, but also perishable.

Watts believed that, as a matter of survival, primitive cultures were more instinctively attuned to the physicality of the world around them than to the pleasurable effects of that world on their imaginations. Today we have almost given up on instinct altogether and have opted for the intellectual and emotional pleasures of our increasingly sophisticated technological world. Our imaginations soar and our progress speeds ahead, yet for every growth of consciousness or heightened sensitivity there is a consequence. "We cannot," in the words of Watts, "be more sensitive to pleasure without being more sensitive to pain." Away from the demanding work of survival, woman today has time to look at herself in labor, and the environment in which she gives birth greatly affects her perception. For 98 per cent of American women, this environment is the hospital, the very center of pain, disease, illness, and suffering. While at one time in history she did not have words to describe these most strenuous sensations, many generations later she began to find them uncomfortable. As civilization progressed and more generations passed, discomfort turned to pain and woman focused more and more intently on the uterine contractions working so hard to

When I began labor, it came fast and hard.
Terrible pains. Just before he was born the doctor
put a mask over my face and I went right to
sleep. I woke in the morning. The nurse appeared
at the door carrying him in the crook of her

expel her child. And her mother and her mother's mother, her friends and sisters, her church, her teachers, and even the very best obstetricians available all told her it would hurt like hell.

Any attempt to cultivate pleasure to the exclusion of pain is as impossible as returning to a condition of less sensitivity to the world within our bodies. So the modern curse is our inability to reinterpret as sensation what our language has clearly defined as pain, and our refusal to let go of what we remember as pain. The modern woman in labor is at a profound disadvantage in comparison with her ancient sister in that she fully remembers all that her culture has taught her about the dangers and the painfulness of birth. And she has lots of time, lying flat on her back in a labor bed, to magnify every sensation.

Woman gives birth, and she is one with the process. At the time that she is unable to separate herself from her body and watch herself giving birth, she is unable to understand it. The strong, sometimes violent contractions of labor throw woman back to her most instinctual and primitive state. And, like her ancestral sister, she is more likely to turn to someone nearby for assistance and comfort in childbirth than at any other time in her life. Traditionally she has turned to the midwife, a woman who brings to the process an empathy and sharing that only personal experience can provide. Since in America the midwife has been replaced by the doctor, woman now turns to man for assistance, reassurance, and knowledge of what is happening inside her during birth. But the doctor can hardly provide firsthand experience. Rather he will

arm. His eyes were open and huge. I wondered what he thought of me. "I have a surprise for you!" she said. She wouldn't bring him in because it was between feedings. I cried. I'd had my baby and I couldn't see him.
—Rose Galler, *mother, age 58*

offer knowledge based on study and observation, which woman drinks up in her need for confirmation that all is well. At every turn in pregnancy and in birth she sees him as the prime authority and relies less and less on her own knowledge about herself. Close to her at a time when she is extremely vulnerable, the physician offers his skill as a surgeon in rescuing woman from the mysteries of her body and in alleviating pain, suffering, and disease.

So the modern obstetrician's attitude toward birth is cautious to the extreme. When he looks at birth he is waiting for something to go wrong. Pain is the assumption from which he works, for the obstetrician not only believes in the truth of pain in labor, he subconsciously or consciously suggests this pain to the woman he assists. His image of woman is that of a fragile, emotional creature not meant to endure strenuous work or pain. He likens her to a child, and through excessive and misplaced sympathy, he seeks to spare this grown-up little girl any suffering in the course of birth. A kind doctor in 1974 has changed little in his attitude from a kind doctor two hundred years before, for both attempt to protect woman from the strongest sensations of her body. And woman loses in the attempt.

So it is that an obstetrician can easily misinterpret a woman's request for assistance as a desire to be relieved of the entire responsibility in birth, i.e., to be knocked out completely. A fine example of this kind of misunderstanding of the doctor's role is a popular book written by an obstetrician on his experience as *Woman's Doctor*. In irreverent language and with infinite kindness, a lack of

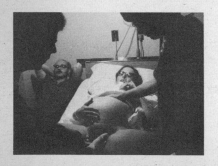

false modesty, and a sense of humor, Dr. William J. Sweeney set out in good faith to tell his story of women. His book lacks smugness and is uncommonly frank in its portrayal of the good obstetrician. He admits that doctors, especially obstetricians, have been spoiled into believing that they are little gods.

> It's not just that we're idolized by our patients. We also work in offices and hospitals where we're waited on. Especially as surgeons, we don't get anything for ourselves . . . We drop a white coat and a nurse picks it up . . . We never clean anything . . . If, God forbid, a scalpel is dirty, we throw it at a nurse and say, "This one's dirty!" Do that at home with a fork or knife and your wife has a right to kill you!
>
> We're tough to live with because we're spoiled. And we're egotistical . . . Don't let anybody tell you that a doctor doesn't *enjoy* his work, the success and the adoration he gets.

He is even willing to admit the lengths to which some doctors will go to retain control of the birth scene, even if they have missed the delivery.

> When the patient is ready for delivery and her doctor isn't there, she's given some anesthesia that puts her out and she is delivered by a different obstetrician. Then her own doctor comes roaring in with his white coat on, takes some blood—there's always plenty of blood around, with the placenta and episiotomy—and he smears it over him and acts as if he's just finished the delivery. He walks out to greet the father and says, "It's a boy."

Pain is a psychosomatic phenomenon. It flourishes with fatigue, loneliness, fear, tension, and bodily dysfunction.
> —NILES NEWTON, Pregnancy, Birth and the Newborn Baby

154

Women are not always unconscious of such happenings. Some have reported that their legs were held together to keep the baby from coming before the doctor arrived. Others have complained that they felt they were knocked out against their expressed, even shouted, desires. Still others remember that they were anesthetized after a rapid birth so that the anesthesiologist could collect his fee.

Though Dr. Sweeney provides an example of the doctor at his most truthful and humorous, he nevertheless shares many pitfalls and fallacies with a majority of his colleagues when he displays that kindly condescension of a man who really doesn't trust either nature or women. He bases his beliefs on three assumptions: first, that nature left to its own will mess things up badly; second, that woman wants someone else to make decisions about her birth for her; and third, that woman in the middle of heavy labor is undergoing tremendous pain when she turns to plead for help to the doctor at hand. Dr. Sweeney is willing to say that the whole experience is much too painful for a woman to go through it without "proper medical support," i.e., interference in the process through drugs.

Listen to Dr. Sweeney advise a couple that has planned and prepared for a "natural" birth in the hospital:

> Jean, I know you and Ed are planning to have natural childbirth, but there's no reason for you to be a martyr. If you're hurting badly, tell Dr. Richards. You're not going to lose face if you take a little Demerol.

Again, Demerol is the pharmaceutical name for meperidine hydrochloride, a narcotic compound used as an

---

The topics of death and dying hold a continual fascination for the pregnant woman. . . . It is as though, by being closer to birth, to the beginning of life, these women were automatically closer

analgesic or sedative. It will of course get to the fetus within minutes after it gets to Jean, dimming her perception and reducing her participation, while increasing her dependence upon the doctor and his assistants. In the early states of pregnancy, however, when the couple first visits the obstetrician, Demerol certainly seems far less damaging than the doctor's own advice. To use the words "lose face" or "martyr" is to demean the concept of natural childbirth and to reduce Jean's attempt to take responsibility in her own birth to the mere whim of a child. Since the doctor knows little about Jean's threshold of pain, and since Jean knows nothing about the kind of pain she will experience, neither of them can rely very heavily on what she would like to call a woman's choice. The problem is further compounded—and she will remember this—when Dr. Sweeney draws the line between contractions she can endure and contractions that are "hurting badly," which she cannot endure. With this suggestion, he has implanted the notion in Jean's mind that there will inevitably come a time when she simply can't take it anymore. Having bought this utterly logical assumption, Jean will wait for that moment throughout pregnancy, labor, and delivery.

Sure enough, Jean refuses Demerol up to the moment of transition when she is eight centimeters dilated, and the drama that follows represents what happens to women like her all over the country when the helpful doctor intervenes:

She had a contraction and began panting through the mouth, but suddenly she stopped the exercise, curled

---

to death. And in fact pregnant women are more in touch with their entire life cycles than at any other time in their lives.
— ARTHUR AND LIBBY COLEMAN,
The Psychology of Pregnancy

over on her side and started sobbing. "I can't do it. I just can't do it. Oh my God, it hurts." I sat on the bed and she gripped my hands until it was over. "For God's sake, Jean, why don't you ask Dr. Orsini for some Demerol?" "We wanted natural childbirth. You said the pain might be like this but they (her natural childbirth teachers) said if we did everything it would just be like menstrual cramps." Her hazel eyes looked stricken behind the tears.

And so he heroically steps in to help.

"I'll be right back." . . . I went down the hall and told the nurse to get me 100 milligrams of Demerol and handed her Jean's chart with the order written . . . I said to Jean, "We're giving you an injection of Demerol. It will work within a few minutes, honey." She nodded silently.

The drama continues as the doctor explains his action to Jean's husband.

"Now listen, let's try to understand something . . . Some women have easier labors than others. Jean's not going through with natural childbirth because there's no reason on God's earth for her to suffer like that. It's archaic. Labor contractions are like nothing else in the world."

In response, what can Ed do but give thanks that they have such a humane doctor? He turns to Jean.

"Oh sweetheart, I'm really glad. It looked awful."

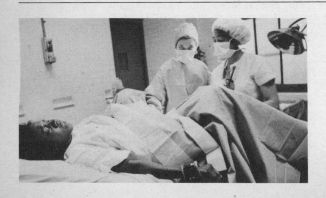

Jean is apologetic, as becomes a person who feels dependent. She is sorry for having cried and made a fuss. The doctor responds as to a child, chiding:

> "Jean, I'm going to turn you over and spank you, baby and all, if you start feeling guilty."

Then Dr. Sweeney, in all good faith, takes off on an attack against the stupid natural childbirth teachers who lie to women about what birth is really like.

> I've had people come in to labor with playing cards or magazines or martinis, all set for a picnic because Mrs. Whatshername who ran the class said it wasn't going to hurt. The husband is there with the powder so he can rub his wife's tummy, and he's got a stop-watch and he's timing every contraction—cheerleader, that's what he is—and everything's fine for a while . . . The wife goes through early labor and she's glowing . . . and BAM! she goes into real labor. Suddenly it's excruciating and she shatters. First of all she didn't get the rapport with her obstetrician that she needed. She got it with the woman who was teaching her how to breathe . . . The poor lady who really goes to pieces has to be sedated. There's nothing else we can do with her.

Dr. Sweeney ends his diatribe against foolish women, an opinion that he has unconsciously let slip, and goes on to say that he always lets his women know what labor is really like, how bad it really is. And he muses:

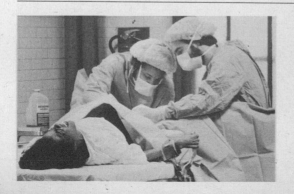

I'll never understand what's so wonderful and modern about natural childbirth. What the hell, if it's going to be really natural, the lady ought to then eat the placenta. I mean, that's what the animals do."

Dr. Sweeney, like many doctors, becomes very hostile when he is unable to control the situation and make everything all right. His last remark about leaving a woman to go back to the animal state is one very commonly repeated by doctors when confronted by women who do not want interference in birth unless there is clear medical necessity.

Even though not all attempted "natural" or drugless births end in medication, the doctor seems to have a moral for women who are stubborn. He goes on to tell how Jean had problems with her labor and how her baby's heart tones, common indicator of infant health, had dropped. There is a great rushing around as the doctor, having waited as long as he could to see if the problem would correct itself, shifts into the role of surgeon.

"Hit the buzzer." The nurse went over to the wall fast and pulled the switch that sets off the emergency buzzer on the floor. When that buzzer rings, everybody comes running because no one knows what's going on, and when you're in trouble in a good hospital everybody works . . .

The infant is delivered with difficulty, with forceps. Jean's birth has now become a medical emergency. The baby, whose heartbeat had slowed greatly, is pallid, almost white, and shows no muscle tone. Does Jean know it may

A doctor anesthetizes himself through anesthetizing a woman, in order to avoid his own fears about pain.

—HERMEIN WATKINS, R.N.

have been the drugs that made the baby function so sluggishly? Does Dr. Sweeney know, and will he learn from this experience and investigate the effect of drugs in order to protect future infants? Probably not.

But the ending to this drama is a happy one. The baby, after great effort by all concerned, pulls around and begins to breathe on his own. Such cases do occur. Even frantic emergencies. But Dr. Sweeney has tied it in so carefully with Jean's foolish desire to endure pain without drugs that we are left doubtful of the ability of the natural process to ever work on its own.

Again, the delivery table is hardly the place for woman to fight for her rights. This is especially true during the transition stage of labor when the muscles looping over the uterus are working with savage strength to pull the unlocking jaws of the cervix all the way open. At this point the woman, nearly sapped of all energy, must rally her reserves to begin pushing the baby out, yet she is now confronted with contractions even more violent than before, coming so hard and fast they seem to meld together in successive waves, culminating in a shattering explosion that overwhelms her entire body. This is the moment Dr. Sweeney was afraid of (and has been waiting for) all along, the moment when Jean and *all* laboring mothers quite literally lose their reason. Suddenly nauseous and chilled to the bone, woman turns to the nearest figure of authority with beseeching eyes and a look on her face that no one who has ever attended a delivery will ever forget. It is a look of shock and disbelief, a statement all its own that woman is never so completely and totally alone than at

this moment. A beseeching, pleading, imploring cry for help, which looks like terror to the uninitiated, it is often articulated as "Do something!" "I can't go on!" "Help me!" or words of similar dramatic power. The response of early Christian man might have been to read his wife the passages from the Scriptures telling her it was her lot to suffer so; the response of modern doctors is to inject drugs to end the suffering. Yet neither reaction is responsible. When primitive woman turned to the midwife with that same look of desperation, the midwife rightfully interpreted the plea to mean "*Assist* me," "Support me," "Tell me this is supposed to happen." The obstetrician reads it as a cry to "Stop it," "Intervene," "Do it for me."

Rare and humane indeed is the obstetrician who interprets the look as a plea for moral support from a woman who is losing confidence in her body, who is enveloped in what she believes is pain, and who has lost faith that her baby will ever be born. If, instead of electing to use anesthesia or analgesia, the obstetrician merely sits down near her and takes her hand, looks into her eyes, and reassures her that all is well (as in fact it usually is, since transition is a most difficult time and usually lasts but a few contractions), he can honestly tell her that the birth is coming and he will stay with her. He can help her regain her calm breathing pattern, tell her how beautiful she's doing and assuage her real fear, which is (ask any mother) neither the pain nor its intensity, but the belief that the labor process will never end. So the problem is not that modern woman cannot tolerate a given sensation at a given moment but rather that there comes a point, as in transition labor, when she ceases to experience the present and lives only in her memory of the past and expectation of the future. The mind's conception of a repetition of a single painful moment, repeating itself over and over and over again through eternity, is truly frightening, and this in itself brings real pain in its wake.

Fear, then, has much to do with the causation factors contributing to what we call pain. And Dr. Sweeney rightfully objects to the lack of rapport between woman and doctor, which could alleviate her fears and prepare the way for a birth process that she always could and still can endure without drugs. If there is a single barrier separating woman from birth in its most natural environment, it is not woman's weakened condition, or the overly refined sensitivity of her society, or her dependence on drugs, or "pain." It is fear.

9
Fear:
Woman's Curse

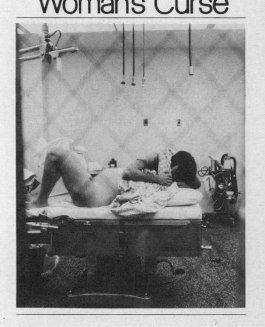

Fear:
Woman's Curse

Most DICTIONARIES define fear as the distressing emotion aroused by impending pain, danger, evil, etc. It has at its base a foreknowledge or anticipation that something bad is about to happen, and its function is to initiate preparation of the body for that event. An animal walking through the forest may be frightened by a threatening sound and stand very still, listening, frozen in its tracks. At that moment, fear sends impulses to the muscles and glands, and tension spreads throughout the animal's body: its adrenalin releases, its urine is voided, its muscles tighten, its breathing quickens, its heart pumps harder, and then, fully prepared for flight, it breaks into a run.

Fear is thus a psychogenic factor, for it originates in the mind and affects the body through involuntary physical responses—involuntary because before the mind can calm its fear, the reactions of the body are already taking place. Fear of falling off a curb, for example, produces involuntary reactions of the legs, torso, and arms to regain balance or to prepare the body for possible injury, even as the mind begins to believe the danger of falling has passed.

Since it is the mind that triggers fear to begin with, incorrect foreknowledge can sometimes set off this chain of reactions unnecessarily. One of Shelley Berman's best

---

I remember when I first came in there was a woman in the next room yelling. I told Chuck I hope I don't act like that. Well, I was a million times worse than she ever thought of being.
                                        —LAURA ROSSITER, *mother*

"embarrassing situation" routines was his impression of a man at a staid cocktail party who begins to sit down, suddenly fears the chair is not there, and reacts bodily by flinging his arms and legs out to either side in preparation for a bad fall. When his arm strikes the seat of the chair and he realizes that it *was* there all along, the flailing activity stops and he sits down, smiling as if nothing happened, knowing full well everyone has seen it and believes him to be afflicted with muscle spasms. The entire bit takes no more than a few seconds, a credit to Berman's talent and an excellent representation of the amazing ways the mind, even when in error, works with fear to serve the body.

Modern society has its own problems with fear and is often more victimized than served by it. Consider, for example, a man with an urgent need to defecate who cannot find a bathroom that affords him much privacy. Fear of embarrassing noises or smells may stop the movement of bowels until he turns on the tap water or waits for everyone to leave. Not so amusing but just as universal is the woman nearing sexual climax who suddenly fears she is too inhibited to reach orgasm and, by the very interference of fear in this natural function, simply cannot reach it. In terms of its long-range effects, when fear of inadequacy or failure results in tension that is not released through flight or immediate action, it can cause pronounced sweating and shaking, backaches, migraines, or ulcers, all of which have no physical basis for cure. Thus, the only way to stop these involuntary physical reactions

is to stop the fear, and the only way to stop the fear is to reevaluate the mind's foreknowledge of impending pain, danger, or evil.

Fear as a natural function in childbirth is best examined through Professor Cornelius Naaktgeboren's studies of psychogenic factors in animal births. In an enlightening film of a laboring red deer, Naaktgeboren shows how the animal's fear of imminent danger creates tension in all muscles and glands so that her uterine contractions actually slow down and stop. Prepared now for immediate flight, she moves quickly away to find a safer place, and, once she feels relaxed and drained of tension, her contractions renew without interference.

Occasionally, Naaktgeboren found that he himself was the cause of such fear-initiated delays in birth:

> In the rabbit I observed that one young was already expelled and I tried to make photographs. Although I waited for over two hours nothing happened, whereas normally the expulsion phase for a litter of rabbits does not take more than about ten minutes. I decided to leave the animal for a short time. At my return, twenty minutes later, I discovered thirteen newborn rabbits.

Anyone who has grown up on a farm may have had similar experiences. A mare will often deliver its foal only when an observer or well-intentioned veterinary assistant disappears from view. Naaktgeboren's studies of sheep consistently show that unnatural disturbance during labor causes such severe delays in uterine contractions that "a considerable increase in the rate of veterinary assisted

---

I was lying on the guerney waiting to be wheeled to the delivery room. The nurse couldn't get the wheels to roll. I was so afraid on that broken guerney, without John to time my contractions.

deliveries" has been noted. Again it can be concluded that the very sight of a veterinary assistant may create such tension in the mother that the assistant ends up resolving the problem that he himself has created. Worse, in his studies of cattle, rats, and dogs, Naaktgeboren has found that such disturbances not only cause prolonged labor, but also result in "a much higher perinatal mortality rate."

Naaktgeboren believes there is definite, consistent proof that the regulating mechanism of labor in the human female is much the same as in animals. This is revealed in cases related to fear, especially in the condition known as "uterine inertia," the phenomenon of unexpected delays or complete discontinuance of labor pains. Diagnoses of uterine inertia are uncommonly high in hospitals; many women will leave home in the midst of strong labor, only to arrive at the hospital and find that contractions have stopped. Naaktgeboren believes a great part of this pathology is due to fear of the hospital environment itself:

> In my opinion a lot of pathology is created. In modern textbooks they write that contractions, when irregular, frighten women. Women then become anxious. This is not true. It is the other way around. Even if the woman herself is convinced of the importance of being in a hospital, the changing surroundings may influence the inner biological rhythms.

But uterine inertia may be only the first sign of a self-perpetuating phenomenon called the "fear-tension-pain" syndrome posited by the English physician Grantly Dick-Read. Considered by many to be the father of natural

---

He was putting on his gown down the hall.
I didn't have a contraction for a full five minutes,
just out of fear.
     —SANDY BROCKWAY, *mother of two*

168

childbirth, Read believed that modern women are not simply magnifying their contractions into painful sensations as they lie in the labor bed engulfed in fear. In his excellent book, *Childbirth Without Fear*, Read explains that fear activates tension in the circular fibers of muscles in the lower part of the uterus, which, instead of relaxing as the cervix opens, now work to close it in an attempt to stop birth until danger has passed and fear dissipated. Meanwhile, however, the longitudinal muscles farther up the uterus continue to contract, for these muscles are controlled by the lumbosacral autonomic system and are not affected by fear-initiated inhibitory tension. Thus the two sets of muscles are working very hard to resist each other, and the ultimate result is actual, physical, overwhelmingly devastating pain.

> So the uterus goes on contracting just the same, in spite of the sympathetic nervous system being activated. We have then a condition of the expulsive fibers pushing against the circular fibers; we have two opposing groups of muscles working one against the other. The normal and natural result of this is that there is excessive tension, and soon a painless natural function is made into an extremely painful and therefore abnormal condition. . . . It is pathological because it is opposed to normal physiological activity. Fear and apprehension mean real physical pain, not only subjective but objective, organic pain, intrinsic and extrinsic in the periphery that is active during labor.

Thus fear and its effects may cause such pain that a woman will panic and begin to believe something has

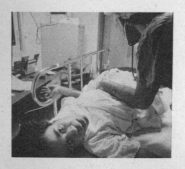

gone wrong, that she will never come out of it, that no one is there to help her—even that what she is experiencing now is a prelude to death. All of this activates even more fear, which again activates tension, which now compounds the muscular battle in the uterus, thus causing more pain. Again, since the function of fear is to prepare the organism for defense, Read notes that blood supply is rechanneled to those organs and muscles of the body most useful for flight or protection. In birth, however:

> One of the organs useless in defense is the uterus. Under the influence of fear the blood vessels and the muscles supplied by the sympathetic or fear nervous system actually limit the amount of blood going to and coming from the uterus. For a short time this can be done without disturbing the well-being of the infant, for it requires a very much lower oxygen pressure in the blood with which it is supplied than the adult musculature. But if this persists for any length of time without remission, it is quite likely fear itself is enough to deprive the baby within the womb of oxygen, and therefore to cause injury to some of its intricate organs, particularly the brain, and sometimes even cause intrauterine death.

So the effects of uterine inertia may lead to a "white uterus," the condition of a bloodless womb, which now acts to starve the infant of oxygenated blood rather than nurture the child through the process until it can take its own life-breath. At this point, fearing damage to the infant, the obstetrician can only prepare for an immediate Caesarean-section operation. He may feel disgusted with

---

It's my first baby. Mama said I'd probably have a hard time.

—ANONYMOUS MOTHER

the laboring woman, especially if he believes that she could have avoided all the problems that her fears have caused if she had only taken "a little Demerol" to begin with. But little does he know that *he* has contributed in a very major way to the problem by not dealing with her fears early on, by not calming her in the midst of labor, by not assuring her that the natural process would succeed of its own accord, and by showing his annoyance when her contractions first showed signs of slowing down. Since he believes neither in the capabilities of woman nor in the integrity of the natural process, he has consistently offered to interfere rather than assist throughout the entire labor and now faces the utterly wasteful necessity of the ultimate act of interference, the Caesarean section. It is no wonder that more Caesarean operations are performed in America than in any other developed country in the world.

For Grantly Dick-Read, the possibility of painless childbirth began with an understanding of the origins of fear, which he studied as a young doctor in the 1920s and 30s. Like most obstetricians of the time, Read was accustomed to giving chloroform to birthing women for the last contractions and actual birth. A woman in a slum section of London, giving birth in the most primitive of surroundings, caused him to ponder this practice when she refused his offer of interference through anesthesia. She said to him afterward, "It didn't hurt. It wasn't meant to, was it?" Read searched for the answer to the painfulness of civilized childbirth, and after many years and many births, he concluded:

Superstition, civilization, and culture have brought influences to bear upon the minds of women which have introduced fears and anxieties concerning labor. The more cultured the races of the earth have become, so much the more positive they have been in pronouncing childbirth to be a painful and dangerous ordeal.

Read was one of the first physicians to differentiate between natural birth in the primitive state and natural birth in the civilized state, calling the first true natural birth and the second a "cultural labor," in that it is greatly influenced by societal attitudes. Cultural birth includes the vast majority of women who are physiologically equipped to give birth unaided but emotionally unprepared for birth. They are products of centuries of fear.

It is not a simple matter, then, to allay a woman's conscious and unconscious fears about the childbirth process, and Dr. Read is joined by many obstetricians in stating that effective prenatal care must be largely instructional and only partly medical. The physician especially must understand the ease with which he may inadvertently plant a fear-initiating suggestion in the mind of a pregnant woman, and he must attempt to provide a wholly positive image of the birth process and its aftermath for both father and mother. The American physician, Robert Bradley, whose *Husband-Coached Childbirth* creates an immensely valuable place for the husband in pregnancy and labor, also believes that the obstetrician's primary role is one of educator.

We advocates of natural childbirth point out that prenatal teaching of a patient and her husband how to work to-

---

Growing up I heard things like: "I'd like another child. But I couldn't go through that again!" And I thought having a baby was a big secret. I wonder why I wasn't afraid at my births.
> —KENDRA DAY, *mother, after second home birth*

gether to give spontaneous birth is the *primary duty* of a doctor. Most training centers teach budding doctors only the mechanics of abnormal obstetrics (six per cent) and ignore the psychological management of normal obstetrics (94 per cent). Pregnant women should be looked upon not just as baby factories but in a total sense as complex human beings with a mind, a soul, and a body.

The problem, however, is that most doctors do not have the time, patience, or knowledge to deal with the many personal and physical problems with birth that every woman must have answered if she is to know how to deal with her own fears during the process. In America, where continuity of care is essential because of a heavy overlay of cultural attitudes suggesting pain and danger in childbirth, no single person has yet been authorized to take responsibility for working with the birthing woman throughout the entire pregnancy, birth, and postpartum period. Although physicians who advocate natural birth are much more concerned with the vital prenatal period than others, all too often the birthing woman ends up alone in the labor room, striving desperately to deal with her fears, while strangers wander in and out to give pelvic exams, monitor machines, or record notes on her chart. This is a time in a woman's life when she is uniquely impressionable and vulnerable, when she desperately needs the finest supportive care and emotional assistance possible. Yet nobody is there.

In recent years, the lack of care provided by doctors and hospitals has of necessity given rise to an entirely new professional, the childbirth teacher. Today this educator

---

By the time I was eight centimeters dilated I couldn't take it. My husband came in and held my hand. I was sure I was dying.
—EUNICE MITCHELL, *mother*

may be the only knowledgeable person available to offer women and their mates the information and care they so desperately need. The childbirth teacher provides many answers to the questions constantly voiced by pregnant women who will speak out loud, as well as to the many women whose needs go unspoken: What happens to me during labor? What will it feel like? How will I be sure I can make it okay? What can I do to prepare for birth so that I don't panic from fear and pain? After I have my baby, what then? What is breast-feeding like? What if I become depressed when I leave the hospital and find myself all alone with this strange child? None of these questions have been fully answered by doctors or other hospital personnel, who have neither the time nor often the knowledge in such matters. They are very important questions to a woman giving birth in a society where women feel they have lost the "knack" of mothering. Childbirth teachers also teach fathers how to take responsibility in their mates' births, and in many hospitals they have become the greatest impetus for getting fathers and labor coaches into labor and delivery rooms. They offer a wide variety of techniques and systems that enable any woman who makes the effort to give birth without fear and without intolerable pain.

But the American childbirth teacher, who is "outside" the medical profession, is often poorly paid for her vital service. Sometimes she works out of a physician's practice and is paid by or has referrals made by him; sometimes, in communities where there is a need and little money, she works for free while carrying a full-time salaried job.

The childbirth educator has vastly improved the quality of birth in America. Still, she has no authority or responsibility for following a woman through the entirety of birth. Many hospitals leave her outside the labor room doors. And if she offers to lend information and emotional support to women after they have given birth, it is either out of her devotion to the mother, or because she knows that no one else in the community will take such responsibility.

So it is the dilemma of the childbirth teacher that the methods she teaches are not always in accord with hospital procedures, and that obstetricians such as Dr. Sweeney will condemn her for making birth sound easier than he ever believed it could be. Although she may know more about normal childbirth than the doctor, the natural childbirth teacher continues to work on the fringe of the medical establishment, preferring to assist women to accept the way things are rather than to assist them to make demands for change. Laboring mothers are beginning to make the demands themselves, but it is asking a great deal of a woman surrounded by the sensations of her body, working to give birth, to suggest that she should question the authority of doctor and hospital to do as they wish, once she enters their world. Leave her at home and she would, according to many women, feel much easier about speaking up.

The midwife would speak up for the woman, because it is her function to serve as a birthing woman's alter ego and a doctor's conscience. In countries where she is recognized and licensed, she is the only one with the power to stand between the woman giving birth and the medical establishment. She alone protects the normal progress of a healthy woman's body in childbirth.

10
Natural Childbirth?

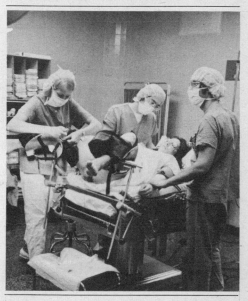

Natural Childbirth?

First of all, *natural childbirth*. That is best defined by the childbirth in which no physical, chemical or psychological condition is likely to disturb the normal sequence of events or disrupt the natural phenomena of parturition.

GRANTLY DICK-READ, M.D. *Childbirth Without Fear*

ASK ANY TEN people what the term "natural childbirth" means and you will probably receive ten different answers. A mother who watched her second birth in a tilted overhead mirror will proudly attest to the joys of "natural childbirth." Questioned further, however, she may reveal that she was referring only to the fact that her eyes were open throughout the procedure, and not to the spinal anesthesia which deadened one-third of her body. Ask any obstetrician who believes that he specializes in intelligent and humane obstetrics and that he caters to intelligent women, and he will try to convince you that *all* his normal births are "natural." What he means to say is that he doesn't believe in giving general anesthesia and that he only practices preventive medicine: the sedatives given early in labor to keep the woman from exhausting herself, the intravenous glucose fluid with Pitocin to give energy and to regulate the contractions, the episiotomy which will prevent needless tearing, and the Pitocin again, as a prevention against hemorrhage, after the placenta has been

delivered. He too is all for "natural childbirth," he says, and recommends all the right methods to his patients.

Natural childbirth in America today may mean anything short of a Caesarean section. We have accepted a product called the "safest," and "best," and now the "most natural" birth possible in civilized society. And each time the sales pitch has been driven home with a lengthy description of why American women, given the condition of their bodies, their intermarriage among pelvic types, and their later age of conceiving, just can't expect to drop their babies as effortlessly as "those naked primitives" did.

Thirty years ago, Grantly Dick-Read first brought new concepts of natural childbirth to enthusiastic audiences in America. So, too, more recently, have the concerted efforts of converts Rosemary Carmel and Elisabeth Bing helped to popularize the Lamaze method all over the United States. Dr. Robert Bradley, whose own method of natural childbirth also won national acclaim, advanced the idea to a new level, that of *husband*-coached childbirth. Yet for all the talk, the popularity, the trendiness and occasional faddishness surrounding natural childbirth, the process itself is seldom achieved.

It would be very difficult to estimate the numbers of mothers who have attempted natural childbirth through one method or another. Many have picked up one of the dozens of books on the subject which detail the glowing experience of other women having painless, fearless, joyful births. Many women have attended at least a few natural childbirth classes, and some have gone all the way into the

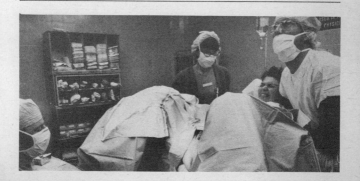

hospital on their husbands' arms, proudly announcing to all the staff that they intend to have a natural birth. But the fact is that while a few women in America may have experienced an undrugged birth, practically no one has ever experienced a *truly* natural birth.

The sad fact is that American women, indeed modern women, are not *expected* to be able to have natural births. They are often encouraged in the attempt, however, because it is a great American tradition to entertain the newest, most enlightened concepts, to participate in the most revolutionary scientific trends—to enter, in fact, every new race. Obstetricians and their nurses coyly tell everyone that their mothers *try* a natural birth. But they all agree that few succeed. They seem relieved to be able to report that at eight centimeters dilation, women usually accept medication. Of course success is not the measure, as Dr. Sweeney likes to say, since there's no sense in being a martyr when "a little Demerol" can make birth "almost" natural and certainly more comfortable.

Authorities writing about childbirth also suffer from the expectation that women will need help through medication. In their popular *Dictionary of Pregnancy, Childbirth and Contraception*, Herbert and Margaret Brant describe natural childbirth as a noble but unattainable goal that any woman should be proud to attempt. But they condemn proponents of natural childbirth for leading women to *expect* that they can succeed.

> The natural childbirth movement has at times fallen into the trap of embracing the success or failure approach, depending on whether labor is complete without artificial

It should be pointed out that natural childbirth, the very inappropriate name for forms of delivery in which women undergo extensive training so that they can cooperate consciously with the aids. This approach is certain to fail in many cases. The accepted and moderate approach is for the woman to be given every help to cope with her labor and to hope for a normal delivery, but to be fully aware that most women need additional help from drugs.

What has led to a "hope" that fully expects failure is the high number of disappointed women who have attempted natural birth in hospitals and found that having a baby hurt like hell, that medication helped, and that the "joy" of natural childbirth was either a lie or an impossible dream.

That many women feel they have failed in one way or another in their births is not due to the method they practice but to the expectation of failure built into every hospital staff. It is this patronizing, negative attitude—more than the technology that spawns it—that makes natural childbirth a deception in the modern hospital. If women were to succeed at having their babies spontaneously and in uncomplicated fashion, requiring only assistance and not intervention, then the hospital staff, trained in crisis and disease, would find itself with nothing medically to do. Complicated and expensive paraphernalia, unnecessary in any normal birth, would gather dust in a corner. Today the modern hospital must treat childbirth as a disorder or at least a *potential* crisis in order to justify its place in the realm of normal birth.

Natural childbirth requires an environment of peaceful and protective calm. The modern hospital is the antithesis of such an environment and must be so as long as person-

---

delivery of the child, is a male invention meant to counteract practices of complete anesthesia, which were also male inventions.
—MARGARET MEAD

nel change shifts every eight hours, rooms continue to be barren of anything soft or personal, and rules are made for the convenience of the staff. The obstetric staff is there to assist the obstetrician, not the mother.

In an effort to erase bad memories from the minds of women who feel they were deceived about natural childbirth, obstetricians, hospital staffs, and childbirth educators reinforce the idea that natural childbirth is impossible and attempt to discredit the term "natural" as used in childbirth. They replace it with such euphemisms as "prepared childbirth" and that winning phrase, "family-centered birth." Some hospitals teach their own preparation classes and force hapless childbirth teachers to send women to the hospital, since there exists no alternative. Such teachers rightly feel it best to prepare the mother and father for what they will encounter at the hospital, rather than lead them to expect a homelike, natural situation that does not exist. So in classes across the country such teachers offer training in one of the methods of breathing and control, or a blend of methods and exercise classes. At the same time they wisely include talks on IVs, vacuum extractors, stirrups, and episiotomies. A woman is reminded to ask for extra pillows during pushing, or to request that she be able to hold her baby on the delivery table. The teacher knows such requests will be granted in hospitals where an effort is made to make the mother feel it is her show. In fact, it is never her show and hospital staffs never intend it to be so.

The progressive obstetrician catches himself before he goes so far as to let the woman know that it is *his* delivery.

Hospitals are no place to have a baby! Babies belong to families, not to a bunch of strangers.
—GAIL REAM, *nursery nurse*

Today he reminds her often that she is an important member of the team that will deliver her baby. If he is in touch with the mood of the times, he will be sure to let the husband know that he too is a needed member of the team. Yes, the team will deliver your baby. With much cheering from the staff and the labor coach of your choice, the woman will be exhorted and challenged and urged to PUSH, Alicia.... PUSH.... PUSH.... HARDER...Now BREATHE...THAT'S IT!...PUSH...PUSH...PUSH! Everyone groups expectantly and enthusiastically around the sweating, panting, pushing mother who looks like nothing more than a trussed-up turkey. That mothers do not consciously remember the experience as silly and downright humiliating is due to their sincere effort to please everyone around them, and to the consuming effort of giving birth. The team approach to childbirth, given a woman's educated determination, can yield an almost drugless delivery, barring the episiotomy and its local anesthesia, of course, and the large doses of' hormones that are routinely administered. For even if the delivery itself occurs without any form of anesthesia or analgesia, it is not to be confused with a natural birth, which can only take place in an atmosphere of calm and quiet faith within a natural environment.

The natural birth is a process so awe-inspiring that it is difficult to describe without becoming intensely poetic or religious. A Danish teacher of midwives, normally not given to the mystical, spoke to me of the "ghostlike presence" that inhabits a labor room in which a woman nearing delivery works in a state of calm acceptance.

How much the current systems of mother and baby care influence what is called "after baby blues" is not known . . . for many American mothers it comes so regularly after delivery that it is to be expected as quite usual.
—NILES NEWTON, Pregnancy, Birth and the Newborn Baby

Between contractions in which she consciously pushes, such a woman can be seen to fall into a deep dreamlike state, only to waken at the next urge to push. Such a delicate environment is easily violated by the mere movement of another laboring woman from one bed to another, or from one room to another. It is shattered by the loud whispers and bustle of the staff, who do not respect the natural process. Watching births in different parts of this country at night and during midday, I am always struck by the *noise* of the hospital obstetric unit, even when no one is talking or moving about. The noise of the bright lights, the noise of all that white and shining chrome. The noise of squeaking, rubber-soled shoes. Hospitals reek of noise and bustle as much as they reek of antiseptics.

That, and a lack of staff. There is always a rush as delivery approaches, even when the staff far outnumbers the patients. In units where there are three laboring women and an empty delivery room, five nurses and a resident are in constant movement from one room to another. No one person can find the time to settle by the side of a woman and take her hand for twenty still and uninterrupted minutes. Hospitals exist at either extreme of frenetic crisis or hapless boredom, and in this environment the presence of a loving husband or a patient labor coach is not enough to insure peace and calm for the laboring woman.

When Marjorie Karmel wrote in *Thank You, Dr. Lamaze* that she believed Grantly Dick-Read but found him too "rhapsodic and mystical," she was responding to the romantic prose of a doctor who had such respect and

---

Although in theory a prepared patient is so completely relaxed and cooperative that locking her arms should be unnecessary, the hospital can't afford to take chances. . . . Perhaps, as more and

admiration for woman giving birth that he could only speak in awe. Read did write of his faith in the birth process:

> It is a belief in the fundamental perfection of reproduction as the greatest and most complete of all natural functions ... Accidents and wastage occur in all forms of reproduction, vegetable as well as animal; in the human race there are fewer accidents and the wastage is incomparably smaller than in any other form of life ...

Dr. Read was not so naive as to assume there was nothing more to birth than letting nature succeed or fail without assistance from man's intelligence. He gave due recognition to the value of obstetrics:

> It is well known that abnormal conditions which are unforeseen, do arise; but this very rarely happens, and it is for such misfortunes that skilled obstetricians exist. But even in the presence of such dangers, the large majority of women and babies are safely treated, and the fact of unforeseen possibilities should not mar the general expectancy of a successful issue.

Read spoke from vast experience with birthing women in Africa as well as in England, during times of bombing and attack as well as peace. He emphasized the importance of woman's knowing in detail everything that happens inside her body during labor. His training was of deep and relaxed breathing to settle the entire body and mind and allow the body to work unhindered by fear of the process, which could in itself result in great pain during a normal

---

more prepared women demonstrate that they can deliver their babies in a relaxed way, the doctor will decide to eliminate handcuffs.
—BARBARA GELB, The ABC of Natural Childbirth

birth. His prenatal exercises prepared modern woman for overall fitness and for the exertion of birth. Given that, he found most women could deliver babies anywhere and alone.

What Dr. Read did not count upon was the way the modern hospital resurrects every anxiety a woman has ever felt about her birth. The Read approach is often too passive to counteract the intrusive environment of the hospital.

The Pavlov method of childbirth, brought from the Soviet Union to France in 1951 by Dr. Fernand Lamaze, offers a program of consciously developed, conditioned reflexes to combat and conquer the intense sensations of birth. Renamed psychoprophylaxis to give it a more scientific ring, the Lamaze method of exercises in muscle control, massage, and breathing does seem aggressive enough to override both the painful fear of contractions and the most intrusive hospital environment. It has the unfortunate side effect of greatly altering a woman's natural experience of birth from one of deep involvement inside her body to a controlled distraction. A woman panting with practiced speed can block out interruption and ride over each contraction with militant control over her body. The Lamaze birth does permit women to have undrugged deliveries, and even "painless" ones. But while primitive woman was at one with the process of birth— and, as such, at one with the natural rhythms of the earth—modern woman practicing the Lamaze method is separate and detached from the sensations, smells, and sights of her body giving birth. She is too involved in her control to notice any part of the basic, sensual (involving all the senses) experience of childbirth.

In 1951 the Soviet government decreed that Pavlovian training was to be the national method of birth. And Pope Pius XII found it possible on January 8, 1956, to fully endorse Lamaze natural birth before an international gathering of obstetrician-gynecologists. He called it a "benefit for the mother in childbirth" that "fully conforms to the will of the Creator." The Lamaze method thus gained endorsement, if it did not in fact gain mass support.

Today Read's approach has been updated to withstand the shock of a hospital environment by Dr. Robert Bradley's notion of husband-coached childbirth. Dr. Bradley claims that of the thirteen thousand childbirths that have come under his care over the years, 93.5 per cent were unmedicated, natural births, and that the rate of infant or maternal mortality was absolute zero. The strength of his method lies in protecting the passivity of the Read method through constant, educated support and encouragement of the husband so that when the hospital environment begins to interfere with the woman's labor or delivery, her mate is right there to help her reinstate a calm and peaceful demeanor. Exercises and classes for both parents begin very early in pregnancy, and Bradley believes that such is their ecstacy that "people watching husband-coached childbirth often say they feel like intruders in a room where a man and a woman are making love." What may also be

---

I felt terrific afterward. But they wouldn't let me touch him. Ten hours later he was brought in for me to look at. It took so long to see my baby!
—SANDY BROCKWAY, *after "natural childbirth"*

the case, however, is that Bradley's method places the husband in a heroic position alongside the doctor, leaving the woman dependent upon both:

> Our men are real men. They finish what they start—pregnancy; and their wives look up to them with respect, love, and affection. . . . Our goal is to make women fall even more in love with their husbands. . . .

For many women, it is difficult to take Dr. Bradley seriously, since he commonly refers to the uterus as the "baby box" and the clitoris as the "passion button," and because he insists that the vaginal exercises of his prenatal program "teach lovemaking . . . our women are magnificent lovers." For all his questionable taste, however, Dr. Bradley's method *is* successful and proves once again that the presence of one person throughout all stages of labor, pregnancy, and delivery, to give the mother constant support and educated encouragement, is one important key to a successful, natural childbirth.

But while method and education are essential to changing woman's attitudes toward birth and reintroducing her to the power and wisdom of her body, method and education transferred to the hospital become less than "natural birth." Natural childbirth is not an aggressive action against the forces of nature. Nor is it a suppression of the sensation and experience of the tremendous effort of the body to give birth. It is simply the full experience of the normal sequence of events flowing without interruption from any external disturbance or interference. Natural childbirth requires a calm and abiding faith and constant

I arrived at the hospital clutching a bath towel between my legs, dripping water. I couldn't find a wheelchair and left a trail all the way down their new, blue-carpeted hall. When I got to the labor room, they put me in a toilet area after giving me an enema. I had my first strong

emotional support for a woman to participate in her body as it births itself.

Most hospital staffs consider their hospitals, above all others, to be humane, comfortable places to give birth. Yet women who have experienced lonely, frightening, and demeaning first births without their mates or a loving friend's attendance, with all the impersonality an ordinary hospital creates, grab at a "family-centered" institution that may loosen some of its unnecessary rules and routines of birth. Most women are grateful to be allowed lengthy visits from their husbands, grateful to hold their newborn babies for a couple of minutes after birth and to have them in their rooms an additional couple of hours a day, grateful to be allowed to wear their own clothes. They would not be so presumptuous as to assume that they should create the rules of the birthing scene or that the attendants at their births should be their own choice of friends. Few mothers question the hospital policy that dictates they cannot fall asleep with their babies in bed with them, or that they cannot establish contact with their newborn and the rest of the family in unbroken quiet and privacy immediately after the birth.

Despite the tremendous effort of childbirth educators to reestablish the normalcy of birth, and despite the effort of some hospitals to simulate the comfortable familiarity of a home environment, natural childbirth is today a gross misnomer. Women giving birth in hospitals are still docile and obedient child-mothers, dependent on the authority of the hospital staff and not at all secure in the process of normal birth.

---

contraction there. I yelled for a nurse, but no one came. Another contraction came and I began doing my Lamaze slow-breathing. I finally went out into the hall and got myself a nurse. John was still filling out the forms downstairs.
                    —SANDY BROCKWAY, *mother of two,*
                              after "natural childbirth"

Today childbirth does not belong to mothers. It is still a foreign experience in a foreign environment, despite the hospital prenatal tour, despite the books and authorities that proclaim the joy of hospital birth. Birth will never belong to the mother and her baby so long as she is not free to choose where she will give birth and who shall be invited to attend.

One of the best sellers in the birthing trade is *A Birth In The Family*. Sold in paperback almost everywhere, it is a blatant piece of public relations, written by that hearty "childbirth coach," Elisabeth Bing, who coauthored this, her second, book with Dr. Gerald S. Barad, Director of Obstetrics and Gynecology at Hunterdon Medical Center, in an effort to promote "family-centered" maternity care at this New Jersey hospital. Sandy, the heroine of the piece, is shown eyeing a hospital tray of food sent up for her husband. She is later seen grinning as she "cheerfully licks" the lollipop between contractions, the only food she is allowed. When Sandy is ready to give birth, Elisabeth Bing launches into rhapsodic but never mystical praise of the delivery room and its staff.

> And now, the wonderful, exciting move to the delivery room! As though a film were speeded up, the nurses pushed Sandy's bed along the corridors; Bill and the doctor, who had left the room a little earlier, had hurried to the doctor's room to change into their scrub suits, to get their masks and caps and gowns. Everybody was smiling, hurrying, and . . . there was the delivery room.
>
> Of course, Sandy had seen it before, three years ago. There was the table in the center of the room, the large

Psychoprophylaxis is not synonymous with laziness . . . a woman must be imbued with the thought that she is essentially responsible for the success or failure of her own childbirth.
—FERNAND LAMAZE

light above it, the stool at one end of the table and another, probably for the anesthesiologist in case he was needed, at the other end; there were tables covered with white drapes, notices on the wall, a big clock; there was the bassinet, with its chromium legs and air of white, clean expectancy for the new baby. In one corner there were some gas cylinders, and in the other corner scales covered with a white sheet, ready to receive the baby for weighing. Sandy took it all in with one glance. It was all familiar to her, reassuring, and beautifully exciting. She felt secure and happy here in this room. . . .

Need we go on! Sandy is obediently following procedure for a family-centered birth, a prepared birth. But by no stretch of the imagination can we call it "natural birth." Sandy is then seen for the next four days shuffling down the hospital corridors pushing little Jennifer in her bassinet home on wheels, still smiling from the experience.

In 1967, Dr. Charles E. Flowers, Jr., Professor and Chairman of the Department of Obstetrics and Gynecology at Baylor University College of Medicine, wrote in *Obstetric Analgesia and Anesthesia*:

The method of Read and the system of psychoprophylaxis of Lamaze and Vellay are being modified in America by being used in conjunction with paracervical and pudendal blocks and/or various analgesic and tranquilizing agents. There are logical reasons why this is so: American women have been delivered by obstetricians in hospitals for the last three decades. Lying-in homes and midwives are not used in American obstetrics, and pregnant patients have been taught to expect obstetric analgesia and anes-

---

People have to realize that life is not a collection of rare diseases. It's colds, hypertension, runny noses, ear infections, and normal deliveries. Hospitals are not normal places. Life is not a hospital.

—RICH QUINT, M.D., *pediatrician*

thesia. Consequently, the average prenatal patient in the United States would like a relatively painless labor even when she desires to actively participate in labor and delivery.

From the first prenatal visit, this is what the doctor expects, and this is what American women are led to believe: that birth can be drug-free but painless; natural but hospitalized; fully experienced but quick and easy. At this point in our history, it is difficult to say who contributed most to this cycle of deceptions—the harried, insensitive doctor who wants birth to go like clockwork; or the uninformed, dependent mother who waits to be told.

Either way, if normal childbirth is to be reclaimed by American women as a natural process for which they bear full responsibility, three things must happen: doctors must learn to respond to the special needs and circumstances of the birthing population; women must address themselves to what they really want in the birthing process and assert their rights to the medical community; and the midwife must be granted her rightful place in the American way of birth.

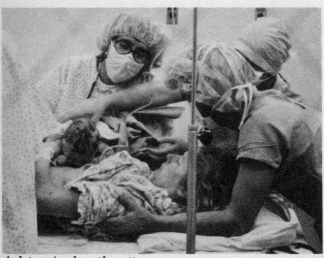

A determined mother attempts to nurse on the delivery table

11
The Return of the Midwife

The Return
of the Midwife

THERE HAVE ALWAYS been midwives, just as there have always been babies, and traditionally this birth attendant has been a woman, often a mother herself. As a trade, midwifery arose from the needs of pregnant women to have a sympathetic and experienced woman sit with them during the birth of their children. The midwife is nothing more nor less than a skilled specialist in normal birth.

The word for midwife varies in different languages, but everywhere the implication is the same. Whether she is called *sage-femme* ("wise woman") in French, *jordmoder* ("earth mother") in Danish, or *midwife* ("one who sits with woman"), she is a person acknowledged as special and knowing. Today, though independent midwifery is illegal in parts of the United States, it continues to be practiced and respected throughout the rest of the world. Whether the midwife is labeled "birth attendant" (the traditional unschooled woman) or "midwife" (the graduate of a special school), she practices a legal profession and she is an institution.

By contrast, the science of obstetrics is a very recent development, a profession made necessary by the advance of civilization and its introduction of new problems into birth. In America, the obstetrician has driven the midwife out of practice and only in recent years has allowed the

nurse-midwife, namesake of but not the same as the midwife, to enter the field of obstetrics. This does not, however, alter the simple fact that the midwife begat the obstetrician, as it was the midwife who practiced for thousands of years in a world where birth was regarded as a natural and normal function of the human body. She has held considerable respect in the eyes of the women she serves because in the vast majority of births the care she has rendered has been enough to insure the health, safety, and comfort of mother and newborn infant. She has merely had to attend nature and to watch and protect the normal process from interference.

It is out of respect for the natural process that the midwife has traditionally worked with only her hands and the simplest of tools. Today, in those countries that prefer the midwife to the nurse with training as a midwife, her tools are still simple and inexpensive. To provide good prenatal care to a healthy woman, a midwife need only keep accurate accounts of the woman's weight, blood pressure, and protein and sugar in the urine; check for signs of pelvic disproportion; measure the height of the womb; and feel for the position of the child. Her equipment consists of a stethoscope of metal or hollowed wood, a blood-pressure cuff, and papers for urine tests. To a birth she brings only a pair of sterile scissors, a clamp for the umbilical cord, and sterile rubber gloves. She can work in the city or in the farthest reaches of the country, and she can work alone. Her sole purpose is to provide support to the birthing woman and to see that she achieves a spontaneous natural childbirth, so long as she is able. To

I still visit some of my babies. You do get fond of them. Don't you!
                    —MISS KENNEDY, *age 76, retired*
                    English midwife

that end the midwife is alert, by training and experience, to the slightest deviation from the normal and is ready at any time to call upon a medical specialist, if the need arises. If the specialist is not available, however, she is fully capable of handling emergencies herself.

I call the midwife the protector of the normal and the conscience of the doctor. Where she is able to practice her trade, she provides moral support for the birthing woman as well. Birth is a straightforward but often lengthy process, frequently accompanied by tremendous sensations in the body and great effort in pushing the baby out. The midwife, as the mother's confidante and guide, holds the key to a normal delivery as much in her positive attitude and her moral support as in her watchful alertness for any sign of difficulty. Most often she is needed as much for what she does *not* do in normal births as for the skill she exhibits in emergencies.

The original village midwife was a woman experienced in birth through long years of practice. She was older than the young mothers she served, and because of her knowledge, she was considered a special friend to all the women in her town or tribal group. During childbirth, her job was to guarantee the mother protection from harmful interference when all went well, to be honest with her, and to proceed with caution when the process indicated possible difficulty. Since she worked only from her instinct and personal experience, her calm and cheerful manner was a natural response to the strenuous exertion of the laboring woman and her need for a safe and quiet environment. She offered soothing words of praise and laid cool hands on a

body tired from its labors, swept up in the pure sensations of bringing forth a baby. She knew the curative art of herbal medicine and offered bittersweet teas and other natural remedies for discomfort and for thirst. She found chanting and singing useful in encouraging the infant to leave its womb home. She may even have learned from her mother or her mother's mother how to halt a pregnancy and start an early labor if the woman's belly showed the baby to be getting too large, or if for any reason pregnancy was to be terminated.

Until recent years, the midwife was guaranteed no income from her work, but she often received a share of the family's food in thanks for her care. At times in every culture she might receive an unwanted child as a gift, too. There are records of many midwives raising these gift children, who were considered special and honored, as their own. It is possible that the midwife also acted as the first wet nurse for women who could not provide nourishment for their babies.

Above all, the midwife *chose* to be a midwife and preferred the company of woman giving birth to any other work. Often the children she assisted into the world became her friends and asked her into their homes to birth the next generation. Through hundreds of births, she gained knowledge of simple ways to keep a mother from tearing or bleeding. She seldom needed to teach a woman how to give birth, for women had not yet covered that intuitive knowledge with layers of learned behavior. When she grew too old to be of service and could not stay alert during the long nights of labor, as was necessary for her

A good midwife never leaves a woman in labor.
She sits and shares and she is patient.
                    —PEGGY EMRY, *midwife, Frontier*
                    Nursing Service

trade, she passed on all her knowledge to a younger woman who chose to be a midwife. That woman may have been her daughter or perhaps one of the girl-children she helped deliver and watched grow to womanhood.

As primitive cultures evolved into civilizations, and as primitive knowledge developed into science and religion, the birth process gradually began to change hands. First the medicine man, then the priest-physician, still later the barber-doctor, and now the obstetrician, all took a turn at the birth process, attempting to understand it, then to control it, and now to manipulate it. Throughout it all, in thousands of years of civilized development, the traditional midwife's role has remained the same. Although in primitive times she was made to bounce the mother up and down to speed labor; in medieval times forced to enter the womb manually; and in early American history persecuted as a witch; and although for hundreds of years in Western civilization she has been ridiculed, scorned, demeaned, and on some occasions executed, the midwife has been secure in her knowledge that she alone attends to the needs of the birthing woman, needs that have never changed.

The midwife of American history continued to practice only so long as there were frontiers to explore and unknown territories to conquer. When settlements developed into stable communities, however, and medical institutions were established in newborn cities, the midwife was driven into the frontier to care for a rural populace that had no access to up-to-date medical health care. Still respected by the

About 80 percent of the world's babies are delivered by midwives.
—Mademoiselle

women she attended but barely tolerated by the doctors who overwhelmed her craft and regarded her as a slovenly illiterate, the midwife was destined for extinction during the nineteenth and twentieth centuries and would have died out entirely had there not been a resurgence of interest and need for her unique and timeless skills. It is not only the growing shortage of obstetricians throughout the country, but also a renewed movement to home birth in many areas, that has called the midwife back from obscurity. Recently, magazines and newspapers have featured glowing reports of "the midwife's return" to the American birth scene. Unlike the image of her ill-kempt and uneducated predecessor, today's nurse-midwife is crisp, clean, and competent, with two or three years of formal training in both nursing and midwifery. Cropping up in hospitals throughout the country, she has been welcomed by some doctors as an invaluable aid and time-saver in their busy schedules. Expectant mothers—once they are convinced she is a far cry from the midwife of yore—see her as a patient and reassuring presence in the hospital delivery room. The nurse-midwife seems the perfect solution to the double dilemma of physicians with little time for routine births and mothers desiring aid and company during the long, lonely hours of labor.

But, unfortunately, she is yet another deception in the process of the hospital birth.

The professions of nursing and midwifery do not easily combine. We need only examine their natural separateness, their differences in temperament and in training, to see

that the midwife and the nurse-midwife come to birth with different points of view and face each other across a wide gulf called "faith."

The midwife has a deep faith, upheld by experience, that nature has designed a complex and perfect process she could not hope to improve. She knows that birth is a process seldom in need of assistance, and she protects this truth with reverence. Her training prepares her to spot deviation, which she learns to recognize through her knowledge of what is normal. She has chosen midwifery because she prefers to work with healthy motherhood as an independent practitioner. By the nature of her occupation, she is unsuited both to take orders unquestioningly and to nurse sick bodies back to health.

Although the midwife easily defers to the judgment of a specialist in abnormalities of birth, she will always question the necessity of every interference. The midwife takes great personal pride in her ability to keep nature on its own course and in her direct involvement with a laboring woman and her family. She stands quite naturally on the side of woman's free choice in birth, and despite her personal preferences, is unwilling to limit unnecessarily a healthy woman's decision as to where and how she gives birth and what she asks of her chosen birth attendants.

A nurse-midwife, on the other hand, is a person preselected by her interest in helping others through illness and disease. In America, where there are no schools for midwives, an independent-minded woman who wants to work in childbirth may opt for nursing rather than a long and arduous study of obstetrics. But nursing school, like

---

As a nurse, I never interfere in what doctors are doing. It's their prerogative. Being a nurse and a woman under a male physician is double trouble.

medical school, teaches that pathology, not the normal, is the expected. In her education as a nurse, the nurse-midwife is taught to expect anything and everything to go awry during birth, and she has a lusty respect for modern forms of interference which will protect woman from her own working body. It is a rare nurse who leaves her training unscarred by that emphasis and expectation of disease or disorder. Thus, examined closely in light of her history as a nurse and the harsh reality of her hospital surroundings, the *nurse* takes her place on the growing obstetric team, but the *midwife* has changed and lost her essence in the process. The reason is a simple one. She is no longer the guardian of normal birth and watchful servant of mothers. She is a registered nurse with a post-graduate degree in a speciality called midwifery. And she looks and acts much like the physician authority whom she is licensed to assist.

Further, a nurse is trained not to make decisions but to accept the decisions of others and to defer to the authority of rank. She believes that the physician, not the birthing mother, knows best and holds the power to heal. By training, she sees life as a physician does, full of problems, abnormalities, and complications, a drama full of risk and danger, diseases and disorders to isolate, diagnose, and solve —a losing battle to fight to the end. Since the United States has chosen to use only nurse-midwives and physicians to attend normal childbirth, the American woman cannot expect to find in her birth attendant either a protector of the normal or a cautious critic of interference.

Although the majority of nurse-midwives reflect a con-

When I want to talk about my feelings and opinions I'm not well-received, and often blatantly so.
        —BETTY CAHILL, *neonatal nurse specialist*

servative education and lack of authority in the medical profession, a small core of liberals has begun to fight for recognition of the nurse-midwife as an entity, separate from both the nursing and the obstetric staff. Recently, Rugh Lubic, a prominent nurse-midwife and director of the Maternity Center Association, has begun to write articles in nursing and obstetrics journals and the public press, in an attempt to carve out a new position for the nurse-midwife. She believes it is important for the nurse-midwife to remain independent from other areas of medicine so that she can serve the mother and not the physician.

Lubic's position becomes weak and defensive, however, when she declares that nurse-midwives have "willingly entered into a colleague relationship with physicians," and that the new relationship of colleague is not meant to surrender a nurse-midwife's integrity as a nurse. This is a sticky position for the nurse-midwife, who must respond on the one hand to criticism from nurses from whom she is separating herself as "midwife," and on the other hand to aloofness from physicians who have yet to consider her, or anyone else outside their medical fraternity, an equal colleague. Because of this, the nurse-midwife's claim that she is not exploited by physicians, that she is not physician dominated because she receives her training from other nurse-midwives, and that she is separate is not altogether convincing. Historically, physicians, especially obstetricians, have shown no desire to allow anyone decision-making power in normal birth. It is true that many obstetricians appear to be welcoming the nurse-midwife into their practice as someone who will shoulder a large part of the burden of parent education, labor coaching, and general patient contact. But they are not suggesting that midwives be allowed to practice independently, or to secure their own "clients," or to refer only abnormal cases back to doctors.

Some obstetricians admit that signing a birth certificate is not proof they have attended a birth. They agree that as many as 20 out of every 100 hospital births may be delivered by someone other than the physician. In support of this is Ruth Lubic's article, "Myths About Nurse-Midwives," in the February 1974 issue of *American Journal of Nursing*, which states that:

> The de facto situation in this country is that nurses educationally unprepared in intrapartum [delivery] midwifery skills, are practicing them in delivery rooms. One only has to talk with labor and delivery-room nurses away from teaching centers (and sometimes within them when educational activities are not continuous) to know that often, due to pressures in the delivery suite, nurses must conduct deliveries. Therefore, should we not be preparing maternity nurses through an educational program to be of the greatest possible assistance to mothers and babies?

No one would deny that midwifery training could be most useful for a nurse. But training as a nurse-midwife does not make her worthy of responsibilities equal to those of the doctor. In the United States, the nurse-midwife is never far from the true authority over birth, the

---

Let's face it. Hospitals are set up for the convenience of the personnel who work there.
—ROBERTA BALLARD, M.D., *neonatalogist*

obstetrician, and she can never be an independent practitioner.

Dr. Louis Hellman, obstetrician, teacher, and author of popular obstetric texts, has been called the "father of nurse-midwifery" for the active role he has played in obtaining recognition for the American nurse-midwife. When the American College of Obstetricians and Gynecologists finally recognized and endorsed the certified nurse-midwife as a key member of the modern obstetric team in January 1971, it was largely due to the fatherly prodding of doctors such as Hellman. This official endorsement reads that the nurse-midwife "may assume complete care and management of uncomplicated maternity patients" while serving as a member of an obstetrics team. It took almost fifty years of struggle on the part of nurse-midwives to obtain such recognition. But the struggle has not ended with endorsement. As soon as nurse-midwives began to reform their practice to make it truly patient centered, many previously supportive physicians suddenly put on the brakes.

Dr. Hellman, speaking before a meeting of the Armed Forces District of the American College of Obstetricians and Gynecologists in 1973, revealed how unacceptable any attempt at role change is to obstetricians. While he did say that nurse-midwifery "might offer many positive benefits," he declared:

> If it continues to press for a return to the naturalism of the past, with the zealotry that seems to be its present penchant, much progress may be lost and a true team approach may become difficult.

American doctors resist any move to take birth out of the hospital or to make it a woman's event. They resist true midwifery.

In October 1972, at the fiftieth anniversary of the International Confederation of Midwives, held for the first time in America, Professor G. J. Kloosterman from Holland was asked to speak about the midwife's role in a technological world. He was particularly qualified to make such an address because of his many years as chief of the prominent Amsterdam training school for midwives before becoming Chief of Obstetricians and Gynecologists at the University of Amsterdam Hospital. Kloosterman began by describing normal birth:

> Spontaneous labor in a healthy woman is an event marked by a number of processes which are so complex and so perfectly attuned to each other that any interference with these processes will only detract from their optimum character.

Faced with a spontaneous birth, he said, the attendant must only:

> show respect for this physiological birth and therefore comply with the first rule of medicine, that of "nil nocere": injure nothing.... The doctor always on the lookout for pathology, eager to interfere, will much too often change true physiological aspects of human reproduction into pathology.

Many Western doctors, he said, hold the belief that:

we can improve everything, even natural childbirth in a healthy woman. This philosophy is the philosophy of people who think it deplorable that they were not consulted at the creation of Eve, because they would have done a better job.

He reminded his audience that the midwife cannot be replaced by even a very sophisticated battery of instruments, because her work consists of "protecting the completely healthy woman from unnecessary interference, impatience, over-estimation of technology, and against human meddlesomeness." She is there "to inspire self-confidence and to stimulate the expectant mother in such a way that she changes her reproductive task from a burden into a creative deed accepted by free will." And third, she is "constantly on the lookout for abnormalities." To do the latter she needs to carry out simple procedures at every check-up: weight, blood pressure, urine, height of the fundus (the top of the pregnant uterus), the position of the child, signs of pelvic disproportion. She takes blood and sends it to the laboratory for necessary tests. In this way she can divide women into categories of high risk or good health and pass high-risk mothers on to physicians. She can also be responsible for birth control. It is Kloosterman's opinion from experience that over 70 per cent of all pregnant women, thus screened, would deliver naturally and should be attended only by midwives. Further, he stated that during delivery only 3 to 5 per cent of the healthy mothers would ever require consultation from a doctor. Given such midwife care, for healthy, low-risk mothers, the infant mortality rate would be 2 to 4 in 1,000, Kloosterman said, a figure markedly lower than any other birth statistics in the world.* So too would the maternal mortality rate be lower, as Kloosterman explained that for midwife-attended, low-risk mothers the mortality rate is less than 5 in 100,000 cases.** He added that a group of 20,000 deliveries by midwives in Holland produced no case in which an obstetrician could have done any better than the midwife.

> In quite a number of situations, it is difficult to draw the line between normality and abnormality. In these situations, the obstetrician needs an experienced midwife who can act as his partner in the discussion and sometimes even as his conscience.

What was of special interest to Americans in his audience was Kloosterman's recommendation that nurses and midwives be kept separate to minimize the natural differences between science and routine. And he cautioned that a nurse-midwife is not necessarily a real midwife.

> The obedient female assistant who needs the doctor's presence at the end of a normal childbirth in a healthy woman can be called a nurse or a nurse-midwife, but a real midwife she is not, no more than the experienced surgical nurse is a surgeon.

* In 1971 the infant mortality rate in Holland was 11.1; in the United States it was 18.5; both figures include healthy and high-risk mothers.
** In the United States in 1973, this rate was 20.5, which includes both healthy and high-risk mothers.

> We've had a dozen med students from the best med schools in the country come to watch us work. They all have their doctors' faces well on when they arrive. It takes weeks before they finally drop the impersonality and get involved.
> —HELEN SWALLOW, R.N. and midwife

Kloosterman ended his speech with encouragement to lay midwives.

> Throughout the world there exists a group of women who feel mightily drawn to giving care to women in childbirth. At the same time maternal and independent, responsive to a mother's needs yet accepting full responsibility as her attendant, such women are natural midwives. Without the presence and the acceptance of the midwife, obstetrics becomes aggressive, technological, and inhuman.

Today, this "natural midwife" *is* emerging from obscurity in some parts of the United States, even where she has to practice illegally.

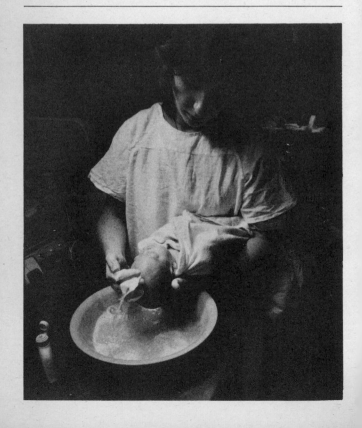

An Irish Nurse-Midwife
Looks at the American Hospital

Ann saw her younger sister's birth. It was her mother's ninth baby, and the doctor accompanied the midwife in case of hemorrhage, because Ann's family lived ten miles from the nearest town. Ann trained and worked as a nurse-midwife in Ireland and England, then traveled to America where she has been a nurse in labor and delivery rooms and intensive care nurseries of several city hospitals for the past nine years.

I THINK there are risks going to a hospital for a normal birth. I've seen quite a few things happen there. Last year we ran a very busy unit, a small city hospital with 20 post-partum beds. There were often nine or ten deliveries a night.

I saw doctors rupturing membranes before it was necessary, and epidurals given far too early. They gave one woman an epidural when she was only three centimeters dilated. She labored nine more hours and they kept re-administering the drug that whole time. One of her twins went into fetal distress, and both twins were in intensive care for three weeks. Some doctors routinely deliver the placenta manually; in fact one doctor did it on every delivery I attended—brought the placenta out in little blobs.

One young girl received a routine epidural, and when she was completely dilated the nurse called the doctor on duty. It was 5:00 a.m. and he was sleeping down the hall. He didn't get up and he wouldn't get up. With the epidural, the woman couldn't feel her contractions and had no urge to push, even though she was fully dilated for three hours before the shifts changed at eight. One of the doctors who came on tried to deliver her, but he couldn't because contractions had stopped completely. So they induced labor and she delivered at 9:20. The baby was in the nursery that night when I came on duty again. It looked a bit bluish, but then all the babies there looked a bit bluish. Anyway, it died on the tenth day of life. The doctors never did decide what happened. And the mother was in isolation, treated for spinal meningitis. I thought, "oh, we could have delivered you at home and you'd have both been fine!"

A doctor who was in a rush tried to deliver a first mother when she was only eight centimeters dilated. I had just examined her myself and there were two centimeters of cervix all the way 'round. I told the doctor that and he said, "Nonsense. There are little tricks you can play." He tried the vacuum extractor but couldn't get it to go on the baby's head, because the cervix was in the way. He asked for a smaller and smaller attachment and couldn't get one small enough to avoid the cervix. Then he tried forceps. He went up inside the cervix and must have clamped onto the cord because suddenly the fetal heart beat dropped. The woman had to have an immediate C-section.

When a woman doesn't have any medication she'll deliver at her own pace. But an undrugged birth is a frantic event in a hospital. The doctors get very nervous. They're not in control and never quite prepared. "Get this!" "Get that!" "Oh! Move this here!" "Quick! It's coming!" Nothing is ready! But usually, when there is anesthesia, the doctor is prepared. He slits the perineum, just so, and he casually looks around to see: yes, his bulb syringe is right there, and his this and that are there, everything is ready. Okay, he brings the head out, there. . . . the baby is delivered, just so. . . . he cuts the cord, and everything is done in nice and easy fashion. After a normal, undrugged birth, the doctor usually turns to me and says: "Well! That was fast!" And he thinks, oh what a good boy am I. This baby didn't fall out.

12
The Practicing Midwife: Nancy Mills

The Practicing Midwife:
Nancy Mills

NANCY MILLS *is a midwife. She serves the parents of her community who choose to give birth without medical interference, parents who prefer to have their babies at home rather than in the hospital. Her clients—for they are not patients—live in the county of Sonoma, a semirural area north of San Francisco. Nancy has been practicing for four years, and assists about seventy births a year.*

In a profession of uncertain legal status in California, where anyone practicing it is liable to legal harassment and criticism from organized medicine, Nancy Mills is in a position of solitary responsibility. She has worked on her own for five years with no doctor to shelter her, no insurance to protect her. Nancy is not a trained medical or paramedical person, but an independent practitioner and lay midwife. Her education is largely self-acquired.

Nancy epitomizes the best traits of a midwife, for she is committed to nothing more nor less than helping women give birth safely and in the way they choose. She is respectful of birth as a natural process that will succeed on its own in the vast majority of cases, and she has acquired the rare gift of patience and constancy in waiting out the long hours with a laboring woman. She spends extra minutes watching, ready to let a seeming difficulty straighten itself out. She practices midwifery with her hands, not instru-

---

I think a place must be made for those lay people who are truly competent and are "naturals" at shepherding a normal birth.

—MICHAEL WHITT, M.D.

ments, and if a medical problem occurs she immediately consults a doctor. In cases of emergency she takes the woman directly to the hospital and provides a written case history to the attending physician. Nancy has created a relationship of respect and trust with her community hospital and with some of the community doctors, despite their disagreement with her and continuing refusal to assist home birth. She seldom complains about the disinterest of the medical community in recognizing the needs of some parents. She believes simply that there is a gap in the medical services available to women in Sonoma County, and that she is most capable of bridging that gap. She does not see her work either as revolutionary or as utopian, and she is neither cynic nor idealist about human nature. She recognizes the great many reasons why people choose to have a child, and why they may choose not to deliver in a hospital. She has tremendous respect for the ability of women to know what they want, and offers them only the service of her craft. She recognizes too that not all of her clients will take full responsibility in bearing a child and in giving birth at home. She does not believe that home birth is for everyone, and is more interested in educating women to all the possible choices and sources of information that exist than in proselytizing clients to her own care. Nancy is simply the county midwife, a shoulder to lean on, another woman to confide in, a constant source of support, a trained attendant, and a protector of the normal process of birth.

Nancy did not grow up intending to be a midwife, although she now feels it is her natural calling. When she had her first child, at the age of sixteen, her doctor was in favor of an undrugged birth and assured her that everything would be just fine, that she was "built" to have babies. Since the hospital lacked the necessary forms that would have allowed drugs to be administered to a minor, Nancy had no medication for the births of either of her first two children. Looking back on the experience, she remembers feeling lonely during labor but recalls that delivery itself was "terrific."

Nancy's interest in birth began to focus at the age of twenty-three, when she went to visit a friend one day and found her in labor. The husband had planned to assist his wife in delivery, and Nancy stayed to watch and give psychological support to the mother. Everything went fine until the baby's head began to emerge. The husband fainted, so Nancy slipped into position just in time and "caught" her first baby. What happened after that, how word spread throughout the community about "Nancy Mills, the midwife," is best explained in Nancy's own words, excerpted from conversations with her at her home. Nancy had her third child at home, and her husband Barry caught their baby.

Growing up in Alameda, California, I never even heard the word midwife. I guess I read about it somewhere later on. But I think I first heard it applied to me when someone said, "Are you Nancy Mills, the midwife?" What could I say except yes. I was delivering babies.

I did half a dozen births before I ever consciously thought about being a midwife. I was referred to as "the only person in the neighborhood who'd seen a baby born."

The birth of a child is a family event and as such should, ideally, take place at home as a normal part of life.
> —SHEILA KITZINGER, The Experience of
> Childbirth

Then as "the only person who'd seen two babies born."
Then three, and four, and so on. I was the only person
around who had some information and experience. At one
point in my first months of work I had three or four births
coming up at once. People were calling to say, "So-and-so
told me you'd delivered their baby. You've seen some home
births. We're planning to do it ourselves. Would you come
and help?" Maybe I knew a slight bit more than that
family who'd already read quite a bit. It was actually the
families themselves who turned me on. They passed books
on to me, such as the *Rural Midwifery Handbook*, and the
handbook put out for police and fire departments, *Emergency
Childbirth*. Then I started reading natural childbirth
books and books on breast-feeding. I learned from mothers,
who'd tell me their problems. And I'd go and look up a
little more about it and relate it to their needs. Pretty soon
I gained some knowledge. Then these three or four births
came up around the same time, and I became conscious
that I was actually becoming a midwife. I was still thinking
I was just someone there to help.

At the same time that I began to attend home births, I
met a nurse working on a master's project on home birth.
She was active in the medical community and had heard
about me from some families. She was trying to find out
how many people were having babies at home and why,
and what the problems and the sociological implications
were of a movement to home births. I helped her work on
a grant for that project. And she helped me get obstetrical
textbooks and taught me what she could, and she introduced
me into the medical community.

So I became the first person practicing midwifery in Sonoma County. Then a doctor in Marin County started responding to local requests for someone to attend home births and began using a nurse as his own midwife (he was the only one in the state I know of). He would use me for his calls in Sonoma County. He would come to the births, but he wanted a midwife there first for several reasons: to evaluate the home situation, to call him when it was time for the mother to deliver, and to deliver in case it happened before he arrived. His time was very pressed, going all over four counties delivering babies and running a general practice as well. He encouraged me, and his nurse taught me how to palpate [feel for the position of the baby in the uterus], and how to do a thorough vaginal exam. Another doctor actually referred patients to me, because he didn't want to do home births. He'd give prenatal care and then I would deliver them. That was our relationship. And if I found any problems I would call him and ask his opinion.

Doctors aren't answering the needs of some parents, but someone must. I've always felt I am doing what I was called upon to do and that I was born a midwife, not made one. A million times I've been asked, "Aren't you afraid of being busted, of getting sued?" I don't want to live with fear, so I try not to have fear about what I am doing, on any level. I didn't start out to break any law. I didn't know what the law was. And I do call myself a midwife now because I'm not afraid of the law, of someone coming to get me because they think I'm practicing

medicine without a license. I gave up worrying a long time ago. Maybe I never did worry about it.

I don't like to think of home versus hospital birth as a controversy. I don't want it to turn into an argument. It seems so silly, nurses getting up at conferences to defend their hospitals. I think people ought to be able to deliver where they want. I think what you get out of a home birth depends on what you are looking for. If you're not into the importance of bonding between mother and child, or nursing your baby right away, of wanting your husband and other children there, of being in your own familiar environment—if you're not into all of the emotional and psychological parts of childbirth—then it doesn't matter where or how you have your baby. It won't mean any more to you. On another level I'd like to turn people on to these things, but I can't, anymore than I can get them to change any part of their lives. Nor would I want to.

I've always held the philosophy that people need to make their own decisions. Some people want me to do it for them. Then my job is to give them information so they can make up their own minds. I have forgotten my role on several occasions and felt myself telling them what to do as a doctor would. But I have faith in what I'm doing when I stick to my basic philosophy of helping people do what *they* want to do. When I get all fouled up in the medical trip that it's too risky and that I should advise people this and that, then I get off the track from what I feel is right.

If I could do it again, I wouldn't have my baby in a hospital. Each time my baby wasn't really mine until I went home with it.
                    —ALIX DOHERTY, *mother of four*

At first when people asked me to come to their births, I was there as a friend only. I would go back afterward to help women with breast-feeding problems, to help them take care of their kids, to help them clean house. My first birth I spent most of my time washing dishes, cleaning house, changing the sheets after the birth. I felt the mother should rest, so I had her lay back with her baby and I cleaned house and took care of the other kids. I became aware of the need for someone to help at home after a birth. Now I think I should be reimbursed for my work, as a craftsman is paid for his craft. Midwifery's been that for me, a craft.

At first most of the people I saw having their babies at home were doing it very simply from an aesthetic viewpoint. The experience of childbirth was very important to them. They wanted to "attend" their own childbirth. It was as simple as that. Now that midwives are available here, many people expect it as a service and aren't really thinking of the responsibility of a home birth.

Yes, of course there is some risk at home. But there are risks to every aspect of life, including the hospital. So I never hesitate to inform the family what it really means to have their baby at home. I make it very clear to them what I'm capable of doing and what I'm not capable of doing. And the decision to have a baby at home is their decision, not mine. I do not want to influence them toward hospital or home. I am aware of my responsibility and I accept it. I can evaluate problems that come up at home, and then I always consult a doctor.

I think obstetricians are essential to problem births and

If you tied 95 percent of women in labor to a tree in Golden Gate Park, the baby would fall out. . . . But I would never do a home delivery because it wouldn't be safe.

—FRED OSTERMANN, M.D.,
quoted in Newsweek

emergencies. They can do Caesarean sections in seconds. Doctors do deserve a lot of money. But on some level what they do gets blown way out of proportion. They deserve respect and admiration and money comparable to what they do. But how much more?

I sat and talked with an obstetrician at lunch one day who said to me at least ten times in the course of our conversation, "Time is money." I said I try not to discriminate against people and give help to whoever needs it. He said he tries not to discriminate either. "But if one comes into my office with money and one with none, I would prefer to send the one who doesn't have any money somewhere else." And he went on to say that he supposed if he continued to take on a few of our patients it wouldn't break him. But it was so apparent how important time and money were to him I can't help but wonder how he can offer quality care to women. What's he in it for?

Doctors are so unrespectful of a woman's body. Take breast-feeding. They know nothing of it. And not only because they've not done it themselves. They don't get into it. They don't have any interest in it. A doctor doesn't sit on a woman's bed and teach her about breast-feeding her child and talk to her about ways of handling problems in the family, or how to eat properly, or how to take care of her two-year-old now that there's a baby. Doctors don't take the time to sit and talk with a husband about what kind of emotional problems they may have in the weeks after the birth. Doctors don't know how to talk about sex, and about how to reestablish sex life after a baby is born. They routinely do the same things to all women and tend

to see the same results. We midwives probably see more variation among women because we don't treat them alike.

There are very few doctors in the community who will tell a pregnant woman, "You are completely healthy and there's no reason why you shouldn't deliver normally and easily at home." Only a few will take the time to inform women of the risks involved at home, which I always do. But there are doctors who freak out and tell women horror stories about home birth and kick them out of the office. There are still no doctors in the county who will go to home births. But maybe that's not a doctor's place. Doctors should not deliver babies at home unless they really want to get into it. Even the few I've seen who feel they want to still leave the talking and counseling to the nurses. But I feel critical about the doctors for talking about "all those people out there." They have no familiarity whatever with those people. They are inside buildings eight to twenty-four hours a day. They haven't the time to look around. How can they? They go straight from school to med school to practice without any experience "out there."

I think a midwife can handle a normal childbirth best because she takes into account all the needs of the family. Midwives are compassionate people, there to help women, and not merely in childbirth. Midwives are taken in by families, loved, called back for years. Women with sexual problems who would never talk to a doctor will talk for hours with their midwife. A midwife, as a woman, has also had the same kind of emotional experiences. She understands womanhood, what it's like to grow up woman, being a wife

and a mother. I've always felt great respect for the human body, and for a woman's body in birth. I don't like routine episiotomies and the unnecessary use of forceps. I don't think anesthetics are ever necessary in normal childbirth. And they are so harmful to the baby. Women never ask for drugs at home. No one has ever said, "I wish I'd had something."

I'm glad the hospital is there when I need it. It happens very rarely, and usually I can stay with the mother all through her birth, even if she requires a C-section. There was a time when someone would meet me at the door and say, "Get lost; we'll take care of it." I think now the feeling is that they may not like me, but they accept me. And that's an achievement.

I have been to several hospital births where the couple has said, "Our baby will not go to the nursery. You may examine her here on the bed." Then they leave the hospital together in a couple of hours with their baby. It's real hard to do this. It depends a lot on how strong the husband is, how willing to stand up for his wife and baby. He's the one who can affect what happens. Usually the woman is more vulnerable and emotional then. If he knows what she wants, he can do it. I've seen some really good experiences at hospitals this way. I think it is where your head is at when you have a baby, not where you are located physically.

Sure, you can affect a lot of people and a lot of births if you make changes at the hospital level. Our hospital has loosened up in the last four years by allowing husbands into deliveries. Now they've gotten a wedge, similar to the

Every time I enter a home to attend a birth, I look around and wonder, where will she choose to give birth? In her bed, on the floor, in the corner backed up against the wall, crouching on all fours, squatting?
—RAVEN LANG, *California lay midwife*

British one, for their delivery tables so the woman can sit at a forty-five-degree angle during pushing. They now allow the woman to deliver unstrapped. Women can also nurse on the delivery table if they demand it. By telling parents what to expect from the hospital and what they need to demand to get what they want, I am a help. But no hospital birth is as natural as a home birth. Hospitals are for sick people.

I think one reason I work in childbirth is that I see and learn so much about people. I'm very interested in relationships. The way people act together. The way women are when they are alone. At home I spend a lot of time writing notes on everything about the family, the birth, the kids. At some births you can see the tremendous love and respect a man has for his wife. He is learning so much about her.

Very few women have to be hospitalized to give birth. One case where the hospital was necessary occurred when I was with a woman who had a prolapsed cord. That is, the cord came down before the baby, a situation that is life threatening to the baby. I put the cord back inside and I kept my hand on it as we drove all the way to the hospital, with the mother on her hands and knees. I had her pant all the way, to keep the labor stationary and prevent damage to the baby. I explained to her what was happening as she panted, and told her she'd probably have to have a Caesarean section. Since it was her second child, and the first had been at home, she accepted it well. All the way to the hospital the baby's heart tones were fine. We took her in. The doctor did an emergency C-section. After the operation he came out and took me aside. "You know," he said, "those heart tones were fine until you took your hand out. And then they dropped to forty." Then he gave me a funny look as if to say, "What is this you're doing?" And he shook his finger at me: "One of these days the statistics are going to catch up with you!" He was saying I was just lucky this time. I said, "Think positively." And I really think having a positive attitude has something to do with it. A hospital thinks in statistics and anticipates emergencies, and I think this affects their births and the number of problems they see.

On another occasion I took a woman with fetal distress to the hospital and the attending staff refused to take my word on anything. The woman labored needlessly for nine full hours before a decision was made to X ray her pelvis, as I had requested on entry. I felt helpless. They finally had to deliver the woman in emergency high-forceps procedure because the heart tones had stopped altogether. Then the baby was sent to the intensive-care nursery and the mother couldn't see her. There was nerve damage and there was infection. I went to the hospital the next day and spoke with the nursing supervisor and the doctor on duty, because I was so upset. The whole situation could have been avoided. They called me to a meeting later of the nurses and residents who had been on duty. The women at the meeting kept saying to me, "You can't be emotional." As if I should be detached. The doctor admitted their work was in error. I said I thought it was a pretty rotten way for a baby to start out life.

I've had several cases where I walked in the door of a home and found a girl just two centimeters dilated. Yet I'd instantly known this birth wasn't going to work at home. She was holding back too much. Then I had to make the decision to take her to the hospital unless she could relax. Some women just simply can't deliver at home, for emotional reasons. Physiologically there is no problem, yet they need to be in a hospital for security. As soon as they get there they feel relieved and ready to deliver the baby. Other people can't cope with hospitals and deliver much easier if they stay at home. I'm sure some women end up having Caesareans just from their inability to dilate because of being so frightened and upset. Sometimes it's hard to know how a woman will react in labor and where she'll feel safe. And it's too bad most women are afraid of such a natural and beautiful experience as home birth.

At one birth the baby came out and didn't breathe. We worked and worked for minutes to get it to breathe. The woman's brother and her mother were in the room with us. Her brother is a physician, but he didn't interfere. He didn't know what to do. There was a total silence as we worked over her baby. It came around finally and today, two years later, is fine and healthy. I sometimes wonder what that doctor thinks of us midwives, having watched his own sister at a very difficult time. The family lived up in the country, 1½ hours from the nearest hospital.

Another time a doctor watched his sister give birth to a nine-pound boy at home with no problems. It was her first baby and he was real concerned she might tear if she didn't have an episiotomy. I reassured him that with vaginal massage and controlled pushing we wouldn't have a tear. And we didn't. This is most often the case. He was delighted and is today attending home births himself.

I delivered a baby for a Korean girl who didn't speak a word of English. She was on a plastic sheet on hands and knees when I arrived, with her mother-in-law forcing raw eggs down her throat. My sister and I tried not to say anything because they couldn't have understood us anyway. And the girl had a fine birth. We smiled and giggled a lot, she and I. That's how it happened. I did have to stop the mother-in-law, who'd had twelve children of her own, from doing some interesting things. She was in there with her fist on the abdomen, trying to knead and pull the placenta out the second after the child was born. I discouraged that.

The older woman cried when the baby was born. It was the young woman's second girl child. She cried too, and we immediately picked up that there was something very wrong. We found out that her husband was the first son of twelve boys and is supposed to produce boy children. As a wife with a second daughter she was failing him, and in Korea, evidently, a husband might go on to another wife for such an offense. It's thought that if you have two girls in a row, you always produce girls. I learned this through her brother, the family interpreter, who arrived later. I asked him, "Is she going to resent this child?" And he spoke right out: "Oh, yes." I just said, "Oh." I felt really bad. You know, I wanted to take that baby home. I told the brother that they were living in America now. And here in America we think that women are just as good as men. He told them and they all tried to smile. You could tell, though, that they thought they knew better.

I've had so many unbelievable experiences. I had one woman, a perfect stranger, knock on my door at midnight, in labor. Her husband was there too, with a shotgun in his hand. I couldn't turn her away.

Midwives are characteristically unaggressive, gentle, and patient people who work quietly in their community for the women who seek their service. Because in America the medical system neither supports nor understands their function, midwives are left to learn by their own experience, or by whatever textbooks, films, and other resources they can find. As much as they have seen the process of birth, assisted it and attended it for many years, the midwives are always in need of more information and must seek support and advice wherever they can find it. For some, this is an anxious and difficult experience at first, because it forces the midwife to become aggressive, and to find other midwives in the area to share information about the many nuances of her craft. So Nancy Mills began to organize.

We first got together as a group for the sole purpose of sharing information, all kinds. The women at those first meetings came from all sides. Some were very revolutionary. Some heavily political, some into the women's movement. And there were some, like myself, who had no particular consciousness of the women's movement or anything political, but who felt we were in a helping profession. I respect the women's movement a great deal and now that I'm older I find I make friends with more women and I see how much I care for them. That is a new experience for me. When I was younger, although I'd always liked women, I often found myself accidently in competition with them. And years ago there were always some who got nervous when I let them know I cared. So I thought I wasn't supposed to show affection for other women. Midwifery, the women's movement, the hip movement, the natural foods movement, the antiwar movement, all came to me about the same time.

The lay midwives I associate with are much more radical than other women, I guess. But I know I started out with no consciousness of breaking any law. I didn't know what the law was. In the early days there were four practicing lay midwives in Northern California that I knew about. We found out that each one of us started practicing the same year, all without previous training, all working independently. We found incredible similarities in how we got started as midwives. Myself, I have a very definite philosophy and spiritual attitude about it. But I don't feel fight, fight, fight, change the laws. When you get so involved in fighting to change the laws, you're no longer delivering the babies and helping the women. It's hard to do both. Those midwives who have strong political feelings have them inside. They don't go running to the state capitol. We get our work done. We go to seminars, classes, meetings. We share information. Three of us started the midwifery group and went to see if there were more of us around. We found a couple of licensed nurse-midwives who are teaching but not attending birth. Everyone came out of the bushes. I can remember feeling apprehensive at the first meeting, scared of where I stood in regard to those other women, especially in my knowledge of deliveries. But it was unanimous that we would meet again. And the next meeting we returned with our past months' experiences to share. Someone had delivered a complicated breech. We all sat on the edge of our chairs to hear each other's stories. And that is the kind of knowledge that is best.

We also talked a lot about books we'd studied—Margaret Miles' English midwifery text, obstetric texts, pediatric texts. Whatever we saw or learned we turned each other on to. One had access to the medical libraries and brought more books and an occasional film. And we all had our little home movies of some birth we'd taken part in. It was a beautiful interchange of people and ideas. One of the midwives who was a nurse and practicing with a doctor has gone back East to train in nurse-midwifery at Yale. Another one has moved to Hawaii and has managed to get a license to practice there. We no longer have meetings, and I miss them.

Although a midwife will spend a great deal of time counseling her client on the realities of home birth, no one has yet explained to the midwife exactly what the realities are for her. In time she may discover that midwifery, if not illegal, has become tightly constrained by ominous pressure from the medical community or law-enforcement agencies. Yet because fear of legal or social entanglements will only impede her work, the midwife attempts to maintain her delicate position by gaining the trust of local authorities, even though they are aware that she is working outside the law. Occasionally a local or state group may work with her to help the community and gain information about home birth, but here the midwife may be deceived by the prospect of security and find herself even more constrained by society's fear. For Nancy Mills, a woman who had built an enduring rapport with doctors and hospital staffs in her community, a perfect opportunity seemed to present itself when she began working for a state-funded project designed to bring pre- and post-natal care to pregnant women—but no home deliveries. Some months into the program, she was still excited with the way it was working out.

We provide free care at the health center. The people who funded us know that I'm a midwife. The head of the department of maternal and child health is new and has spent three years in Africa working with midwives. He gives lay people in the community whatever responsibility they show they can handle. Another woman there, who has been in maternal and child health for years, also loves midwives and has wanted them all along in California. So between the two of these officials they think I'm great. The state public health department wouldn't bust me, I don't think. Their attitude is that it's better that someone's out helping people, whether we're illegal or not. Plus that they have confidence in me and realize that my relationship with the hospital is fairly good. They've said to me, "Now don't get in trouble." So it's a quiet, unspoken thing. I'm not getting paid to actually deliver babies; I do that on my own time. So it's two totally independent jobs right now.

In March of 1974, when law-enforcement agencies in other areas of California did begin to arrest midwives, Nancy received several communications from doctors in Sonoma County warning her to seek legal protection or stop her midwifery practice. By April, officials of the state-funded project under which Nancy thought she had found

226

*the perfect compromise informed her that she must either
stop her practice or leave the project. That summer obstetricians in Sonoma County brought charges against Nancy
for practicing medicine without a license, and in September
she was ordered by the court to terminate her practice or
face prosecution by the state. As of this writing she quietly*

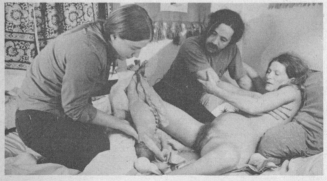

continues to attend home births. The meetings of mid-
wives that Nancy once respected so much have now
resumed no longer to share information but to consider
ways in which midwives in California can educate the
public and fight the law. Meanwhile, many more "birth at-
tendants" are beginning to practice in Sonoma County and

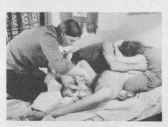

throughout California, and each of them faces the difficult task of education and training for a profession which has no legal status and no formal training provided.

13
Home Birth

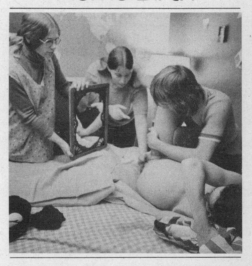

Home Birth

To HEAR PHYSICIANS and obstetricians expound upon the need for hospitalization for each and every birth, one would think the Bible ought to be revised to read: "And on the eighth day God created hospitals; and he saw that it was good." Despite the modern notion that birth is unsafe outside a fully equipped hospital, nature continues to design the birthing process so that it seldom needs a hospital.

Why defend home birth? Why not ask the medical profession to defend hospital birth? The fact is that American hospital statistics have never been good enough to serve as a defense of hospital birth (see Chapter 5), nor has it ever been disputed that under normal circumstances, without socially produced fears, a woman who chooses home birth feels safer and more comfortable among friends and family in her own surroundings. Home birth *is* the safest for women who choose it, when it follows thorough prenatal care and is carefully assisted by trained attendants.

The safety of home birth has been amply demonstrated by the successful record of the Chicago Maternity Center, an organization that has sent skilled birth attendants to home births in severely depressed areas for over seventy-five years. Headed by Dr. Beatrice Tucker, who has presided over 100,000 births herself, the Center's staff was often called to attend the births of women who had never

It couldn't have been better!
—ANONYMOUS NEW MOTHER *after home birth*

received prenatal care and whose only preparation for birth was a clean sheet on the kitchen table. "In the 1930's we'd deliver babies in rooms with dirt floors, no toilets and no electricity. We'd work by candlelight," Dr. Tucker recalled to a *Life* magazine writer in 1972. Yet in spite of poor facilities, unsanitary conditions and last-minute complications, 90 per cent of the 150,000 births attended by the Chicago Maternity Center have been delivered at home. Only one out of every ten mothers had to be removed from her home for a hospital delivery.

As a result, "I am committed to home births," Dr. Tucker has said, noting that "in a hospital, the isolation is devastating." As *Life* reported it, "more and more people, particularly well-educated young people, are having their babies outside hospitals. Childbirth, they feel, is a happy event which has nothing to do with the sterile impersonality of a hospital. Mothers believe they get more attention during labor at home and recover faster afterward; fathers like participating fully in the birth."

So the question was not a matter of poverty, the article stated, but of choice: "I believe a patient has a right to choose where she wants to have a baby," Dr. Tucker said.*

Anthropologist Lester Hazell, author of the popular

* Sadly, the Chicago Maternity Center discontinued care for home births in the fall of 1973, due to a shortage of obstetricians and medical residents. Also, during its last ten years of operation, requests for home births from community residents declined from 300 a month to 30 a month—probably, as one staff member has suggested, because families in poverty areas have come to regard hospital birth as more prestigious than home birth.

If home birth creates healthier children, if it provides a more loving and sounder bond between the child and its family, then it should be available as an alternative for any families who want it.

—RAVEN LANG, *California lay midwife*

Commonsense Childbirth (1969), is studying the socio-logical impact of the movement to home birth in the San Francisco Bay Area in California. She has gathered data from over 300 home births, the majority of which were attended by the father of the baby, or by a lay mid-wife. Of these 300, there were no cases of maternal death and only one case of fetal death, a stillborn. Only two instances of maternal hemorrhage occurred, one caused by an inexperienced doctor pulling on the cord, the other in a mother who had been diagnosed during pregnancy as a poor risk because of excessive fluid retention and bruising. This woman was an exception, however, as most high-risk mothers had been referred to hospitals early in preg-nancy. Doctors may say that it is unfair to compare such a low rate of infant mortality (3.3 per thousand) from this small sampling of 300 basically normal births, to the national rate (in 1972) of 18.5 per thousand. But they are still astonished to discover that no medication of any kind was administered in all 300 births, that there were no episiotomies, no use of forceps, no separation of mother and child after birth, only one postnatal infection, and of course, no exorbitant doctor or hospital bills. Most of all, what this study and others (see Chapter 15) prove is that home birth can be a reasonable and successful choice for any mother whose prenatal visits during pregnancy indicate a normal, healthy birth.

Nevertheless, when doctors are asked to state their reasons for being against home birth, they often describe terrible things which can happen so quickly that the lives of mother and child are endangered or lost. Specifically,

I say, bring the midwives back!
—EUNICE MITCHELL, *mother*

they focus on the dangers of hemorrhaging for the mother, a problem that many obstetricians believe requires immediate hospitalization because "minutes lost may mean lives lost," as one doctor likes to say. Yet the record of the Frontier Nursing Service (FNS) in Kentucky (see Chapter 17) shows that with minimal equipment the skilled and attentive midwife can stop hemorrhaging. During the twelve years that the FNS attended home births, not one mother was lost from hemorrhage or any other complication, a fact that is especially interesting because much of the birthing population of Kentucky's mountain areas has been traditionally malnourished and is therefore considered to be a higher risk than the birthing population of the rest of the country. Another interesting aspect of the FNS was that no ambulance was available to follow the midwives deep into the mountains, and often there was no doctor to assist in emergencies.

Physicians also describe the dangers of respiratory problems for the newborn infant and point out that brain damage will occur if the baby does not begin breathing immediately. Such cases are rare with unmedicated births, but if they do occur at home, generally the mildly depressed infant, left alone at its mother's breast, will establish normal breathing patterns on its own within minutes. In cases of severely depressed babies, the quick-thinking midwife can bring about normal breathing patterns through simple manipulations with her hands alone. Doctors who pay so much attention to acute respiratory problems should also note that hospital nurseries are filled with "mildly" depressed and "blue-tinged" infants suffer-

Birth is too important to be left to obstetricians.
—MICHAEL WHITT, M.D.

ing for days and weeks from the effects of drugged and artificially stimulated births.

Where problems do arise at home births, good back-up care in the form of specially equipped, mobile birth units, such as England's famed "flying squads" (see Chapter 18), can bridge the gap between home and hospital and carry surgical help directly to the mother at home, or move the mother and infant to the hospital in a short time. Proper back-up care has never been available in the United States, and during its years of home-birth service the Chicago Maternity Center had to transport as much specialized equipment to the home site as possible, adding its own precautions (such as routine hormone injections), which would not have been necessary were back-up care available. The American consumer needs to ask why such precautions have never been taken in this country and what has prevented community fire departments from including an American version of the "flying squad."

The argument that dirt and bacteria in the home will lead to infection is seldom voiced by doctors today, since the public is now aware that attempts of hospitals to maintain sterility have not prevented the spread of cross-infections which zip through their wards. Staphylococcus infections, a great danger to the newborn babies in hospitals, are almost unheard of at home. Infections of nursing mothers' breasts, which have caused many hospital staffs to suggest that women give up nursing, rarely occur in the home. A baby acquires a certain degree of immunity to the organisms present in its home while still in the womb. And the germs in the home are familiar to a particular family

---

A woman has as much right to choose how and where to have a child as she has to choose what kind of tampons to wear.
        —ROBIN BAKER, *coordinator, Midwives'*
                Defense Committee, Santa Cruz

and are less likely to be dangerous to the infant than the unfamiliar collection of germs found in any hospital maternity ward or infant nursery. The family home can be made clean enough for birth with little effort.

Finally, doctors offer the argument that liability insurance does not cover home birth and that a lawsuit resulting from home delivery could conceivably cost them their careers. If this is true, it is a product of the sorry lack of trust that exists between mother and obstetrician in the United States today. Certainly it is the doctor's problem, not woman's, and it cannot be solved simply by hospitalizing each and every woman who gives birth. As in other areas of health services, it will only be solved when physicians and patients alike see to it that individuals are held responsible for maintaining their own states of health. The best doctor exists only to assist the healing process, not to assume personal responsibility for another human being. Thus the choice of method and place of birth must ultimately rest with the mother, so that her attendants function only to carry out her desires wherever possible. By making home birth seem totally unreasonable, physicians are robbing American women of a vital choice in the function of their own bodies.

At the same time, doctors fail to point out that there are many arguments against routine hospitalization for birth. Besides the threat of damage to mother and infant, hospital birth causes strain on the average family's budget, enforces rigid separation of family members and of mother and child after birth, and results in long isolation of mother and infant from siblings, all of which place unusual strain upon the healthy family unit. Since birth is a time of emotional crisis and change, hospital-created strain upon an already-strained family can be enough to weaken even the strongest ties.

But the greatest problem in the controversy over home versus hospital birth is that these arguments tend to polarize groups into factions of absolute belief in one place or the other. Midwives continue to stress that neither can be made so safe as to guarantee that every mother and every child will survive the process. Just as no device or medical interference has yet been created to insure total safety in any process of life, so does birth always entail a small degree of risk.

Home birth is thus a natural choice, not for all couples but for *many* couples, and today doctors either deal honestly with this fact or avoid the issue entirely and forget they are in a service profession. Home birth is a safe choice for healthy women who consciously prepare for birth, who receive careful prenatal care and screening, and who call in a skilled attendant to assist them. The only reasonable argument left today that can be stated against home birth is that it is too simple and inexpensive a solution for such a complex society as ours. And perhaps that is the real reason why home birth is no longer a choice in America.

Karen and Skip Schmidt chose to have their second child born at home. Their daughter Lorien had been born in a nearby hospital. There the obstetric resident on duty had made an incision for an episiotomy that cut completely

---

Women who want home birth want their babies with them from the moment of birth. Most of these parents are taking full responsibility and are accepting the possible risks. The proportions of this movement are growing too big to deny.
—HELEN NAIL, *California lay midwife*

through Karen's anal sphincter. By the time the obstetrician on duty arrived at the scene, the baby had been pulled out with forceps. There was blood all over the room and the embarrassed resident had to admit that he couldn't sew Karen up again. The obstetrician quietly called the resident aside and criticized him for "botching the job." That was the only mention of the damage Skip and Karen overheard. They were offered no apology. Karen had hemorrhaged over a quart of blood and there was talk of a transfusion. Left alone to handle their feelings in Recovery, the couple felt thoroughly disgusted with the staff. Their new baby had disappeared into another part of the hospital, and Karen did not get to see her for another twenty hours. They left the hospital as soon as possible.

Skip has guilt feelings about the experience of their first birth and wishes he had known more about what to do. "Karen had to have an IV in her arm for two days," he says. "I felt it was just another punishment for her having yelled in the labor room and not having been a model patient. I blame myself for not having wanted to go along to preparation classes with her ahead of time."

Karen knows she was not prepared for Lorien's birth either. She says she lost control early in labor, screamed for "dope," and it was given immediately. But, she adds, "He didn't have to cut me that way. After the hospital experience, I never wanted to have a baby in the hospital again. I didn't even want to have a baby again. I just wanted to get out of there. We left in three days, but it

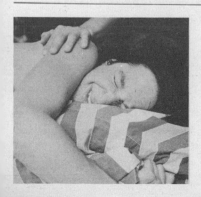

seemed like an eternity. And I couldn't sit down for a month after."

Karen and Skip's first daughter weighed eight pounds and twelve ounces at birth. Karen nursed her successfully at home, and eventually the hospital experience faded into a bad memory. But they were determined that their next birth would be different. They talked to Lorien about the new baby, who would be born at home. And she, at 3½, said she wanted to watch her brother being born. (She was sure it would be a brother for her to play with.)

Nancy Mills and her sister Joan had visited the Schmidt's house before the birth to assess the home environment and to help the couple make preparations. Karen had had her prenatal checkups at the local clinic where Nancy was employed at the time, and this time both she and Skip were well prepared for the birth.

Birth was already under way by the time I arrived at the Schmidt's home in late evening. Nancy called to me from the front door that labor had progressed so rapidly that Karen was already getting ready to push. When I walked into the bedroom, Karen was leaning back in bed on checkered sheets against Skip. She remained there encircled in his arms during the long hour that she pushed. Joan was on the edge of the bed, with a stethoscope around her neck. She was seven months pregnant herself and this birth would be another experience in her education as a midwife and a mother. Joan went into the kitchen to fetch the sterilized instruments that she and

Nancy had brought earlier and had boiled in a covered pot for fifteen minutes: scissors, hemostat (the clamp for the umbilical cord), and a three-ounce rubber ear syringe. They also had brought with them a quantity of disposable sterile gloves, stethoscope, fetoscope, blood-pressure cuff, antiseptic soap, thermometer, sterile cotton pads, paper pads, and diapers: their standard home-birth kit.

Karen and Skip were prepared, too, with a supply of newly laundered receiving blankets, a pot for the placenta, and clean baby clothes. They had made the bed with a plastic sheet underneath to protect their mattress. The room had been warmed to about seventy-five degrees by a small heater. It was a bit hot for all of us, but it would be the perfect temperature for the new baby. Karen had shed her clothes in the efforts of labor.

Nancy made one more vaginal exam during a contraction to check dilation. The cervix was open to ten centimeters and completely thinned. She checked for presentation and the position of the baby's head in the pelvis. The baby was lying in posterior position with its face looking up toward the pubic bone, rather than the more normal face-downward position, as it began to descend into the birth canal. This would result in greater effort for Karen in the second stage of labor, but it was not cause for alarm. Although a doctor often responds to posterior position with a large episiotomy and pulls the baby out himself, Nancy decided to wait and see.

Normally, Nancy makes hot compresses to lay across a

woman's abdomen to soothe her during transition. For women who feel the sensations of labor concentrated in their lower backs, she uses the same sort of compresses, made of soft towels, laid across the lower spine to ease pressure. She also uses compresses on the perineum during pushing to help it stretch and give. But there was no time for such amenities tonight.

Karen began to push with tremendous enthusiasm. Between contractions she would drop her head back against Skip and look at Nancy or Joan to see how she was doing. "Am I all right?" Next time she would ask, "Is the baby all right?"

For two minutes during the latter part of pushing, Nancy lost contact with the fetal heartbeat. This is not uncommon as the baby moves down the birth canal, and since the placental sounds remained loud and clear, she was not worried. The room was silent, except when Karen asked a question or when Nancy gave her praise for relaxing and pointers for slackening the muscles in her pelvic floor. As the baby's head began to crown, Nancy suggested that Karen lie on her side and that Skip support her leg. She explained that this would help prevent tearing from what was obviously going to be a very large head crowning, face up.

Nancy began to massage coconut oil gently into the stretching perineum, smoothing and soothing the skin. Just as the baby's head reached full crown, Nancy called to me to come quick and see. It was a first in her experience:

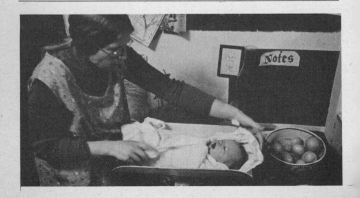

the baby, completely on its own, was rotating its head a full ninety degrees from posterior to anterior position. No sooner had the head completed rotating than it began to slip out toward Nancy's hands, which gently and firmly restrained it from bursting through and tearing Karen. Nancy maintained constant communication with Karen, reminding her how to breathe and explaining everything that was happening. At the very moment that the head slipped through and out, Karen shouted, "Go back in!" Everyone laughed. At that same moment, the tremendous urge to defecate she had felt passed, the burning sensation around her clitoris passed, and her baby's head was born. The rest of the body came out with the next easy contraction, and a little girl was there, a large baby, surprisingly clean. She arrived with one arm crossed over her chest and the cord wrapped loosely once around her neck. Her birth was followed by an initial gush of blood, which stopped suddenly. This often happens as a normal accompaniment to birth, but as was her practice, Nancy kept a watchful eye and prepared to act immediately if there were any signs of hemorrhage. She began to massage the fundus and to feel for the separation of the placenta inside Karen's abdomen.

The baby cried at birth, then stopped and looked quietly around the room. Joan helped Karen put the baby to the breast, then dried and wrapped it in a clean cotton blanket. Nancy and Joan did not attempt to wash the baby, as the creamy vernix (a natural secretion of the fetus) on her skin

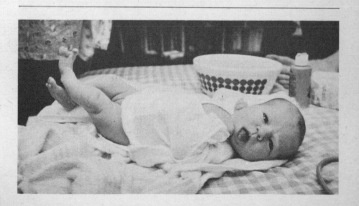

would soon disappear on its own. Nancy watched for the placenta. The uterus began to work again and delivered the placenta with one strong contraction. Nancy began to massage Karen's belly in earnest to keep the uterus tight, a precaution against further bleeding.

Karen lay back, smiling at everyone. "I don't know how to thank you enough." Nancy smiled. They both remembered the hospital experience. After five minutes of bustle and cleanup, the room quieted down. Lorien, still asleep, had been carried into the birthing room by Karen's friend in time to wake for the birth. She had cried a bit at being thus awakened, but watching her mother during the last few pushes, she had been enrapt. There was no fear in Karen's manner, nor great pain, and Lorien was calm. She now snuggled next to her mother on the bed and watched her little sister nurse.

Nancy took Karen's blood pressure and carried the placenta to the kitchen to examine it fully, making sure it was intact and checking for the three vessels in the cord. Skip came in too, carrying Lorien, to look in wonder at the afterbirth. He asked what it would taste like if cooked. "Liver," Nancy said.

Back in the bedroom, Nancy performed a thorough examination of Karen, noting she had torn just a short way down her old episiotomy scar—a superficial, first-degree tear. She took two stitches in the outer layer as the baby continued to suck and the uterus visibly contracted. Karen needed no local anesthesia, since the area was still numb from birth. Nancy talked with Karen about the birth and Skip and Lorien listened.

She said Karen must take it easy for a week and do no housework, because of her previous hemorrhage. She spoke to Lorien about her new sister and how she could help her mommy. Karen needed lots of rest for a few days and Lorien could bring her tea and help Daddy. Nancy said the birth had been slowed a bit by Karen's unconscious tightening of her pelvic floor, but that as soon as she had really let go, as if to defecate, the baby had come right out. She then reminded Skip that he should stand by and watch Karen whenever she took a shower over the next week, since she might feel weak. She was not to take a bath for at least three days, because of the danger that hot water might bring on bleeding.

Nancy then showed both of them how to massage Karen's fundus to keep it firm over the next few hours. Karen should check it every fifteen minutes and, if it was soft, massage it until she fell asleep. The baby was given a complete newborn examination as it lay next to Karen: head circumference measured, heart rate noted, lungs checked to make sure they were clear, reflexes and the stability of the hips examined, respirations counted. Joan brought the baby into the kitchen to weigh her. At the end of tidying up, Nancy asked permission to put silver-nitrate drops in the baby's eyes, a precaution against gonorrhea-produced blindness practiced routinely in American hospitals. She then arranged a time to return the next day to check on Karen and the family. Nancy explained that she found it best to make an appointment, since several times she had returned a day after a birth to find a family already out. She reminded Karen to make certain she urinated before going to sleep so that a full bladder wouldn't get in the way of her contracting uterus, which was returning to its prepregnancy size.

Nancy remarked to me that she always finds it important that a man and woman spend time alone together after a birth experience to give each other love and attention and to reestablish the relationship that birth strains. She always tries to leave the room for a while so the couple can be alone.

The Schmidt's little baby weighed eight pounds and eleven ounces at birth. She was given an Apgar rating of 10 one minute after birth by the nonattending midwife, Joan. Five minutes later she was still given a rating of 10.

Three Country Doctors
Talk about Home Birth

Drs. Michael Whitt, Ed Kosinski, and Wes Sokolosky established the West Marin Medical Center in the rural community of Point Reyes, California in 1970. Having experienced a "disenchantment with the whole delivery scene" in American hospitals early in their careers, they "specifically excluded obstetrics" from the Center. But it was not long before they realized they had settled in a part of California where more and more mothers were giving birth at home without the assistance of the medical community. Recognizing the need for this service, the doctors soon began attending home births when they were called. Today they employ nurses as midwives, and they consider their own attendance at home births a form of traditional midwifery. In the last four years they have attended over five hundred home births.

What was your attitude toward birth when you first began to practice?

KOSINSKI: I was scared for the woman, for what she must be going through. At school I never saw an unmedicated birth, except for one breech that came too quickly. Then I watched *one* woman push her baby out naturally, and I was flabbergasted. She showed no pain. Of the forty or fifty births I had done, that was the first time I'd seen the woman completely in control. The obstetrical service at the hospital where I studied regarded women as slabs of beef. I approached birth in private practice with trepidation, because I didn't feel I'd been properly trained. I felt like I'd been dabbling in some sort of occult science.

If you felt so unprepared for natural birth, how did you train yourselves to attend home births?

WHITT: Mainly we learned by doing; and we learned from the women we attended. People forget we *can* learn

from our experiences, and that experience is the hallmark of science. We have never minced words about the dangers of home birth or the limitations of our experience. We tell mothers that we have no backup help. If women still choose to ask us to attend a birth, it seems ethically imperative that we go.

What about some obstetricians' belief that women don't know enough to be able to make decisions about their births?

SOKOLOSKY: I don't think women are nearly as ignorant of their bodies as doctors make them out to be. They can, however, be scared out of perceiving what's going on inside. This is a functional ignorance. But I don't know of one instance in our experience where the need to *do* something wasn't clear to the woman long before it became clear to us.

WHITT: I think obstetricians are, by training and by temperament, generally unfit to attend a normal birth. Certainly the hospital, in a normal or slightly difficult labor, is not the place to be. It does seem to complicate things. A woman opting for the hospital may have asked for a normal birth, but she is going where she should know normal birth is least likely to occur.

You talk to every woman beforehand about the risks of a home birth. Do you think physicians inform women of the risks of hospitalization?

WHITT: They imply a guarantee that nothing can happen in a hospital, but that is totally false. People talk about "the hospital" as if they're always talking about the high-risk center. There's really very little advantage to the infant in a small, community hospital, with only one doctor and one nurse on night duty.

KOSINSKI: I think you're making a mistake if you believe the hospital is responsible for the quality of care you receive. It's not the hospital, or the nurse, but the doctor. What we're really talking about is a deficient relationship between the doctor and "patient." Authoritarianism among physicians.

Is home birth a responsible choice to make?

WHITT: I think the woman who chooses to have her baby at home is perhaps more responsible than one who abandons herself to even the "best" obstetrician. When a woman goes to the "best" physician, she is getting the "best" physician when crisis develops, not the best one to prevent crisis and attend a normal birth.

KOSINSKI: I think there's a kind of truth of "Murphy's Law" in hospitals: if anything can go wrong, it will, because a hospital has a crisis-orientation.

WHITT: We see very little toxemia at home, almost none. We see very little prematurity. Women at home never ask for medication. I think our whole emphasis in birth should be to get mothers to take care of themselves, instead of simply providing all of these materials and personnel to take care of emergencies *after* they arise. Crisis-oriented care will not lead to a healthier and better-cared-for population. Most of the people who are pontificating against home birth and natural birth have *never* had any experience with it. If we found home birth excessively reckless, we would consider reevaluating our stand. But from our work it may turn out to be safer to deliver at home.

14
An Anonymous
Midwife Speaks Out

An Anonymous
Midwife Speaks Out

Often, legal and social pressures may reach such an inten-
sity that the midwife, especially if she is practicing in a
suburban or middle-class community, may be forced to
keep her trade a secret from all but those who seek her
craft. For Carol, a forty-year-old midwife who has attended
over eighty home births in such an area, midwifery became
such a constant sources of anxiety to her family and
friends that she finally decided to leave the profession. Her
story, told in her own words, represents a common plight
of the midwife in many areas of the United States today.

MY MOTHER is afraid. My brother, who's a lawyer, would
send me up himself. My husband is a school teacher and
this is a very square community. He's afraid it will affect
his job. Everything does around here.

I've got two more births, which I'll complete. One is
with a doctor, whose wife is having a baby, and he wants
to attend as a father.

I have to quit. My kids are great. They've all been to
births with me, from the nineteen-year-old down to the
six-year-old. Five boys and two girls. I had to tell them I
was quitting, because of the legal thing. I would certainly
like to go out and carry a banner for midwifery myself.
But I've made a different life here and it doesn't fit.

I worked in a maternity hospital in Connecticut
when I was eighteen and I vowed then I'd
never have a child if I was going to end up

I first started working with mothers when I began doing childbirth classes six years ago and started going to hospital births with single mothers. I'd attended 179 before I ever did a home birth. The mother would tell the hospital I was her labor coach. Around here I could get in since I had taken Bradley training and was certified.

After I'd done all those hospital births I decided to help women. The first one had privately decided to have a home birth and had told no one; she called me already in labor. She'd also called a public health nurse, since her labor was so long. When I arrived, the nurse was trying to convince her to go to the hospital. The woman just said no. So the nurse said she legally could not stay. She said, "You'll have to get your friend here to help you. I can't." So I stayed with the couple. It was so beautiful, that birth. I couldn't believe the difference. Watching them with their baby. The next thing I knew, everyone began to hear of me and wanted to have me be at their home birth. They started coming like crazy. Somebody recently came down from Oregon to ask if I would deliver their baby. People know me.

I've never charged a fee for my work and people realize I can't charge. But I've received fantastic gifts. Months after the birth people remember how I helped and want to thank me. Earth shoes, handmade dresses, all kinds of good things. The nicest was the loan of a cabin so my husband and I could go away while the family baby-sat all my kids for us.

We are awfully poor. I've never been into money. But I grew up in a very rich home with a maid. Money just

---

*like those countless women I saw coming down
from the delivery room—still knocked out—
not even knowing they'd had a child.*
                    —DORIS CLARK, *California lay midwife*

doesn't seem to matter. I make eighty to ninety dollars a month from my childbirth class.

I would say half of my couples have home deliveries now. I have four doctors in my class. Three have pregnant wives; one is just there to learn. He wants to know why my women are so different in labor from his patients. But his wife is a nurse and is very antagonistic. She saw me delivering two babies on films I showed. In both cases doctors happened to be there too, but they did not show on the film. That woman made me nervous.

A man from the State Board of Medical Examiners called me last month, just after the Santa Cruz midwives were arrested, to find out about my work. I told him I was too busy to talk to him and hung up. As soon as I hung up I got rid of all my birth stuff, put it in other people's homes.

I have more confusions about my work. One woman called thinking I was doing abortions.

I'm going to college to be an R.N. I'm hoping to find a doctor into home deliveries who I could work for. Someone I can support. Then I could do it legally.

Two families in my class are going to deliver their own babies. Sometimes I turn down three women a day. About seven every week. I know I'm not responsible for finding another midwife, but I do feel guilty that I can't help.

Another reason I'm quitting births is that I have no baby sitter now. I just can't be away from home. It got so that there just wasn't enough of me to go around.

Doctors have taught me a lot. Also the midwives group. Suturing, handling shock. I've never had a rush to the

---

My first birth? I missed the whole thing! This time I had my baby at home. If I had to do it over I wouldn't change a thing.
　　　　　　　　　—CAROLYN BOGEL, *mother of two*

hospital when I've decided we should go. I've gone to more than eighty births at home. And I've taken maybe eight into the hospital. Three of those cases I had a doctor with me at the home, and the doctors were even more reluctant than I to go to the hospital. Because they'd never seen a home birth and wanted so much to watch one.

I represent suburbia in a way. I've been volunteer teaching for years. I just need to put on my PTA duds and I can pass. But I've always wanted to be legal. And I've always found myself not quite legal.

I feel that if we are well fed before and during pregnancy, our bodies take care of everything. For home deliveries and when women go to hospital, I suggest they make ice cubes of strong mint and raspberry leaf tea with honey. And crush it up in a thermos. I've been to some hospitals where the staff call that medicine and take it away from the mother. I was surprised to find that prescribing yogurt for a yeast infection is considered to be practicing medicine. During labor I try not to do any vaginal exams. But I do like to let the husband feel the baby's head just before it is born.

One time the local hospital wanted to withhold prenatal care from a mother because the couple planned a home birth.

I had another woman who couldn't decide whether to have a home birth. This was her second child and she was nervous after her first long labor and posterior birth [variation of normal birth, in which baby's head is down but face is up]. She only lived two blocks from the hospital and decided she'd stay home unless during labor she changed her mind. She decided to go to the hospital after all. Some women just don't feel safe at home and can't relax. She was not the sort for home delivery.

When she got to the hospital they wanted to examine her, and the baby was already coming. She told the nurse, but the nurse told her to hold the baby's head back with her hand while they shaved her and washed her and moved her from the labor to the delivery room and put her up on the delivery table. The whole time the baby was crowning almost ten centimeters. When they finally said she could let go, the baby and the placenta rushed out together—and along with it she began to hemorrhage. The hemorrhaging stopped, but they IV'd her with hormones to keep the contractions up and wouldn't let her touch the baby because she wasn't in any condition to nurse. So she spent the night at the hospital with sandbags on her stomach, to keep her uterus down. She was not allowed to nurse and the baby was taken to the nursery. She said she wished she'd never gone. I really do believe they took that baby away and wouldn't let her nurse it to punish her for coming in to the hospital so late.

I had one lady who had six boys. She had labors of twenty-one hours at least at every one, and she'd hemorrhaged after each. Each time there was a question of her even living. Her labors were a cycle of Demerol followed by Pitocin. Demerol for the pain of the induced labor. Then more Pitocin. And more Demerol. A doctor sent the woman to me, because she desperately wanted to have one good birth. It took me three months to brainwash her that she could handle birth with my support, without

Pop. The head came out. I felt it turning . . .
Slurp, the shoulder, then. Fast..I could feel the
arms and legs and feet slipping through me. God,
what an experience! I immediately went into

medication for pain. Her husband stood behind her in labor and wrung his hands the whole time. He is in animal husbandry and artificially inseminates cows. And he was worrying himself sick over his wife giving birth while this "crazy woman," me, tried to have her do it without drugs. She had two hours of labor after she came to the hospital. And delivered with no episiotomy and no tearing. The doctor said, while he was scrubbing up for delivery outside, "Are you sure you can get her through this?" And after her birth, her seventh, the woman said to all of us, "I just can't believe that's all there is to birth!"

If the drugs aren't there, you don't expect them. And there are no drugs at home births. I've never had anyone give birth at home who asked for drugs for pain.

I know that one reason I had seven kids is that I never had the perfect birth. I try to provide as close to that as possible for women. I know if you really have a satisfying experience you may never need to have another child to prove yourself. A lot of people I know who had home births are happy with just one. I think home birth almost always profoundly changes the woman. At the least, her eyes are opened.

When my doctor at the naval hospital, who was young and very new, asked me what I wanted for my first birth, I answered, "Oh, whatever's newest." Well, it just so happened that Grantly Dick-Read was newest then and I said, "I'll take it." (The doctor told me where to get the book.) That doctor was an unusual man. There wasn't a party we went to during my pregnancy that he didn't have me squat on the floor to practice. This was to be his

an extremely satisfied, peaceful, fulfilled frame of mind, and felt a peace that's still with me. That's it!

—ANONYMOUS MOTHER *after home birth*

first planned natural birth. And it changed him. He told me afterward that when he got married his wife would have her baby that way. I was just lucky to have him.

I had my six other babies at a large medical group. They were a variety of Chinese fire drills—all short labors, being rushed to the hospital and having my husband ripped away from me to sign papers, while they quickly shaved and cleaned me up. With the seventh one we decided to have him in the labor room, my husband and me. We were taking movies of that birth. The nurse was appalled at what we were doing. The baby started to be born and the nurse heard us shout excitedly. She ran in the room and grabbed the foot of my bed with one hand and ran out of the room with it and me. Out the door as fast as she could go, pushing and pulling. Well, my husband was standing there with lights and camera and twenty-five feet of extension cord. I remember he looked so funny. She was yelling at him, "Get away! Get away with that camera!" And as she yelled, she ran right into the wall across the hall. And right then the baby's head and shoulders came out. I was shouting to my husband to come and bring the camera. The nurse wanted to get me to Delivery. My last sight of my husband was him standing

there with lights and camera in hand as the nurse slammed the door in his face. She locked the delivery door. And then made me move onto the delivery table, with that baby already half born.

I was really disoriented and irritated. I kept saying, "I want my husband. I want my husband here," over and over. The doctor stepped in and pulled the baby out and said to her, "Open the door for her, will you!" The view my husband got on film was of me up in stirrups, looking at my rear, with the placenta coming out. He asked, "Is that the baby?", referring to the placenta. The doctor turned to him and said, "I thought you went to natural childbirth class." The doctor reached up inside my uterus and manually explored me right there. I had never had that done before. My husband wanted to hit him. But he just stood there and looked at the baby on the next table. The doctor finished and said, "Well, no stitches, no problems. Three minutes. That's the quickest one I've done yet!" and walked out. I remember he had white shoes.

Since the time of this interview, Carol has begun to work openly in her community. Several local physicians are learning home birth skills from her and provide medical backup for each birth.

15
Birth of a Movement: Raven Lang

Birth of a Movement:
Raven Lang

ONE OF THE *most memorable experiences of Raven Lang's childhood occurred one day when, at the age of nine, she happened to catch sight of a cow giving birth in the middle of a clearing. Fascinated, she watched the entire process and came away feeling that it was "all so simple, natural, and enriching, like an apple falling off a tree." Three years later Raven fell ill with rheumatic fever, a condition mistakenly "diagnosed" by her family doctor as nervousness and fatigue related to the onset of puberty. Finally taken to a different doctor, Raven spent a full year in the hospital, where she began to understand "the fallibility of human beings, even those who are represented as people of special knowledge."*

Pregnant herself at twenty-five, Raven studied natural childbirth and adopted an extremely positive attitude about her pregnancy and approaching birth. During labor she discovered that contractions truly were much easier than people had led her to believe, but once in the delivery room, her doctor took over and, much against Raven's wishes, performed an episiotomy. Suddenly someone called in that the delivery room was urgently needed and the doctor had to hurry, so he made a second incision to enlarge the opening even further and in his haste cut through Raven's anal sphincter. The doctor never told her what

---

I cannot say there is anything challenging about delivering a normal baby to a normal mother. There is not. The challenge comes in the complications.
    —ANONYMOUS GRADUATE, *"prestigious medical school,"* quoted in the New York Times

had happened, and for two weeks afterward Raven could not straighten up to walk, could not sit on anything but a soft cushion, could not carry her own baby, and was in a state of diminishing but continual pain. Later she moved to the country, where she began to observe birthing animals. It was then that Raven realized something abnormal and/or unnecessary must have happened at her own delivery. And when neighbors began to invite her to witness home births, she found it exhilarating to see that a normal birth could proceed smoothly without complication or need for medical interference. She began to question all hospital practices related to pregnancy, labor, and delivery.

Raven did feel uneasy that no one attending births at home seemed medically competent to handle problems that might occur. She spent many hours talking to a local doctor named Peter, who had attended home births until the medical community in town had criticized him for veering away from "standard medical practice" and had forced him to stop. It angered Raven that at that point not a single doctor in the entire area of Santa Cruz, California, would attend a home birth, and when she learned that educational classes or organizations for pregnant women were nonexistent as well, she decided to offer her own services as a natural childbirth teacher. Still believing that hospital births were safer than home birth, she advised her pregnant students to deliver in the hospital and that she would accompany them as labor coach. Although many women were afraid of the hospital—sometimes drugs or incisions were administered against the mother's wishes, at other times husbands were not allowed in the delivery

Many doctors and women agree that obstetric procedures at U.S. hospitals are probably the principal reason for the current home-delivery trend.

—Newsweek

room—Raven stuck to her belief that "hospitals are safest." Then the following incident occurred.

One day an eighteen-year-old single woman came to my class. She was extremely healthy, with good spirits and a quiet and strong personality. She was undecided as to whether or not her child would be born at home or in the hospital. Toward the end of her pregnancy, she asked me if I would help her at home, but I didn't feel ready to share the responsibility of her birth with her unless there would be someone more knowledgeable with us. Since we couldn't find anybody to assist her birth at home, she made arrangements to have her baby at the County Hospital in town.

One morning around 4:00 A.M., she called and told me that her labor had started some hours ago. We met at an appointed place, and together went to the hospital. When I first saw Kathy in labor, she was so relaxed and happy that I thought her to be in the very early stages of labor and almost felt she should return home until labor got a bit stronger. Within minutes, though, it became apparent that Kathy was already well into labor and simply handling it with great relaxation.

When Kathy was first admitted to the hospital, she was examined by my friend Peter. He told her that her baby would probably be born by noon that day and that her labor was moving fast and well. We were excited. She was then taken to the labor room, where she continued to labor peacefully, happily, and strongly for a few hours. Around 9:00 A.M. the nurse telephoned Kathy's doctor, a specialist in obstetrics and gynecology, to tell him that

things were moving fast and that Kathy was nearing the
end of the first stage of labor, which meant her delivery
would be sometime before noon, just as Peter had pre-
dicted. However, Kathy's doctor had a luncheon appointment which he very much wanted to keep, so over the
telephone he ordered a heavy dosage of Demerol to slow
things down. I followed the nurse to her telephone call
and listened to her repeat the instructions. The nurse never
protested about the doctor's orders, even though I knew
it was bad medical practice. I pleaded with the nurse to
leave Kathy alone, but orders were orders, and the nurse
was of no mind to question or break them, even for the
sake of Kathy and her baby. She told me that I better not
be too nosy, or I would be told to leave. So Kathy, who
was then in good strong labor and nearing the end of it,
was given a large dose of Demerol against her will. In a
few minutes her labor began to slow down, and in about
twenty minutes she was nearly asleep, with not much labor
happening at all. The shot had been given at approximately
9:30 A.M. At 12:45 P.M. the doctor called again to say he
still couldn't make it to the hospital and to give Kathy
another shot of Demerol. Kathy was almost sleeping without this second shot. Her labor had made no progress
since the initial shot, and with this second shot of
Demerol Kathy truly fell asleep; her labor came to a halt.

Hours wore on. At 3:30 P.M. the doctor called for the
last time to tell the nurse he was coming in and that she
should get things ready for him. The nurse then brought a
table and put it right outside of Kathy's room and began
to fill it with needles, tubing, bottles containing fluids to

*Our strange society will not hold it against you if
your baby is palsied or has his intelligence
stunted by too much anesthesia in the hospital,
but if he is born at home with a birthmark
or a club foot, the fault will be called yours!*
—LESTER HAZELL, Commonsense Childbirth

be dripped into veins, gloves, and other very surgical-looking paraphernalia. I asked the nurse why all of these things were being put there, and she said that this doctor's procedures usually included these materials and that he had just ordered the table and contents. At 4:00 P.M. the doctor arrived. With a big smile, taking off his coat and then proceeding to roll up his sleeves, he said, "We're going to get this show on the road now." He ordered me out of Kathy's labor room and for twenty minutes or so Kathy was alone with him and the nurse. I listened for what I could but there was silence. After the door opened and I was admitted back to the labor room, the doctor said to me, "Well, this baby should be born within the next hour." Then I saw Kathy. The last I had seen her she was on her side completely sleeping with labor at a halt; now she was alertly sitting up, actively breathing with what looked like a good contraction, and a bottle of something was slowly dripping into her vein.

"What did you do to her?" I asked.

"Oh, nothing," he said.

"What do you call that IV drip?" I asked.

"Oh, that. That's just sugar water. It'll give her some energy and get things going for us," he said.

I had known about sugar giving energy, but this I thought was a bit extreme. Then I asked him if he had broken the bag of waters (this is a common American interference that doctors traditionally use to get things going). "Yes," the doctor said, leaving the room with a smile.

Kathy and I were finally alone again, and I must say that

I gave birth. I wasn't delivered. The difference between doing and being done to.
— Doris Clark, *mother and California lay midwife*

I felt happy to see her back into active labor. She seemed to be in about the same stage she had left off at before the initial shot. Her contractions came about every three minutes for the next ten minutes, but then they seemed to stop. Four minutes passed and then five and then six and then seven, and I asked Kathy what had happened to those nice contractions she was just having. She said that they had just stopped and she didn't know what happened. I put my hand on her uterus and sure enough, Kathy was having a good strong contraction that very minute. I asked Kathy what else the doctor had done and she said he had given her a shot somewhere in her vagina. You can imagine how I felt toward that doctor at that moment. Kathy had been given a shot to dull her uterine and vaginal sensations, so that she could no longer feel anything, and as a result could no longer actively respond to her labor. How and if it was affecting her baby was a very real concern for both of us.

Meanwhile, every ten minutes or so a nurse or aide would come in and check Kathy's blood pressure and the baby's heartbeat, record it on Kathy's chart, and leave. The whole morning and early afternoon we had been left virtually alone, and now we were being plagued with visits. The third time someone came in to get the vital statistics, I told her what the statistics were and that there was no need to keep interrupting us and why did they persist so? She answered by pointing to the sugar water and saying that when a woman is given a drug like that, a constant check must be made. I said to her that what was in the bottle was only sugar, and she then corrected me by

turning the bottle around and showing me the prescription, PIT 1 AMP. I was stunned. Kathy had been given a powerful hormone called Pitocin, which is usually excreted in just the right amounts by the body during labor, as long as you don't interfere with the body. This IV Pitocin drip had been the drug used to speed up her labor. I wondered how many other things the doctor had done to Kathy while she lay sleeping in her bed.

The nurses continued their frequent vigil on Kathy's vital signs until one of them, while monitoring the baby's heartbeat, made a furrow on her brow, listened to the baby's heartbeat more closely, and quickly walked out of the room without writing on Kathy's chart. Within minutes the doctor came into the room and listened for a long time to the baby's heart. He then demanded that I leave Kathy's room and shut the door after me. The doctor had originally given Kathy some heavy downers to slow things down for him, then he had given her some heavy uppers "to get the show on the road." Things seemed to be going bad.

A few minutes later, the doctor came out of the room and told me that Kathy's baby was in severe distress and that he had about an hour to save the baby. I tried and struggled to get back to Kathy, but I was kept away from her. Soon I saw someone on the staff wheel Kathy out of labor and into the delivery section. On her way into the delivery she shouted to me with great giant tears all over her face, "Oh God, this is so fucked!" And she went into Delivery along with the large staff. With everyone gone

---

The delivery should be exactly as the woman desires. But we all know this is impossible in a hospital. Hospitals are self-serving.
—MICHAEL WHITT, M.D.

from the halls, I was free to sneak past the barriers set up for me and into the little space which had a large window viewing the delivery room. Kathy was being strapped down to the table; that is, each leg and arm was strapped down, and a green mask covered her face. Seeing Kathy there like that after having worked with her and knowing her expectations and dreams for herself and her baby made my heart scream. It was then that I vowed to help the next pregnant woman seeking an alternative method of birth.

The baby was born vaginally with the use of forceps and much pulling. He was then hit hard and often on the buttocks and given to the staff who awaited the newborn. Kathy was unable to hold or touch her baby at all. The only time she got to see him was when the baby was being hit. From that moment till I left the hospital two hours later, there was no reunion with Kathy and baby. I was allowed to see Kathy for a few minutes and then I was told to leave. Kathy had felt the violation they had done to her, but mostly at the moment she wanted her baby. As it turned out, Kathy's baby had a concussion on his head with a swelling the size of a tennis ball. By the second day after the birth, no one knew yet whether or not there would be any permanent damage. The third day after the birth, Kathy took her baby from the hospital and flew to her parents' home. I got a sad note from her the following week, and I have never heard from her since. That experience cost Kathy approximately seven hundred dollars, the going rate for a "normal" birth in California at that time and cheap by today's standards. This particular story is a nightmare, and although the baby's concussion is extremely uncommon, the treatment of Kathy during labor and delivery is unbearably common:

> According to the National Association for Retarded Children there are now 6,000,000 retarded children and adults in the U.S. with a predicted annual increase of over 100,000 a year. The number of children and adults with behavioral difficulties or perceptual disfunction resulting from minimal brain damage is an ever growing challenge to society and to the economy. While it may be easier on the conscience to blame such numbing facts solely on socio-economic factors and birth defects, recent research makes it evident that obstetrical medication must play a role in our staggering incidence of neurological impairment. It may be convenient to blame our relatively poor infant outcome on lack of facilities or inadequate government funding, but it is obvious from the research being carried out that we could effect an immediate improvement in infant outcome by changing the pattern of obstetrical care in the United States.
>
> —*Doris Haire*, Past President
> International Childbirth Education Association, 1972

Raven continued her classes and attempted to acquaint pregnant women and their mates with their rights in the hospital birth process. She also began collecting data on hospital versus home birth, such as the quotation above, and became more and more knowledgeable—and vocal— on the subject. Soon the inevitable pressure began.

One day I was visited by two public health nurses at my home. They told me that they had been aware of my

---

I believe I am the only certified nurse-midwife now doing home birth. I've trained and have skills, and there are people who need them. There was a lay midwife in our area who needed help so we set up a home birth clinic, with a

teaching classes for some time and had come to find out
if I was properly certified to do such teaching. I told them
I certified myself by my experiences and interests. They
didn't agree with my analysis of certification and told me
that I should stop teaching because of lack of proper credentials. At that time I had approximately fifteen women
coming to me for classes and had a list of about eight more
ready for the next one. I told the nurses that surely they
could see the need for these classes. The nurses truly
understood the reality of the situation. One was already a
mother, and the other was thinking of conceiving in the
near future. But their jobs allowed little room for personal
feelings. They implied that things would soon be better,
because the Public Health Department was currently involved in trying to set up a childbirth-education program.
I told them that the current pregnant women and their
babies could not wait; their time had come. And I had
also come to know by now that I was the captain of my
body, my mind, and my activities.

It was only a matter of time before parents from my
classes asked me if I would attend their births as a kind
of midwife. They wanted someone to attend them who
had at least given birth and witnessed a few. The parents
and I were all aware of our inexhaustible ignorance and
lack of experience, but we were also aware of the harm
done in hospitals through interference and insensitivity.
One risk seemed to outweigh the other. I felt, along with
others, that if we didn't start taking responsibility for what
we believed in, there would never be freedom. For myself,
this meant I would follow a study in obstetrics so that I

*pediatrician-turned-family health practitioner.
We provide complete home delivery service and
we attend about 10 deliveries a month.*
—JUDY GOLDSCHMIDT, *mother and
California nurse-midwife*

would have more knowledge of the possible dangers inherent in home birth and how to deal with some of these dangers, such as hemorrhage, prolapsed cord, asphyxiated babies, and so forth.

I began to attend home births. They were special, always, and superior to hospital births. The couples at home births seemed to fully perceive the significance of the act of becoming parents. Women were experiencing self-realization through their own strengths. Men were learning about the birth process and experiencing it with a sense of responsibility, enthusiasm, and interest. Children were not being kept away from this natural process of life. They were relating to it with pleasure and excitement. Births were sometimes long and difficult, but the spirit of birthing was loving and self-directed.

In January 1971, one of the public health nurses who had paid me a visit some months earlier called to tell me of a meeting that the obstetricians and public health officials were having in order that they might understand the reasons for the increasing frequency of home birth in our area. They wanted to reach an agreement on what they should do about it. I asked if I could be included in this meeting so that I might express and represent some of the ideas and desires of the pregnant community and myself. I also wanted Peter, the young general practitioner, to attend. After I finished talking with the nurse, I sat down with a pen in hand and began to list my requests and grievances. Peter prepared for the meeting as well.

The closed union behavior of the medical people and their failure to recognize and respond to expressed needs has caused the home birth movement to occur.
—LESTER HAZELL, *anthropologist*

Within a week the meeting was held. Peter and I were not allowed to communicate on behalf of the pregnant community because we were not obstetricians. As a result, there was no discussion of philosophical differences and, ultimately, no understanding. It was apparent that the obstetricians didn't really want to understand, or they would not have excluded the two persons who might have been able to shed some light on the matter. The result of this meeting was that the OB's decided to cut off all participation with those wanting home birth by denying them future prenatal care.

By this time, early 1971, I had become aware of at least eight other women who were teaching childbirth preparation, attending births, or talking to pregnant women about childbirth. Three of these women were nurses; all but one were mothers. I called each of them and invited them to my house so that we could become acquainted. With warmth, energy, and conviction, we met and communicated. It became apparent that we could reach many more people in our community and probably do a more comprehensive job by unifying our energies, complementary knowledge, and experiences. For the people wishing home birth who were being refused prenatal care from the doctors in town, we would provide alternative prenatal care. There were, after all, three nurses who knew how to give prenatal care. It was a necessary step to take, for it was vital to the understanding of ourselves as free people. Meetings continued, preparations were made,

dreams were talked about, and the energy continued to mount. By March of '71, a Birth Center opened. We hung a short philosophy on the wall, which read:

> We are a sisterhood concerned with birth and its process. We feel positive attitudes are never too great for the mental, spiritual and physical well being of the child and mother.
>
> We are finding out about natural capabilities of women.
>
> We emphasize the importance of pre and post natal knowledge as well as birth itself. As a birth center we will share our knowledge and love of pregnancy, lactation, and infant care. Classes will be available for instruction in body building exercises, physiological and psychological changes in pregnancy, nutrition, relaxation, breathing, the mechanics of labor and birth, care of the newborn, and related subjects.
>
> We are a group of people who have taken our birth-right—freedom, and decided for ourselves what our rituals of birth will be.

The opening day of the Center was busy and exciting. We worked from the time we opened our doors at 11:00 A.M. until we closed at five. In a few days we scheduled educational meetings for ourselves. It was clear we had much to learn. Besides the study of physiology and anatomy, we examined social, political, and moral questions.

The community continued to support the Birth Center, and indeed, it was truly a community center—with pregnant women, younger and older women, many children,

---

The Santa Cruz arrests raise the basic question, "What is medicine?" said Dr. Sheldon Greenfield of Primex, UCLA's paramedics program. "What is diagnosing? If you look at some woman's big

men, and teen-agers. There began to be a strong and solid identity among the participants.

Home births were happening with greater awareness all over the county. Birth Center personnel were going to more and more of them. Sometimes a woman from the Center would be asked to deliver the baby. The doctors had warned us not to continue because they considered it illegal to practice this kind of medicine without a license. But we could not abide by that kind of thinking because we saw it robbed a woman of the right to give birth, and that could never be taken from anyone. And, we thought, surely knowing how to properly transport someone to the hospital who is bleeding too much is not practicing medicine. The birth attending continued. Within three years a staff of approximately eight women attended over three hundred births.

How did the Birth Center's results in home birth compare to national birth statistics? Although midwives at the Center kept accurate records and charts on each of their clients, no one had thought to do a comparative analysis until Lewis Mehl, a fourth-year medical student at Stanford University, and his wife, Gail, had their baby at home with a Birth Center midwife attending. The experience so revitalized the couple that they decided to study the Birth Center in an effort to see if home birth might be made more available for everyone. They also hoped such a study would help prepare a case for legalizing midwifery in California. The following is Lewis Mehl's report, with his conclusions, which has been submitted to a national medical journal.

---

belly and say, 'You're pregnant,' is that diagnosing? I suggest it's not. If you stand around and offer a woman advice while she's giving birth, is that treatment? Not in a medical sense."
　　　　　　　　　　　　　　　　　　—Rolling Stone

289 women [in this study] came through the Birth Center planning to deliver at home. 231 delivered without problems at home. 13 more delivered at home, but with slight complications. 45 delivered in the hospital, and there were 7 Caesarean sections. 1 baby was stillborn in the group; it had died prior to the onset of labor. Thus, the extrapolated perinatal mortality is 3.2 per 1,000 total births, at a time when this figure for the United States is 27.1. When live births are considered, there is no comparison, since the Birth Center did not have a single live mortality. All of the women except 10 gave birth without analgesia or anesthesia, and the average Apgar (a 0 to 10 rating of the viability of the newborn) rating was 9.4 at 1 minute and 9.7 at 5 minutes. These are impressive scores. Of interest also is the low level of prematurity (2.2% compared with 6.7% for the national average) and the decreased risk of fetal distress and respiratory difficulties in the home-born infants.

Why is this? First, the women giving birth at home were better prepared and had much less fear than women delivering in the hospital. Studies have shown that fear reduces uterine blood flow and decreases the amount of oxygen the baby is receiving (fetal hypoxia). Newton studied the birth of mice in an artificial environment similar to a hospital and showed that labors were 72% longer and that the female mouse lost 54% more pups than did control mice giving birth in normal settings for mice. Goodlin from Stanford has shown that giving birth in the supine position results in fetal hypoxia because of compression on the great vessels. He has gone so far as to recommend that no woman give birth in a supine position. At home, most women were on hands and knees or squatting. It was also found that there was no real need for routine episiotomy. Only 6.6% of the women tore when the delivery was conducted by experienced midwives. The greatest factor contributing toward the success of the Santa Cruz women, however, was the absence of analgesia or anesthesia. Analgesia depresses the baby at birth, resulting in a lower Apgar score; anesthesia results in fetal hypoxia, as do forceps deliveries, which cause a high risk of cerebral palsy.

The statistics were impressive but relatively unimportant to the many men and women of the Santa Cruz community who knew only that midwives at the Birth Center were warm, knowledgeable, and trustworthy about every-

thing from contraception to home birth. And so the Center continued to grow. Raven continues:

Within a year after the Center was functioning, we became aware of people in other communities involved in similar activities. Some women were childbirth educators, some were lay midwives, some were professionally trained and certified midwives. Most women were working independently and outside the system. A list of names was brought together, meetings were held, and within a few months the group represented an area approximately 150 miles north and south of Santa Cruz. Meetings were held once a month. At first people became acquainted with one another and shared experiences and techniques. Then we decided to invite someone to our meeting who would present a topic of mutual interest. But most of the time, the most obstetrically knowledgeable member of the group prepared a talk. The members steadily grew in medical knowledge. I was exhilarated by this experience in self-reliance and self-control. It reminded me of the irregular schools* that once existed in the states before monopolistic licensing and accreditation procedures were established. Our group was taking the power to form its own growth by collectively gaining knowledge through our own efforts, by our own desires. We took the license to create ourselves, all the while continuing to deliver babies in our respective communities.

Within one year of the coming together of this group, we had gathered statistics of our own which covered the delivery of four hundred babies. Our once-a-month work-

* In the U.S.A. in the 1800s, a growing number of formally trained doctors took great pains to distinguish themselves from the host of lay practitioners. Closing their schools to the main society of medical people, they admitted only people of wealth or of the ruling class. All other people practicing medicine or healing the sick were called "irregular doctors." In time, the "regulars" developed into the American Medical Association and made it illegal for anyone not of their training, or from their schools, to practice medicine. Many of those who stopped working, or worked silently, were herbalists, midwives, birth controllers, and abortionists. Many of those practicing were women. Also practicing were groups of mixed races and nationalities. All of these people shared one thing in common; they were members of the working or poorer class.

shops resembled the format of a school, although the majority of the group was reluctant to call themselves or identify themselves as a school. Even though the group was in fact already functioning as a school, or, more clearly stated, an irregular school, I felt that the use of the word seemed too audacious for a group made up primarily of lay women. And for those women who possessed certification, there was some concern that participation in our group might endanger the loss of this hard-earned certificate, especially if we had publicly called ourselves a school. Nevertheless, it was clear to me that within the year we had become a significant and recognized group on our own; indeed, we had dealt with the lives of some eight hundred women and infants, and affected many other people as well.

At times I talked of starting our own school, but felt the majority of the group was waiting for a more powerful or a more acceptable "someone-else" to authorize or sanction us. And the incorporation of a school would mean facing many problems that would take time away from the actual practice of midwifing. Among these problems would be a system of certification to people who had dealt with all the aspects of education for midwives. These people would have to possess knowledge, experience, and understanding of the job. The membership of this kind of organization would be open for anyone wishing to follow it, providing that certification would come only after a completed study. Setting up a school like this might eventually mean a confrontation with the law and a confrontation with the American Medical Association.

Who is to say who can or cannot create a school for oneself? Who is to perpetuate absurd standards that are irrelevant to the practice of midwifing, or medicine? The need to educate ourselves and our children seems overwhelming to me. We have already set up alternate schools for our children because we find that those offered by the system are unacceptable. The Birth Center provides an example of an alternate method of dealing with birth, because some people believe that what is given by the system is unacceptable. And, in the same vein, when medical schools and midwifing schools continue to close their doors to the thousands wanting to attend and open their doors to only the few, then the growth and development of alternate methods of educating ourselves is the next and necessary step to take.

At present there is no school for educating midwives in California. There is no license to practice midwifing for those who possess proper certification earned from other states. The schools in this country that do exist for the licensing of midwives do not accept people who are not already certified nurses, and the nursing programs in this country are so degrading and sexist that people like me would not submit to such a form of education. It is unjust to require so much time from an individual to practice what realistically takes approximately one to two years' preparation. Licensing regulations need to change so that those who do fulfill the existing educational requirements in midwifing can be certified and those who have learned the art and science of midwifing through other methods can be given equivalency tests and then be certified upon examination, providing the test is truly relevant for delivering babies.

Just before noon on March 6, 1974, Linda Bennett and Jeanine Walker drove from the Birth Center to the nearby town of Ben Lomond to assist in the home birth of a woman named Terri and her mate, Peter. Even before reaching the house, the two women sensed that something was wrong; they had, in fact, conferred with other midwives about this couple the night before at "rounds," a meeting in which current files of Birth Center women had been reviewed. One of the midwives attending the meeting expressed feelings shared by the group when she said, "These people are just clouded with fear." Others stated that Terri and Peter seemed too nervous to make it through a home birth. The midwives had also been concerned that Terri had insisted she would deliver in May when all her symptoms seemed to indicate a June due date. Now, on March 6, Linda Bennett and Jeanine Walker hurried to what they feared would be a premature birth.

They were met at the apartment by several men in hippie clothing who told them that Terri was in the shower and would be out any minute. One man asked Jeanine if she were the midwife, and Jeanine, an apprentice who did not consider herself a midwife but still a student, told them no, she was just learning and had come to observe, learn, and assist. Then they turned to Linda and offered her fifty dollars in payment, which she refused, surprised at their conduct. They pressed the issue of money so much that finally she put the fifty dollars in her purse. As Linda turned toward the bathroom to see what had become of Terri, the men moved in and identified themselves as undercover agents. They confiscated her kit of birth tools, arrested both women, and drove them to jail.

Terri was later identified as Terri Johnson, an undercover investigator for the State Department of Consumer Affairs (SDCA), whose supervisory arm in medical activities is the Board of Medical Examiners. It is this Board that directs investigations of groups or individuals in California who are suspected of practicing medicine without a license.

But the situation began to resemble a scene out of Keystone Kops when, at the same time that Linda Bennett and Jeanine Walker were being taken to jail, officials from the district attorney's office, the sheriff's department, the state police, and the SDCA converged on the Birth Center for a grand "sweep" of arrests. They found and arrested one midwife, Kate Bowland, and confiscated "evidence" such as gauze pads, diapers, files, notebooks, birth kits, films, slides, tea, stethoscopes, blood-pressure cuffs, and hemostats. They also charged Kate with possession of marijuana, even though she was not carrying it on her person at the time of the break-in. Raven, who had called the local newspapers and radio stations in an attempt to protect the Birth Center from illegalities on the part of

Kate Bowland, left

the investigators, arrived and stood on the sidelines writing down the agents' license-plate numbers. Kate, unable to leave the house, sat at the front window describing events inside the Center to local radio station KUSP and the local alternative newspaper, the Santa Cruz Times. *Another midwife spotted "Pete," the man who had played the role of Terri's husband, and attempted to talk with him but without much success; he did show her his badge and she said later that he felt "very bad" about his part in the arrests.*

Besides the chaos and the threat to their livelihood, the midwives were also concerned about Terri. "What they did," Raven said later, referring to the SDCA, "was wait until they had a woman in their department who became pregnant so that they could use her body. That's right. Think about that lady. She's still pregnant. That's a heavy thing to do, using her body and her baby against us." And Kate Bowland told KUSP and the Santa Cruz Times *that she hoped Terri could still have positive thoughts about her birth after all that had happened.*

The Los Angeles Free Press *reported a few weeks later:*

All in all, the massive conflagration of undercover agents and uniformed authorities employed 13 people, 8 cars, innumerable facilities and untold expense to charge three women with a misdemeanor.

Why all the fuss? It may be that state authorities are planning more "raids" of midwifery centers, clinics and homes in the future, and that they want an air-tight case in the first trial in order to have a more powerful hand with the next and the next and the next. But the mid-wives in Santa Cruz may outsmart them yet: since the Birth Center personnel believe the real issue is not of a violation of law but of human rights, they may file an injunction which will stop the criminal proceedings, pending the outcome of a civil case.

If this happens, the entire fabric of the law regarding home births and midwifery will come into public scrutiny: and for the first time, so will the current over-technologized procedures of hospital births and obstetricians' care.

As of May 1976, the case of the Santa Cruz midwives was still unresolved. In an initial ruling earlier in the spring, the district court of appeals held that the women could not be charged with a crime, stating that childbirth is not an illness, deformity or disease, and that therefore midwifery does not constitute the practice of medicine. Just two months later, the same three judges granted a re-hearing on the case and reversed their decision. It can be assumed that they were under great pressure from the medical community and the state attorney general's office to reconsider the implications of declaring unlicensed midwives free to practice their craft. The case is expected to go to the state supreme court, which will have to decide whether midwifery is practicing medicine without a license and whether expectant mothers have a right to choose the setting and attendants for birth. In the meantime the majority of obstetricians in Santa Cruz and other counties in the state continue to attempt to coerce women into the hospital for normal childbirth, refusing to provide any prenatal care to a woman planning a home birth.

16
The Midwife Goes to Trial: Norman Casserley

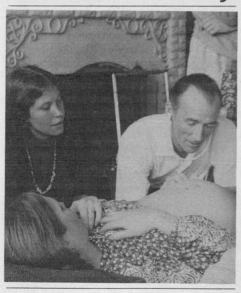

The Midwife Goes to Trial: Norman Casserley

Because home births have always been regarded in America as a phenomenon of the frontier, where doctors and hospitals were simply not available, our image today of the female birth attendant is of a dirty, illiterate old "granny," shuffling through the back country to administer primitive care to pioneer mothers. During the last fifty years, as the American Medical Association has attempted to incorporate all health services into its own domain, a concerted effort has been made by physicians to educate the public to the dangers of childbirth and the need for hospitalization under an obstetrician's care, and, once and for all, birth has become equated with sickness. Case law of the last thirty years has reinforced the modern deception of physicians and legislators alike that pregnancy is an illness and childbirth too risky to be handled by anyone but the obstetrician inside his institution, the hospital.

Unlike other countries, the United States never allowed the midwife to become an integral part of the social fabric of her country. With no possible way for her to defend herself, no institution to train her formally (as in Holland), and no national organization of midwifery to fight for her rights (as in England and Denmark), the

Why do we need doctors to tell us everything?
—GAIL REAM, *nursery nurse*

American midwife became an easy target. Her status, her numbers, even her traditional role as *un*medical birth attendant have all but disappeared.

In February 1974, the American College of Nurse-Midwives (ACNM) announced the results of a state-by-state study that investigated the legal position of nurse-midwives and lay midwives throughout the nation. It found that Arizona, Washington, D.C., Florida, Kentucky, Maine, Mississippi, New Jersey, New Mexico, New York, Ohio, Pennsylvania, South Carolina, Utah, Vermont, and West Virginia now give legal recognition to nurse-midwives, but only as members of an obstetrics team, not as independent practitioners.

Nurse-midwives are allowed to practice under permissive laws but are given no specific legal recognition in Illinois, Indiana, Louisiana, Maryland, Minnesota, North Carolina, Oregon, Texas, and Wyoming. In these states the practice of midwifery, even under the direction of obstetricians, could easily be jeopardized if the authorities were to give the state law a more restrictive interpretation than they do now. A few states—Delaware, Hawaii, Idaho, and Alaska—also have permissive laws, but ACNM could find very few lay or nurse-midwives practicing in these states.

Michigan, Missouri, and South Dakota have made special exemptions to their state laws for institutions where nurse-midwives are allowed to practice under careful restrictions. Lay midwives are permitted to practice in Alabama, Arkansas, Oklahoma, Tennessee, Virginia, and Washington, but in most cases these midwives are rare

---

I've wanted to ask my doctor how he'd *like to have a baby, after delivering them. A doctor just wipes his hands and walks out!*
     —EUNICE MITCHELL, *following first birth*

284

"grannies" who still exist in rural areas where the medical community cannot or will not provide health care.

Today, Colorado and Nebraska clearly prohibit the practice of both nurse-midwifery and lay midwifery. California, Iowa, Kansas, Massachusetts, Michigan, Missouri, Montana, Nevada, New Hampshire, North Dakota, Rhode Island, South Dakota, and Wisconsin all have laws that do not allow the midwife to practice fully, and in many cases these laws are so vague and confusing that it is as if midwifery were outlawed altogether.

California is the most notorious of those states with confusing laws because in many areas of that state alternative lifestyles have spawned a network of independent, self-trained midwives who attend home births as a direct response to consumer demand. Indeed, to look at home birth as anything other than a consumer issue is to fall under a deception perpetrated by the government, the American Medical Association, and insurance companies, whose main concern is the protection of doctors and hospitals, not mothers. The question is not whether American hospital births are safer than home births (they are not), nor whether doctors and nurses in hospitals are "better" than lay midwives at home. The real question is whether a woman has the right to decide the manner and place in which she gives birth to her own baby, and whether American medical services can be truly responsive to community needs. In California they obviously are not; in other states they only seem to be, for "granny" clauses and nurse-midwife laws only deceive the consumer into

© Mister Midwife

thinking she still has a choice in selecting her own birth attendant. In most states, women are unaware that they have any choice at all other than the hospital birth.

In a way, it is fortunate that midwifery and home birth are basically illegal in California, for it is there that the movement to home birth has emerged as a consumer force, and there that no palliative, watered-down laws have clouded the real issues. With no legal route yet available for those who choose to give birth outside the hospital, and with crackdowns on midwives in California occurring more frequently in 1974, the issue of home versus hospital birth and of lay midwife versus obstetrician has been forced into the open. This has enlightened many women who never realized that medical interference may not be the safest practice, and that alternative methods to the hospital birth can indeed be available to anyone.

Midwifery was made legal in California in 1917 under Section 2140 of the State Business and Professions Code, which says:

> The certificate to practice midwifery authorizes the holder to attend cases of normal childbirth. . . . The practice of midwifery constitutes the furthering or undertaking by any person to assist a woman in normal childbirth. But it does not include the use of any instrument at any childbirth, except such instrument as is necessary in severing the umbilical cord, nor does it include the assisting of childbirth by any artificial, forcible, or mechanical means. . . . A midwife is not authorized to practice medicine and surgery.

I came to America when I was 13. Being Chinese, I am very modest. But the exposed breast is seen everywhere in China and we think nothing of it. The breast is sacred. By the time I had my own baby here I was too embarrassed to nurse in public.

—KATY SID, *nursery nurse*

Under sections 2260–2266 of the same code, the State Board of Medical Examiners was given sole authority for issuing certificates to midwives. In 1949, this authority was revoked when the state legislature repealed sections 2260–2266, although it did not repeal section 2140, which is still on the books today. So California holds the dubious distinction of having laws which state, in effect, that midwives are legal if they carry a certificate that does not exist. When "caught," the midwife is not prosecuted for practicing midwifery per se, but for violating Business and Professions Code section 2141, generally referred to as "practicing medicine without a license." This section reads as follows:

Any person, who practices or attempts to practice, or who advertises or holds himself out as practicing, any system or mode of treating the sick or afflicted in this State, or who diagnoses, treats, operates for, or prescribes for any ailment, blemish, deformity, disease, disfigurement, disorder, injury, or other mental or physical condition of any person, without having at the time of so doing a valid, unrevoked certificate as provided in this chapter, is guilty of a misdemeanor.

Basically, then, to practice without a license is to diagnose or treat a condition of ill health, to prescribe medication, or to perform surgery. That the violation constitutes little more than a misdemeanor does not lessen the fact that conviction of this crime would surely damage the midwife's reputation in her community.

Nevertheless, by prosecuting midwives for practicing

I arrived at 3:00 a.m., had one more good pain which seemed to last forever. Then one after another. I said to the nurse, "I can't take an enema because my baby's coming!" She said, "Everybody gets an enema." Then she saw how close it was and ran to get the doctor. I was

medicine without a license, California law-enforcement agencies are creating a new platform through which the midwife can openly defend the legitimacy of her craft, of home births, and of the right of women to choose the manner and place of the birth of their babies. Since midwives contend that pregnancy is not a condition of ill health, that labor is a natural function of the body, and that attending a delivery in which neither medication is given nor surgery performed is simply assisting nature, not treating sickness, they state that practicing medicine has nothing to do with practicing midwifery.

One midwife who claims to have statistics and who does have experience to prove this is Norman Casserley, a forty-seven-year-old bachelor who is probably the only male lay midwife in the United States to maintain that he has "officiated" over thirty-five hundred births in his twenty-five-year career. He also claims that in all of those births there has never been an instance of infant or maternal mortality, that he has never had to take a woman to the hospital due to last-minute complications, and that not a single client has ever suffered from perineum tears, hemorrhage, or infection. His specialty, he contends, has been difficult births of high-risk women as young as eleven and as old as fifty-five, women with a history of hemorrhaging in previous births, and women who had been told by doctors that their pelvic measurement was too small to accommodate a normal baby's head—a condition for which most doctors will perform a Caesarean section. Yet at no time, he claims, did he ever use forceps, perform episiotomies, or give medication to any of the

---

left alone, pushing. I watched a crucifix on the wall. I'm Jewish, but I prayed to it. Zip, the baby slid out. I was afraid to move, that I might hurt it. They came and took him away.
— ROSE GALLER, *remembering first birth 30 years ago*

mothers under his care. As *Prevention* magazine pointed out in June 1972, if an M.D. were to achieve such a perfect record, "it's a good guess that doctor would be something of a legend." For Norman Casserley, however, his legendary status has resulted in a three-year battle with the courts of California in which he was convicted on three counts of practicing medicine without a license.

Norman is a slender, crisply tailored man with thinning hair brushed immaculately into place and a soothing, earnest, gentle but authoritarian voice. He was born and raised in Ireland, graduated from premed school at the University of Ireland at Dublin, and attended three years of medical school at Rotunda Maternity Hospital. "Although it normally takes two years to complete the necessary one thousand births to graduate," Norman says, "it took me longer because my births were much slower. I would not do Caesarean or any episiotomies. All the cases scheduled for Caesareans that came my way, I delivered vaginally. I never did do work in Caesarean and left school without my license. I began practicing midwifery without my M.D. degree, and I practiced in European homes, in sixteen countries in all."

Norman states that he met and worked with the late Dr. Fernand Lamaze in the early fifties and that together they learned a great deal about natural childbirth. "We both came to New York to conquer American obstetrics. It was the height of the McCarthy era, and we were failures, of course, for Dr. Lamaze was the chief of obstetrics in the Communist trade union clinic in Paris.

He could not even get speaking engagements here. He went home and I stayed and kept delivering babies quietly." Norman settled in San Diego, California, where he began to build up his practice by working at first with minority clients who could not afford the care of an obstetrician or a hospital birth.

Norman states that his usual practice is to begin midwifery care with prenatal examination and instruction three months before birth, so that he can detect signs of possible complications which might require a doctor's interference. "I start my mothers off with a quick course in anatomy and physiology, the parts of the body and how it functions," he says. "Not just the uterus but the whole body. Then we go into microbiology, bacteria and fungus, and all kinds of things that can cause disease. Then a bit of organic chemistry, body chemistry. I usually spend half a day at each session." Norman believes his further instructions on diet, exercise, and attitude help to provide insurance that even the most difficult births can proceed without complication.

Generally, Norman moves into the home of a birthing couple about a week before their baby is due, using their address as a base from which he travels to other homes on his prenatal "rounds." At the onset of labor he encourages the mother to continue with her household chores right up to the moment of pushing, so that she can use her vertical position to best advantage. During delivery he allows her to find whatever position is most comfortable—

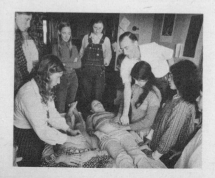

other than lying flat on her back—and will catch the baby whether she is squatting, supporting herself on hands and knees, or lying at an angle, propped up with pillows. Norman teaches the husband to vaginally massage his wife long before birth, to strengthen her tissues, and encourages him to help catch the baby and tie and cut the cord. He attempts to place the baby at its mother's nipple at a maximum of fifteen seconds after delivery, and encourages both parents to sleep with the child in their own bed. If they are too tired or are afraid of harming the infant in their sleep, Norman often takes the baby to bed himself, so concerned is he that the warmth of body-to-body contact be sustained and that someone be there to watch for signs of complication during the crucial first twelve hours of life. He remains at the home at least a week after birth, helping the mother to adjust to her new role and teaching both parents postnatal care. He now charges $1,000 for this care, and is probably the highest-paid midwife in the country.

Norman's statistics have never been validated and probably never will be, as the only person collecting data on Norman Casserley is Norman Casserley himself. Yet it would be next to impossible to refute all of these claims, since Norman's clients are his most vehement supporters and rushed to defend him in the press the moment his court ordeals reached the public.

Other midwives in California seem to recognize him as a respected and knowledgeable authority on home birth, and his lectures and demonstrations at the Santa Cruz Birth Center have been characterized by other midwives

---

*I know a woman who just had a baby at age 34.
Donna said the worst part of it all was when
they wouldn't let her hold her baby except to feed
it. So she left the hospital the very next day.*
—ANONYMOUS

there as "extremely helpful and informative." I think of Norman as a kind of priest of natural childbirth because he is dedicated, comforting, asexual, and authoritarian about "natural *home* birth," as he calls it, which has become a kind of religion to him. In fact, he is often so adamant about the way natural childbirth should take place at home that he can easily take on the very *un*midwifelike tone of a stern and admonishing doctor, even though his qualities of patience, support, and gentle guidance have earned him an excellent reputation with home-birth parents in many parts of the United States. Norman's statements that the sound of the *placenta* is a more accurate indication of the full-term baby's condition than the fetal heartbeat and that it is the fetus which psychically manages the birth process, even more than the mother; and the fact that he started out in San Diego by advertising himself as "midwife to royalty in fifty countries" and as "specialist in firstborns and sub-teen-agers" only seem to have heightened the attraction of this lone maverick and have not detracted from his image as competent birth attendant.

Early in 1971, a sixteen-year-old woman in El Cajon, California, asked Norman about the possibility of a home birth for her child. As was his practice, Norman began a series of prenatal visits with a thorough examination in which he searched for "possible facts that I might refer to a physician" if the need for a hospital birth were to arise. He claimed later that he told the woman nothing of his conclusions, stating only that he "found nothing to refer to a physician."

We are the oldest profession! Not the hookers!
—PAT MITCHNICK, *lay midwife*

In May 1971 the California Board of Medical Examiners filed suit against Norman for practicing medicine without a license, referring specifically to his use of a blood-pressure cuff for the purpose of diagnosing his client's condition. Norman stated that he had no money to hire a lawyer and after researching the laws himself, claimed that attending normal births was not to be construed as practicing medicine because birth was not a disease. He cited well over three hundred court cases on record in which birth was clearly shown, he said, to be a natural function of a healthy body unless such complications arose that placed the body in a condition of ill health. He pointed out that the state of California itself did not consider birth a disability because women taking maternity leave were not allowed to claim state disability insurance for that very reason. He further stated that although he always used a blood-pressure cuff during his prenatal examinations, his purpose was not to diagnose, but to detect signs of abnormality that he would refer to a doctor; besides which, he contended that he had told his client nothing of his findings. Among the many documents he uncovered, Norman pointed to an opinion by the California Attorney General in 1964 which stated that the term *diagnosis* "is defined by the Medical Practice Act as 'any undertaking by any method, device or procedure whatsoever . . . to ascertain or establish whether or not a person is suffering from any physical, mental or nervous disorder. . . .' "

Norman sent out flyers, reprints, statements, and letters to the press and to anyone who would listen, in an attempt to gain support for what was rapidly becoming a one-man crusade. Investigators from the Department of Consumer Affairs approached his ex-clients in an attempt to obtain signed statements that would incriminate Norman as a medical practitioner, but could find not a single mother who would cooperate. Indeed, his ex-clients defended him passionately in the press, and a surprising number of doctors also wrote letters in his support.

But soon this new-found publicity resulted in even further pressure on Norman from other agencies. The U.S. Post Office began checking on his literature after a woman complained that she had been sexually aroused by it. The Internal Revenue Service, after learning that Norman allegedly charged $1,000 per home birth and that he claimed to have attended over thirty-five hundred births, added up the figures and ordered him to pay taxes on $3.5 million in income. Norman protested that a thousand of those births had taken place when he was a medical student in Ireland, and that a majority of the others had either been paid in part or not at all because his early clients had been so poor. That he charged $1,000 per home birth now, he contended, had nothing to do with the fact that his income up to that time had been $5,000 a year, for which he had always paid the appropriate tax.

In October 1971 Superior Court Judge Roscoe Wilkey issued a preliminary injunction barring Norman from continuing his practice of midwifery. Undaunted, Norman returned to his law books and was back in court within two months to ask Judge Wilkey if he could establish a blood-pressure-reading business similar to one that was at the time in full operation in downtown Los Angeles. There, Norman pointed out, any citizen could read his own blood pressure on a device called a sphygmomanometer. If he could be a sphygmomanometrist, Norman stated, he would not give out medical advice, diagnosis, or treatment. The judge reportedly declined to comment.

By this time Norman's desperate attempts to defend himself against all comers seemed only to strengthen his zealotry. Apparently convinced he could turn adverse publicity to his advantage, he rewrote his "business card" (actually a mimeographed square of paper) to include such phrases as BANNED IN SAN DIEGO and UNDERGROUND, and even went in for sloganeering with such statements as FOR HEALTHIER MOTHER & CHILD IN ECSTASY and (as if to validate his $1,000 fee) LUXURY FOR GIRLS WHO CAN ONLY AFFORD THE BEST. And, in an apparent attempt to link his name inextricably with his lifelong career, he petitioned a district court in the state of Texas to change his name legally to Mister Midwife. Norman continued to practice outside California and insisted that those who were writing to him use this name on the outside envelope because even this would be "good advertising for the neighbors and postal workers, etc."

At times Norman's tireless, single-minded, nearly fanatic dedication to the defense of lay midwifery and home birth not only tired but shocked his listeners, who would shake their heads in wonder and dispose of him as a "quack."

Not true: a monumental curiosity, yes; a quack, no. However strange his behavior might seem to be, Norman Casserley has proven time and time again that normal births can be safely delivered at home and that even high-risk mothers can enjoy a peaceful, beautiful, and safe birth experience without need for medical interference. Norman is a man who stood up long ago and defended the practice of traditional lay midwifery at the risk of his livelihood and reputation, and who has fought for women's rights as much as his own. Besieged by state and municipal law-enforcement agencies, the Board of Medical Examiners, the State Attorney General, the Internal Revenue Service, and even the Post Office, he has defended himself alone throughout and has uncovered scores of documents that may one day contribute to the legalization of lay midwifery and home birth throughout the country. That he seemed a bit overly zealous and possibly erratic in his behavior in the process is no wonder.

At his trial in March 1972, Norman based his defense on the premise that the practice of midwifery has nothing to do with the practice of medicine or any of its functions of diagnosis, medication, or surgery, and that pregnancy is neither a sickness nor an abnormal condition. He was convicted on three counts of practicing without a license and as of this writing has taken his appeal to a higher court.

Norman believes he would have won the case if the judge had not instructed the jury that health and physiology had nothing to do with normalcy in childbirth, and that because not more than 50 per cent of women were pregnant at any one time, pregnancy was to be considered abnormal and therefore in the same category of sickness and disease. What a strange state of affairs that such unreasonable logic should set first legal precedent for prosecution of midwives in California.

And why? Why did the state of California wait for over twenty years before prosecuting Norman Casserley and for over two years before arresting midwives at the Santa Cruz Birth Center? One theory is that midwives have always been in existence in rural areas of every state, but that until the movement to home birth in California, they had not threatened the established medical profession. Sometime before his court ordeals began, Norman Casserley received quite a bit of publicity when he wrote to local newspapers, the Better Business Bureau, *Dear Abby*, and the President of the United States about how he had discovered a young woman abandoned in an office of a local emergency hospital who was obviously giving birth alone. His pleas to the hospital staff were to no avail until finally an orderly casually walked into the office and caught the baby in the nick of time. Public response to Norman's letters was immensely supportive. Raven Lang and other midwives at the Santa Cruz Birth Center also became recognized throughout the country for their excellent book on home birth, called simply, *Birth Book*, published in 1972. With such notoriety and its implications that established medical services were not responding to consumer needs, midwives in California suddenly became the target of a concerted effort on the part of local obstetricians, in concert with law-enforcement agencies, to rout out the midwife once again and reestablish uniform medical procedures as the only legitimate service available to the average consumer.

Recently a slight inroad was made by State Assemblyman Gordon W. Duffy, who introduced Assembly Bill 1503 in 1972 and fought for its passage in 1973. In effect, the bill provides for a temporary exemption to current law regarding the experimental Health Manpower Project, which was originally designed to accommodate paramedics returning from Vietnam. The bill states in part that the "legislature finds that experimentation with new kinds and combinations of health care delivery systems is desirable, and that, for purposes of such experimentation, a select number of publicly evaluated health manpower innovation programs be exempt from the healing arts practices acts . . . ." In this bill, "health care services" are defined as "the practice of medicine, dentistry, nursing, pharmacy, optometry, podiatry, midwifery, and psychology," and under this exemption nurse-midwives at St. Luke's hospital in San Francisco have already been permitted to practice under the supervision of obstetricians.

The bill is primarily concerned with training programs for paramedics, however, and does not allow nurse-midwives who have been licensed outside the state to practice in California, nor does it allow lay *or* nurse-midwives to work in concert with doctors in private practice, because it is specifically directed to nonprofit community hospitals or clinics. Such a bill as AB 1503 should therefore be considered only as the first step in a direction which may one day lead to laws that will truly legitimatize nurse-midwives. That it is unresponsive to existing consumer demands for home births and lay midwives is a function of the slow-moving wheels of state legislatures everywhere and of modern attitudes regarding home births in general.

The latest attempt to pave the way for nurse-midwives in California is Senate Bill 1332, introduced by Anthony Bielenson and passed by the Senate in 1973. This bill would permit the practice of nurse-midwifery in organized clinics and hospitals under the supervision of physicians. The bill stipulates that " 'supervision' shall not be construed to require physical presence of the supervising physician," which would at least give the nurse-midwife some allowance for independent activity. Nevertheless, she would still be restricted in her actions by the American College of Nurse Midwives and by the physician responsible for her professional service. He too would be limited by the prejudicial attitudes of his own professional governing body, the College of Physicians and Surgeons, and by his private pressure group, the AMA.

According to Hal Reynolds, Director of Government Relations for the California Nurses Association, "there is

nothing in this bill to prevent the nurse-midwife from operating on a fee-for-service basis, as long as she operates under the clinical direction of a physician and surgeon." Under SB 1332, then, although the nurse-midwife could not function as an independent practitioner, nor attend births outside the conventional clinic or hospital, she could conceivably develop her authority into a highly useful and respected position within the confines of the hospital routine. Yet even if this bill were to pass easily in the Assembly, the fact remains that no nurse-midwife, anywhere, can have any power without the sympathetic support of physicians. As has been demonstrated throughout the nation for several decades, in America it is the obstetrician who has absolute power over childbirth; it is the obstetrician who is paid by insurance companies; and it is the obstetrician who establishes the definition of what is common practice in medicine—and common practice has the power of law. Were the nurse-midwife even to appear to be impinging upon this sacred domain, the obstetrician could move very quickly to "keep her in her place."

It is no wonder, then, that after passage in the Senate, AB 1332 ran aground in the Assembly, where it was staunchly opposed by representatives of the Board of Medical Examiners and the California Medical Association. A fact sheet issued in the spring of 1974 by the School of Nursing at the University of California reported that Senator Bielenson, faced with this powerful opposition, "is not feeling any sense of urgency to get along with pressing for his bill." As to the question of lay midwifery, it has become exceedingly clear that California, like other states

---

Women are very oppressed in childbirth in hospitals. I feel we need to break away and start helping ourselves. I want to learn more about the way our bodies function so I can help pregnant women. I want to be a midwife!
—Kim Sparrow, *left in photograph, age 14, apprentice midwife*

in the union, will not even consider permitting lay mid-wives to practice until consumers unite and present a concerted demand in their favor.

What is most difficult to comprehend throughout all these legal entanglements is how physicians can fail to see that the midwife could make a tremendous contribution to their own profession. With the shortage of obstetricians so keenly at hand (see Chapter 5), and with the oft-stated boredom with which many obstetricians view normal birth, midwives could free doctors from attending all but ab-normal births or conditions of *true* disorder in pregnancy, for which the doctor has specialized his calling. For women who prefer hospital births, the nurse-midwife, working under the close supervision of an obstetrician, could at least humanize the hospital procedure in a way that would give birthing mothers the constancy of care they so desperately need during the crucial periods of labor and delivery. For women who desire to give birth at home and who choose to have a lay midwife by their sides, pre- and post-natal attention would be heightened, support and trust during delivery would be strengthened, and doctors having no time for home-birth visits would not have to be contacted except in cases of emergency.

Since it has been proven time and time again that over 90 per cent of all births are completely normal and require no medical attention beyond the first prenatal examina-tions, and since statistics of home births in other countries compare favorably to hospital statistics in the United States, there is *no reason* for the medical community or governmental agencies to fight the emergence of practicing midwives today. Their continuation to do so can only be attributed to feelings of personal and professional threat from women—and some men—whose intention is only to assist nature, not to practice medicine.

Dr. John Van S. Maeck, chief of obstetrics at the University of Vermont, was quoted in *Prevention* in June 1972 as saying, "There has never been a problem of patient-acceptance of the nurse-midwife, but I believe there is a real problem in doctor-acceptance. We must educate doctors to recognize that they have a potential partner in the nurse-midwife." And in the lay midwife, it may be added.

An even more direct statement was made by Dr. Seth E. Many of Cambridge, Mass., in the same issue of *Prevention:* "Simply put, an attempt to redefine pregnancy and birth as a medical illness, may be considered an attempt to protect and extend a professional domain, rather than the giving of humane consideration to the rights and needs of people everywhere."

That a profession which considers itself so advanced, because of the very medical technology and procedures that are running the birth process for thousands of women across the nation, should so callously dispense with the very birth attendants who can reclaim the process for women and make it safer as well, is no less than a *shameful* indictment of the medical fraternity in the United States today.

Betty Cahill:
A California Nurse
Chooses Home Birth

Betty Cahill is a neonatal nurse specialist and childbirth teacher at a large community hospital where "natural childbirth" is the rage. Her greatgrandmother was a midwife in Hiawassi, Georgia. Her grandma Effie gave birth to Betty's mother sitting "right on Grandpa's lap." But home birth was a very hard decision for Betty Cahill.

BEFORE I MADE my choice I had to completely reevaluate what the hospital is doing in normal birth. I knew what I wanted, but I couldn't be sure I'd get it in any hospital. I wanted this to be *my* birth, not *theirs*. I realized I was making a decision for my unborn child, but I felt the baby would be better off born at home. After all, I'd been in the business of birth myself.

Maia was born a little after midnight, after twenty-three hours labor. We all settled down in bed about three when the midwife and doctor had left. I couldn't sleep. A light came through the crack in the door and I must have watched, felt and smelled her for five or six hours. The most powerful feeling came over me; she was *my* baby.

There was a secret meeting at the hospital to decide whether I should even be allowed to continue to teach, because of the example I had set for parents. They allowed me to stay, but my teaching has changed since then. I feel I must prepare couples for what they will encounter in the hospital. Teach them to communicate what they want in birth. Yet I can't offer something I know they won't be able to get in a hospital.

Still, I am a trained nurse. I can't forget how much I was trained to expect that something *will* go wrong, and the nurse had better be there! I was trained to be afraid. But since my home birth I'm less afraid about life.

17
Granny,
Come Home!

Granny,
Come Home!

We are perfectly willing to look at nurse-midwifery on a pilot basis. But until we are certain that it's in the public interest to have certified nurse-midwives—and I haven't seen any real evidence that it is a state-wide necessity—then we have to oppose this.

—DR. THOMAS ELMENDORF,
past president of the California Medical Association, 1974

FROM JULY 1960 through June 1963, two nurse-midwives were given special dispensation by the state of California to develop a pilot program of maternity care for women of Madera County, a low-income, rural area which was perpetually short of physicians and nurses. Working at Madera County Hospital, these women developed close relationships with the county's birthing mothers and provided a complete program of prenatal through postnatal care. By the middle of the program they were handling most of the pregnancies and delivering 78 per cent of the babies, assisted only by staff physicians in emergencies, and by obstetricians and pediatricians from a neighboring county on a limited consultation basis.

The nurse-midwives achieved startling results. Over the three-year period the incidence of prematurity in Madera County dropped almost by half. Neonatal mortality, considered by obstetricians to be the most accurate

Doctors always act as if they can improve on the process of nature. I think there are things women instinctively know about giving birth. We must know them or the race wouldn't have survived. Yet doctors don't listen to mothers. Their attitude is, "All these silly women—what do they know?
—KENDRA DAY, *mother*

measure of birth care, dropped from 23.9 newborns per thousand to only 10.3 per thousand—less than half of what it had been before the midwives arrived. But two years after the pilot program had been disbanded and the nurse-midwives had left the county, neonatal mortality shot up to 32.1 per thousand. There had been no nursery epidemics, no increase in the number of multiple births, and no increase in neonatal deaths in other parts of the county. The only change in maternity care in Madera County was the absence of the nurse-midwives.

According to Barry S. Levy, Frederick S. Wilkinson, and William M. Marinc, whose analysis of the Nurse Obstetric Aide (NOA) project appeared in the *American Journal of Obstetrics and Gynecology* (January 1, 1971): "The discontinuation of a medical care program that was thought to be beneficial is a rare occurrence in American medicine...." Yet the powerful Council of the California Medical Association "refused to support a permanent change in the state law which would have permitted nurse-midwives to practice as they had during the program." Naturally, the CMA, representing the obstetrical community under the direction of such officials as Dr. Thomas Elmendorf, could hardly permit the continuance of a program that allowed nurse-midwives so much independent authority.

The Madera County midwives were able to give quality care to mothers within the context of the community hospital. Since physicians and complicated machinery were not available to them and since they were too shorthanded to administer the many drugs and interferences routinely used elsewhere, the midwives kept birth simple.

They did not function as doctors arriving at the last minute "to catch the baby," nor as nurses specializing in fragmentary care within the obstetric team. Although state administrators officially referred to them as nurse obstetric assistants, they became, in fact, true midwives in the traditional sense—independent, sympathetic, and patient attendants of the natural process who stayed at mothers' sides throughout labor and delivery. Their conscientious attention to the individual needs of birthing women and their willingness to work within the social and economic conditions peculiar to Madera County gave them a further stature that state officials could hardly applaud: they had combined the best qualities of the old "granny" midwife with the intelligent care of the modern administrator.

For too long, American women have bought the deception that the old granny midwife was exactly as she was described by physicians and politicians—slovenly, illiterate, superstitious, and crudely countrified. That she was also knowledgeable, competent, and supportive in her own way has long been forgotten in light of our modern hospital care with its immaculate staff and starchy efficiency. A true pioneer, the granny faced overwhelming barriers in reaching her birthing neighbors in time, in handling medical emergencies herself, and in raising and supporting her own family. How easily we scoff at her as an ignorant woman, when it is we who are ignorant of the true qualities of the traditional midwife, we who have been deceived by the quick-and-easy modern birth. Who was the granny? Where did she practice? What special qualities did she possess that made her invaluable to the population she served?

Part of the original FNS

The redbud trees were blooming on Big Hill in McKee, Kentucky, when I arrived in March, 1974, to find out what the old-fashioned granny was really like. I was on my way to the tiny town of Hyden, birthplace of the famed Frontier Nursing Service in southeastern Kentucky, the first institution to provide training that combined the qualities of the granny and the nurse, and superior birth care at low cost. The bus dropped me off at McKee, county seat of Jackson County. The front page of the local paper contained two interesting items, placing the town in the past and the present simultaneously. According to the first, "a streaker rode a motorcycle around the McKee County Courthouse and disappeared out the fastest road. . . ." Next to this item Sheriff Hershell Lynch in an interview told how a moonshine still had just been discovered, one that had apparently been in operation until a few hours before: "One of the largest ever found in Jackson County . . . We've probably walked one hundred miles searching for this one."

Independent midwives practiced in the hills of Jackson County, just an hour's drive away from the Frontier Nursing Service territory, until very recently. Delsia Gabbard's grandmother had been the best-known granny in the area, and I wanted to know about her. Delsia and I sat and talked over some brandied fruitcake and coffee about the way things used to be:

> My grandmaw was the real midwife of the whole county. She's been dead eighteen years, but way past sixty-five she'd still go out. Folks paid her with anything. Sometimes

If you put me in a cabin with nothing in it, I'd probably feel secure. If you put me in a large hospital delivery room, I'd probably want to run.
—ANONYMOUS MIDWIFE,
Frontier Nursing Service

nothing. She and my grandfather farmed to live. If families were in real bad shape about something to eat, she'd take sweet potatoes and milk and butter in her saddle bags. She'd take something to eat every time she went out.

Everyone called her "Maw Lear." And she was a sight. A good cook, real handy gardener, made blankets from sheep wool, could knit and card and spin too. She was tough, Mammy was. Everybody put their faith in her. She couldn't even read or write. But she was gifted.

Sometimes a woman'd be up agin it and having a hard tussle. They'd go and get the doctor and he'd say, "You don't need me. Maw Lear can do all I can do."

Delsia was herself born at home, with her grandma as her mother's midwife. And she remembers the many births Maw Lear went out on.

She would go out three times a month at least. She would go out at midnight and ride a horse eight or ten miles. After it was over and the baby fine, after there wasn't anyone left around the home, she'd cook a good meal for the family before leaving. And then she'd go back after a time or two to see if everything was okay.

Maw Lear seldom lost a baby.

They didn't lose a lot of babies in my grandmaw's day. Not at birth they didn't. That just goes to show you— that it was good. Wasn't it?

Jean Fee, McKee's local nurse, heard I was in town and made a special trip to come see the visitor from California who was so interested in midwives. She had trained with

---

We tried not to handle women with obstetric problems. But, in fact, we never turned down a call. We did our best and we never left a mother to labor alone.

—ANONYMOUS MIDWIFE,
Frontier Nursing Service

309

Kentucky's Frontier Service, the origin of American nurse-midwifery. Ten years ago, when Jean graduated, FNS mid-wives, like their granny predecessors, were still driving miles up-county to deliver babies at home.

When I first went to FNS I got everything other than obstetrics. I got to take care of the children with worms, the old people with pneumonia, and the fellow who came in saying he wanted "some of them thar little green heart pills Dr. Schaeffer give me three years ago."

The first year I was there, there was no doctor. We had to rely on ourselves, even after the doctor came back. With the area we served, there was no earthly way you could ask permission before you did something. The emphasis of our midwifery was to know and be able to manage the normal and be able to recognize the abnormal and know in time to be able to do something before it became an emergency. We had parasites of all kinds here, and they pull down your hemoglobin. Anemia was a constant problem, largely dietary and climatically caused. People still ate molasses but it was already being replaced by sugar.

The first evidences of civilization are never the best. Television sets and old wrecked cars and TV dinners were the first to hit. We spent more time trying to get people to leave the soft drinks alone than trying to improve anything else. The second baby I delivered was to a woman fifty years old, number twelve for her. This woman had struck labor when her husband was at work. They didn't own a vehicle so she hit the road with her thumb, because she had been told to get to the hospital. I happened to be standing there when she arrived. She hit the bed and I grabbed the baby. She should really have been delivered at

*The Frontier
Nursing Service*

home, because of the danger of not getting to the hospital in time.

Having attended both home and hospital births before giving up midwifery to practice nursing, Jean had strong ideas about the best place for birthing.

I think where the house is adequate and where there aren't fifty kids to keep Mother hopping, then I much prefer home birth. I don't get all dewy-eyed about it being a great emotional experience; but it doesn't interrupt the continuity of home life. It doesn't expose the patient to nearly as much infection. There's no place in the world as heavily infested with bugs of every shape and size as a hospital. Wait, I take that back. A doctor's waiting room is worse. You don't see staph infections in home-born children. You don't see thrush in home-born children unless they're older and dragging bottles around on the floor. You don't see puerperal infections in mothers delivered at home unless they're absolutely filthy. And you usually don't then. We had a saying that everybody is immune to his own dirt.

We had no phones when I worked at FNS, or if we did they went off. We almost always had someone come and fetch us; called "running the granny race." You ran for the granny to see if you could get back with her before the baby came.

The nurse-midwives from the FNS were not local women. Yet they were accepted everywhere they went because they filled a great need and did no moralizing about the conditions under which they worked.

FNS midwives making rounds

People don't make much of a fuss here about gratitude. But let something happen to one of the midwives and everybody came by to help.

The real grannies were rapidly disappearing by the 1960s, but there were still a few of them practicing far from the main roads. Jean knew several.

There was an old woman on Sam's Branch and she'd been a granny for I don't know how long. And she was shamey-faced about talking about her midwifery experiences to me. She'd been put down by somebody or other for not being a nurse. She wasn't the most sanitary or the most unsanitary person I ever saw. But people have different ideas about sanitation too. You can go into somebody's house who burns coal and their hands are going to be black. Now that's not "nasty." That, by the way, is Kentuckian for "filth."

Jean left me with a pile of old FNS bulletins, going back twenty years. I read until early morning, trying to imagine what it would be like to be a modern nurse-midwife in the rough hills of rural Kentucky, far from any space-age medical assistance, riding jeep or horseback up the hills.

In Leslie County, Kentucky, boys don't play doctor; they play nurse-midwife. The Frontier Nursing Service has provided primary and often total medical care in illness, emergency, and birth to all families in its 1,000-square-mile territory. Doctors are rarely lured to the area. In 1969 there were only fifty physicians for all of the eight-county region in southern Kentucky, which had a population of over 100,000. Leslie County itself had few doctors for its 18,000 residents.

Mary Breckinridge founded the Frontier Nursing Service in 1925. Raised in Kentucky, she studied midwifery at the British Hospital for Mothers and Babies in London, and then returned home. She wanted to help mothers and babies who had the most needs and the least care. She chose Leslie County, the poorest and most inaccessible county in Kentucky, believing that if she could provide good care under the worst conditions it would be an example for others to follow. There were no motor roads for sixty miles in any direction, and the midwives she brought from England arrived at homes on horseback. There was not a single doctor to help them in emergencies, so they had to handle all emergencies themselves. When the British midwives returned home during World War II, Mary Breckinridge began training her own midwives as she had been trained in England. Over the years the community helped the FNS build its headquarters, its hospital, and half a dozen outpost clinics up in the hills. Maternity and pediatric care were the primary services the midwives provided because Leslie County, until five years ago, had the highest birth rate in the country.

Today less than 7 per cent of the home visits involve midwifery. Not only has the family size dropped from an average dozen to three or four, but most births now take place in Hyden Hospital. Horses have given way to jeeps, and the county has changed in other ways as well. Many homes now have electricity, and if they have no phone or indoor toilet they boast at least one TV, a radio, and maybe a refrigerator and range. Modern forms of American malnutrition have reached the county as diets of soup beans, home-ground corn, and salt pork have given way to bleached flours, degerminated corn, preservatives, and sugar. Every country store carries stacks and stacks of empty Coke and Pepsi bottles out front. The full package maternity care that cost a family five dollars in 1935 costs one hundred today, but the Frontier Nursing Service still offers excellent care at cheap prices.

There has been another change in Leslie County. People there are concerned now about their image in the outside world and attempt to follow the national trends they see on their TVs. In the last eight years, they have been hounded by media people looking for a good angle on a story about Appalachian poverty and they have developed a wary self-consciousness. Several people, noting the camera hanging from my neck, told me stories about photographers who had been run off at gunpoint after pictures of the poorest shacks and most disreputable families appeared in national magazines. Still, the FNS was used to visitors from many countries and for the most part accepted strangers.

To get to the Frontier Nursing Service, I had to travel Highway 421, which wove back and forth across narrow bridges over a rock-filled creek. The creek and surrounding hillside were full of bits and pieces of old junked automobiles, and even the tiny manicured family graveyards on the slopes looked like oases in the midst of dumping grounds for cars. It seemed that around every bend a pastel aluminum trailer was parked next to a brick bungalow, its roof blackened all around from burning coal. Next to these stood weathering brown-gray cabins, clean and threadbare shells. One yard slipped into another without fenced boundaries; and in front of every home, as if to mark the territory, sat a late-model car and the body of a worn-out pickup truck. Spiky antennas perched on every roof. The sky was thin and gray and clean.

Hyden Hospital and the midwifery school sit high up on the main hill above the squat town. The snaking narrow road was paved for the first time several years ago. The gray stone and wood-frame buildings sit primly among the trees, like an old-fashioned country boarding school.

Helen Brown is the present head of the FNS and oversees the hospital and the training school, as well as the six outpost clinics which comprise the service. I was invited to meet her for four o'clock tea at the FNS headquarters several miles back of Hyden. Tradition is as strong at the Frontier Nursing Service as the resourcefulness necessary for survival in harsh country. Helen Brown seemed pleased to be able to tell yet another visitor about her work.

I came here in 1938, because you could be a nurse and ride horseback at the same time.

314

In the early years we found it very difficult to persuade women to come into the hospital if they needed it. But mountain families follow a pattern of what families do on the outside. Ten years ago in this country there was a tremendous upsurge in hospital deliveries, so women here now accept and expect hospital birth.

I asked her if that was the main reason home birth had been discontinued at the service.

Not really. Medical insurance, private and government, just won't pay for home deliveries. We tried to change that, because it is cheaper for them to pay us for a home birth than a hospital one. They didn't listen.

Helen fought the move to compulsory hospital births for years, and the FNS makes it a firm policy never to turn anyone down for financial reasons, nor to refuse help to a woman who demands home birth. Nevertheless, home birth is a thing of the past. I asked if she thought it was less safe to deliver women at home.

I think babies born at home did very well when they were all breast-fed, even when women were worn down, anemic, wormy, and had too many babies for their health. The health of the mother is better today. We still see malnourished women, though, because the mother is the last one to eat, after she feeds her husband and her children.

Today Helen Brown reluctantly goes along with the trend toward compulsory hospital birth. She is committed

Helen Brown

to keeping the FNS alive and growing and up with the times. She did suggest that it would be interesting for me to speak with Anna May January, at seventy the oldest nurse-midwife still at the FNS. Anna May is retired now, but lives at the student center. She brightened when I asked her to tell me about the old days in the service.

Winters were worse then than they are now. I remember my coworker and I each walked 250 miles one month. It was too dangerous to get the horses out. I think we had sixteen maternity cases due that month.

I loved the home deliveries. I felt much more at home in the cabin than in the hospital. There your mother *knew* you. Of course, there was no sweeter music than hearing the horse come with the doctor, when we needed him. I had my share of hemorrhages, but I never lost a mother. We had no plasma then. And I remember when a big obstetrician came from England and said that you'd be surprised how the simplest things often do work as good as any IVs. I always remember what Mrs. Breckinridge said to us: "The further away you get from nature the more trouble you get."

She told me how she used her hands during childbirth instead of "fancy" instruments.

I controlled the mother's perineum with my right hand. We were considered very poor midwives if our women had any tears. We kept mothers in bed ten days, and we gave them a complete bed bath and bathed the baby every day but Sunday. And if the mother had fever, we came out on Sunday too. But we didn't get any mothers running fevers.

She said that both the mothers and their babies were healthy at home. It was untrue that home-born babies had more problems.

Most of the children who died, died after they were weaned, their second year. All the mothers nursed then and it seemed to keep the babies healthy. They all slept with their babies and I think that's the way it's right.

I believe it'll take a hundred years for breast-feeding to come back if it ever does. False advertising, I think. Mothers think it's too much trouble. When our babies were all breast-fed, visitors would come and say we had the best babies they'd ever seen. It's all changed tremendously today.

Much has changed with the Frontier Nursing Service. Pressures from modern life have been difficult to avoid. The service now goes along with the prevailing medical attitude around the country that all births should take place in hospitals, so the midwives are more like nurses' now, using drugs with greater frequency, giving routine hormone injections after second stage, and making routine episiotomies in first mothers. The temptations of hospital medicine seem too great to resist, even though when home births were common, until the 1960s, birth statistics of the Frontier Nursing Service could not be criticized. Ten thousand deliveries at home from 1925 to 1955 showed 9.1 maternal puerperal deaths, despite the fact that mothers in

*Anna May January, age 70,
retired FNS midwife*

Leslie County have always fallen in categories of high risk in far greater proportion than the rest of the birthing population. Among white women in the United States during the same period, the rate averaged 34 per 10,000 births. Furthermore, there has not been a single maternal death at FNS in the past twenty-two years.

The Frontier Nursing Service may have changed in recent years, but its record and experience now stand as a model of traditional midwifery. Whether she is called a "granny," a "nurse-midwife," or an "obstetric aide," the competent midwife, left on her own, is the perfect complement to the natural process of childbirth and the best attendant to the birthing mother.

But the role of the nurse-midwife is becoming narrowly defined within the hospital system. In these surroundings, under the direct authority of the physician specialist, can the nurse-midwife of today survive as a true midwife? Can the mother still depend upon her to provide the care she needs, as she depended upon her granny?

Kings County Hospital in New York is the contemporary model and another kind of showcase for American nurse-midwifery. The hospital serves a vast portion of Brooklyn's teeming immigrant population, 95 per cent of which is nonwhite, including Puerto Ricans and blacks from Jamaica and the rest of the West Indies who pass through Brooklyn, the doorway to America. Given the difficulty of administering a hospital the size of a small city and the necessity of providing care and education in different languages, Kings County has many problems the average suburban hospital does not. Yet these problems have worked to surprising advantage in childbirth, because the underbudgeted and overworked staff has never been able to afford the expense or time necessary to administer medication to mothers during normal labor and delivery. Ten years ago such an admission would have been considered a gross failure of services and an example of discrimination against nonwhites. Today, in light of all the evidence now available on the damaging effects of obstetric drugs and other interferences, it is this hospital's recommendation.

Infant mortality has dropped steadily at Kings County over the years, to a point where it is just half of the national average for teaching hospitals its size. Last year 31 per cent of all births were attended by nurse-midwives, most of whom were studying at Downstate Medical Facility of the State University of New York, located just across the street. With publicity from newspapers and national magazines praising nurse-midwives, Kings County now receives a growing number of maternity patients from middle-class and wealthy neighborhoods who want to have an undrugged, midwife-attended birth.

Dr. John Boyce, director of the obstetric services at Kings County, believes that childbirth is a normal process in a healthy woman's life. He admits that his hospital must handle a number of high-risk mothers, due to pervasive problems of poor nutrition and large numbers (about 25 per cent) of mothers under twenty years of age. Because of family-planning education, 60 per cent of these young mothers are having their first child, but some are having their third or fourth. Although Kings County now permits husbands and mates to attend labor

---

A patient would come in labor and one of us was assigned to her. We'd stay with her till after the delivery, no matter how long it took. But administratively and economically it doesn't make

and delivery, the community has been slow to respond to this new policy. As Dr. Boyce stated:

> It will take some time for people to accept our offer at face value, to participate in the births of their babies. You can't shut the labor room door in a guy's face for fifteen years and then expect him to rush in once you open it.

So far, as much as 15 per cent of the mothers have received no prenatal care at all, and only 10 per cent of the registered couples attend the prenatal classes that prepare them for delivery together. Both Dr. Boyce and Nancy O'Donohue, nurse-midwife administrator, are attempting to improve the hospital's prenatal care. They admit the clinic will continue to be a "zoo" until the patient load is decreased and extra clinics are opened outside the hospital to handle pre- and post-natal care. The hospital has already enlarged its obstetric space and broken its nursery down into smaller units. It is now up to the mother to choose who will support and attend her in labor: husband, friend, or relative.

Kings County offers a cheaper birth than do comparable hospitals, with a total package to avoid hidden costs to the patient. A three-day maternity stay is approximately $550, and prenatal clinic visits are scaled to income. This price includes the mother's and baby's room, board, X rays, and medication. At Downstate Hospital just across the street, a family must pay its maternity bill in cash before leaving the hospital. There a three-day stay with prenatal care and private physician costs more than $1,000.

The nurse-midwife is a strong member of the Kings

---

sense to assign someone making $12,000–$13,000, and with our training, to one patient for a whole day.

—Barbara Petersen, *nurse-midwife,*
Mademoiselle

County team. Nancy O'Donohue feels nursing is where the manpower in health care can be found and would like to see many more American nurses trained in midwifery. John Boyce would agree. He adds that the nurse-midwife should be able to move up the ranks of responsibility and authority in the hospital.

I look at the nurse-midwife as a component in the delivery of obstetric care. I think any area that is delivering OB care should give nurse-midwives all the appropriate possibility to develop their potential, not only in normal but also in abnormal care under adequate supervision.

Both he and Ms. O'Donohue want to get maternity care out of huge hospitals. But, from Dr. Boyce's point of view as an obstetrician and administrator, there are advantages to a hospital the size of Kings County.

A benefit of a large hospital is that it can protect large numbers of patients and spot trends quickly among the birthing population. A change here influences an enormous number of lives.

They would welcome the possibility of joint private practice between midwives and doctors, and they would even consider home delivery.

Ms. O'Donohue privately acknowledges that many mothers prefer a nonhospital birth, despite all the amenities a hospital can offer. "If we made home delivery available, people would always want it. You maintain a degree of control which you relinquish the moment you

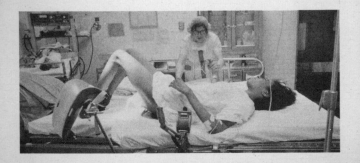

enter a hospital." They both agree that "as a natural course of things, people would want to exclude the hospital from their births." But John Boyce feels it is not good policy for a hospital to pioneer in providing home births, especially when that would imply it is safe to go into homes for birth.

> I couldn't make home deliveries safe for midwives. I would have to vouch for their personal safety, which I cannot. And since the birth of a child in Brooklyn is hospital oriented today, I would be fighting the hierarchy in obstetrics to alter that.

Our talk ended and I was given permission to watch and photograph births for the evening with mothers' consent.

It was just an average night at Kings County, with half a dozen women in varying stages of labor and a ratio of staff to mothers of about one to one, nurse-midwives, obstetric residents, nurses, and one watchful medical student. I shuttled back and forth between two sides of the floor to watch labors and births attended by physicians and by nurse-midwives in their last months of training.

The gap between the best intentions of administrators and the practices of the hospital, especially during evening hours when the staff is on its own, was instantly apparent. Everyone was struggling to do a good job despite changing shifts, professional tensions, and the pressure of time that exists as much in Kings County as in other hospitals. And despite the lack of routine medications, the atmosphere was frenzied and strained. Margaret Strickhouser, attending nurse-midwife, summed it all up as she looked up at me from behind her sterile face mask and said:

> There's too much interference here. They don't leave people alone. They don't have the patience to wait for nature. There are too many vaginal exams. They use rountine IVs with glucose and give routine Pitocin after delivery. If mothers breast-fed, I don't think we would need oxytocics at all. They rupture routinely here at about five centimeters. It speeds up labor. As a nurse, I would never deliver a patient in stirrups if I had a choice. I would let her deliver in the labor bed. If we think it's going to be a nice delivery, we do sometimes let them. But we don't tell anyone. I don't buck the system while I'm learning. As a student I can get away with a lot more experimentation here than as a staff nurse.

Margaret delivered on one side of the corridor as the resident and his staff delivered on the other. Both gave early episiotomies; both left mothers alone in recovery for an hour, with their babies across the room under electric warmers. On neither side was the mother allowed to hold her baby after birth. In the midwife section I saw a great deal of attention and contact during labor. Across the hall, the doctors spent an entire labor trying to reach a distraught and frightened mother. To gain contact, they cajoled, threatened, and shouted at the unlistening young woman who screamed with every contraction. The resident made an episiotomy which cut through the anal sphincter. "Fourth degree median," he wrote on the woman's chart later. I asked him about episiotomies.

> The bigger the better. Listen, we try to keep it natural, but we really have to rush the patient to Delivery so someone else can use the room. The women tend to come in fairly late in labor, often six or seven centimeters; there really isn't time to medicate them when it would still be safe for the baby.
>
> I plan to do mainly gynecology when I get out. Obstetrics is too much pressure, it's hard on the body. You smoke, you drink. I'm not gonna spend the rest of my life up all night. We don't even have time to talk to the women in clinic. A regular monthly checkup I have just two minutes to spend. I can't talk with a woman. If I spend fifteen minutes with one woman, I'll be there twenty-four

hours just finishing the day's appointments. Maybe 120 patients each day. I talk to them in labor; but by then it's too late. They are scared of the baby coming.

Back in the physician's lounge for a brief moment, Norm Schneiderman, a third-year medical student, commented on the scene outside and on his impressions of childbirth.

This is my second day. I walked in the ward and met this resident and knew I was going to learn something from him. I will be getting no formal training in natural childbirth. Our six-week rotation in obstetrics used to be twelve weeks five years ago. Its function is to teach three things: how to do a good normal delivery, how to give a good pelvic examination, and what to do in complications. We're not taught much about prenatal care.

Then he changed the subject to his own feelings and his wife's.

My wife says when she's ready to deliver she's going to lock herself in the bathroom until it's too late for me to take her to the hospital. She wants to have the baby natural. And I'm all in favor—except for the one-in-a-hundred chance of a complication.

In private practice physicians are worried about their patients' well-being and are concerned that women come back to their practice. So they tend to ease women's pain with something. And women want something for pain. It's normal in the twentieth century, where the layman looks to the doctor to take away his pains, cure everything, instantly. People today don't want to put up with any discomfort.

Despite the personal beliefs and intentions of residents and midwives alike, both are caught in a system that moves women through birth too quickly to permit closeness with any patient. The harried nurse-midwife of Kings County is unable to humanize the hospital maternity system. If nurse-midwives are ever to function as true midwives, they must be free from pressure to rush and alter the natural process. The average hospital is not conducive to normal birth experiences, even with the finest nurse-midwives and the finest intentions.

18
England and Denmark: Midwifery on the Brink

Charlotte Truscott, British District Midwife

England and Denmark:
Midwifery on the Brink

> I loved my job. We used to be on call twenty-four hours a day because we wanted to. Now it's not the same at all. I miss home deliveries a lot.
>
> Midwifery used to be a vocation—a calling. Now, sadly, it's a job.

THE WORDS are spoken quietly by a former domiciliary (home-birth) midwife as she stands in front of the Royal College of Midwives in London. She is a small, middle-aged woman who wears the traditional blue uniform with its dark blue pillbox hat and black walking shoes. On her hat is the pin that distinguishes all members of her profession, a profession most of the world admires. She is a British midwife, a member of that sturdy tradition of birth attendants who in England have been fully trained, officially sanctioned, and nationally honored for nearly one hundred years. Today British midwives continue to attend 80 per cent of the nation's births each year. Yet the domiciliary midwife is a practitioner of a displaced and dying craft.

That home birth and independent midwifery is no longer an option for most English women is not the result of a conscious choice on the part of mothers. British obstetricians, working under the national health plan with

---

People often write me from the States about how to have a baby at home. They know I'm very much in favor of home confinements. Because of

governmental agencies, have made every attempt to move birth into the hospital, and to replace the domiciliary midwife with the obstetrical team. In the last decade, as the bureaucratic machinery began to mesh together to institutionalize midwifery and as obstetricians gained more control over normal birth, the midwife became a part of the hospital team, a step that limited but secured her position. Today there are 70,000 midwives in England, but only 20,000 are engaged in active practice, and less than 6,000 attend home births.

Inside the British hospital, the modern nurse-midwife is dressed in white. She continues to wear her traditional midwife pin, but she is actually part nurse, part midwife, and part doctor. Assigned to an obstetrical team, she administers specialized care in particular phases of the birth process, such as prenatal care, or postnatal care, or labor, or delivery. She does not follow a single mother through the entire course of birth. In the delivery room, she is allowed to administer drugs and perform episiotomies, and although the conduct of the delivery is technically under her care, an obstetrician "consultant" often takes over when transition begins.

Twenty years ago, more than half of all British babies were born at home, the "proper environment" for normal birth. An excellent back-up service was available at all times through England's famed Flying Squads. These were specially equipped ambulances stationed at local hospitals which could be reached by midwives through an emergency telephone number. The ambulance carried intravenous fluids, blood, plasma, an incubator, an oxygen tank,

---

the lack of a back-up system in America, I advise them about the tremendous risks.
—SHEILA KITZINGER

anesthetics, instruments for emergency forceps or Caesarean deliveries, and sterile gowns, masks, and drapes. An obstetrician always accompanied the ambulance, so the Flying Squad was able to bring a mobile operating room to the birthing mother's door within minutes of the midwife's call.

Today the Flying Squads are seldom used, as home births have declined from 50 per cent of all births in the mid-1950s to only 5 per cent today. The remaining domiciliary midwives work for local authorities who assign them to particular geographic districts (usually in poverty areas), and who pay their salary. These district midwives follow pregnant women from the earliest prenatal visits, through labor and delivery, to as many as four weeks after birth, but they are required to work closely with hospitals and local obstetricians throughout.

So the bureaucratic machinery surrounding the practice of midwifery in England seems to have contributed to a compartmentalization of the midwife's duties. Basic to this direction is the Royal College of Midwives, the official training, licensing, and standard-setting body of English midwifery. Its objective, established in 1881, is "to promote and advance the art and science of midwifery and to raise the efficiency of midwives." In the past, the RCM supervised the training of both midwives and nurse-midwives, but today the nurse is preferred, and training is designed to offer midwifery as an advanced degree for the low-salaried nurse. Over 80 per cent of all English midwives are now nurses first, and most of them have opted to work

Maternity ward at large London hospital. Note children are allowed in wards.

in hospitals under the close supervision of obstetricians. Midwives train at the 240 midwifery schools scattered throughout the country, and they are required to take a refresher course every five years to avoid becoming rigid and narrow-minded, a criticism leveled at some midwives in the past who had acted more as stern authorities than compassionate attendants.

While the RCM acts as the licensing and training association, the real governing body of English midwifery today is the Central Midwives Board, which is comprised of obstetricians, midwives, and governmental authorities. Both groups constantly feed information to the British headquarters of the International Confederation of Midwives, an organization formed (in 1922), largely through British inspiration and maintained through British zeal, to raise the standards of midwifery around the world. By working closely with the World Health Organization and the International Confederation of Obstetricians and Gynecologists, the ICM has been in the vanguard of modern midwifery to both underdeveloped and developed countries. So, while traditional British midwifery is on a gradual decline on the home front, the international organization, largely through the efforts of its executive secretary, Marjorie Bayes, continues to adopt the modern British view of midwifery as part of the obstetric team.

At the ICM headquarters in London, Ms. Bayes and her assistant, Ms. F. Margaret Hardy, expressed both a pride and a sadness in the way British midwifery has changed over the years. According to Ms. Hardy:

It was an enlightened band of women, educated women, in the 1880s who formed the Midwives Institute [later called the Royal College of Midwives]. They organized instruction for midwives, and they tried on eight occasions to get a bill through Parliament governing midwives. It finally passed in 1902 and resulted in the formation of the Central Midwives Board. So the midwives themselves were responsible for their governing body. By the time of the First Midwives Act, all people practicing midwifery had to notify the board. They were called "bona fide." Then by 1905 every new person practicing midwifery had to have special training and receive a certificate from the Central Midwives Board.

But as Ms. Hardy explained some of the duties of the British midwife today, it became evident that the midwife has lost a great deal of her independence and her authority somewhere along the way.

At about thirty-six weeks, the pregnant patient is referred by her midwife to be seen by a doctor a second time to see whether she's physically fit to receive inhalation analgesia, which can be administered by midwives in the home. Midwives working in hospitals must obey the rules of the hospital. And it is the doctor there who takes ultimate responsibility for any drugs given. A midwife in the domiciliary field carries drugs she's permitted to use, provided she's been instructed in their use and dosage, and then she replenishes her supply by an order from her supervisor or the medical office of health in her district.

As she spoke about the duties of the midwife, it seemed as if woman's traditional birth attendant had become little more than a specialist in modern obstetric aids. But Ms. Hardy insisted that midwives still practice a separate art, and that they work *with* obstetricians, not for them. "Obstetricians here will tell you they couldn't practice obstetrics without the service of midwives," she said. Ms. Bayes agreed, but admitted that modern midwifery does have its disadvantages.

It's very difficult today to have simplicity in maternity care. We have all these ultrasonic rays and monitors. It's the doctors who have brought them in. They are the senior members of the team. It is often the doctor who makes something abnormal in birth. To me, midwifery is becoming too scientific. The attitude of midwifery was always: whenever in doubt, wait.

I did my training in 1936. I used to deliver mothers in their own homes. I would go and sit with a mother in labor. And I wouldn't rush to fetch a doctor. I would just wait a little while. Well, you see, those days of being patient seem to have gone. People today don't believe in simplicity. All these ICM meetings we're having—I don't want them to be complicated. If we don't keep to simple things, we don't get anywhere. Miss Hardy and I are talking about the next midwifery congress. Well, I am tired of scientific subjects. It's time we got down to something more basic than having people come to talk to us about these wonderful scientific developments. It's the quality of life we're talking about, isn't it?

In Ireland and England most of us who give birth at home were ourselves born at home. Women I've seen in America seem more afraid and less relaxed about giving birth.

—Irish nurse-midwife

Like many midwives I met in England, Ms. Bayes and Ms. Hardy bow to the undisputed authority of the obstetrician "consultant" in all phases of childbirth. They do not agree with many "modern" practices in obstetrics, particularly the trend to "nine-to-five obstetrics"—routine induction of labor for the purpose of keeping all births within the normal work week.

> When a woman goes into a hospital antenatal clinic, she comes under the authority of a particular consultant. It all depends on that physician's attitude whether she will be induced or not. And it is out of our hands.

Much about birth today *is* out of the midwife's hands. Yet midwives all over England are quick to remind foreign visitors that there is still a great difference between the practice of midwifery and the practice of modern obstetrics. "Obstetrics is done by doctors and midwifery is done by midwives," said Ms. Hardy. The words ring a bit hollow, because the difference may be lost on English mothers, who have lost their traditional birth attendant and remain confused and alone—and dependent on the hospital obstetric team.

While midwives may feel that decisions are "out of our hands," the National Childbirth Trust, England's most "radical" childbirth organization, is attempting to show women that birth and all decisions surrounding it really belong to the mother. Gwen Rankin, childbirth educator and former chairman of the National Childbirth Trust, helped found this organization back in 1956 when she and a dozen other women came together after hearing a speech

Nursery at London hospital

by Grantly Dick-Read. They decided to work for the purpose of helping educate other women to both the process of birth and their rights as mothers. The trust began by answering requests for information through correspondence, then provided classes in natural childbirth. Soon there was an overwhelming response to the classes, combined with a profound and outspoken disapproval from physicians and older midwives who saw the trust as somehow subversive. Ms. Rankin talked openly about the storm of protest which continues to rage about her work to this day.

Soon after the trust began there was enormous distrust felt by doctors and midwives for us. They thought we were unqualified people teaching something we knew nothing about. The fact that many of us are qualified as teachers or are in other professions doesn't ease their anxiety. I am a biologist and a teacher. And I'm a mother. This gives me quite a lot of skilled approaches which midwives and doctors maybe don't have. The fact that I communicate information to women really alarms them, particularly doctors, and particularly if I'm taking any money for doing so. They don't want their patients influenced by anybody but them.

The important thing they must realize is the trust is not attempting to teach obstetrics. We are teaching about birth as a process and labor as an experience everyone can understand and cooperate with. We've seen a need for education and worked our guts out to fill it.

The midwife, Gwen feels, is in no position to defend the needs and rights of parents in childbirth.

Midwifery is a threatened profession. Midwives feel they might be dispensed with. Now actually the whole of British obstetrics really depends on the British midwife. But midwives feel that the obstetricians make all the decisions and they cannot protest in the best interests of the mother. Of course, where the midwife is left out today, the parents feel even more left out. They come even further down the scale of involvement in what decisions are made for them.

I think this has really occurred mostly since the growth of so much technology for birth. Doctors are going great guns for the quality of life in the physical sense, monitoring the unborn child, increasing the efficiency of the placenta through hormonal injections, making sure babies never go beyond term, doing a lot of external controls. But the emotional climate into which the baby is going to be born isn't yet regarded as very important. In England we used to have a system similar to Holland, with home birth and simple procedures. We've abandoned it in recent years. And I believe it's due largely to the passionate devotion of the medical profession to drugs, drugs, and still more drugs as the answer to the problems of time and personnel and everything else.

I would say a fair proportion of our midwives in their thirties and forties are really frustrated doctors at heart, women very keen about taking control of labor and extremely enthusiastic about obstetric techniques. They are superb deliverers of babies, wonderful at giving injections, and they approach birth as obstetricians do.

Younger English midwives are more interested in serving the emotional needs of birthing women, but the hospital

Retired English midwives pose under picture of the Queen at reunion in The Royal College of Midwives

structure makes it difficult for them to respond fully. Gwen Rankin's niece Julie had just finished training at a famous midwifery school. Her conversations with her aunt seemed to reflect the difficult bind midwifery finds itself in today.

Julie says in her hospital "a thousand opportunities a day are lost" for contact with the patients. There are lots of times when, she says, she knows she should be sitting and talking with a mother for five minutes. But the hospital is not run for her or anyone to do that. The most important thing she was taught to remember in training, she says, is that once labor has begun it must be completed as quickly and efficiently as possible! She has said, "If the uterus begins to flag in its work we speed it up. It's the safest way." I say to her, "What are you talking about; women have been delivering babies behind hedges for countless years and the uterus has done its job perfectly well without being 'picked up.' Give it a chance, for goodness' sake!" She says that may be so, but if she had to deliver a baby in someone's home without cyntocin and pethidine and blood on hand she would be petrified. And she adds, "And that's my training talking. I know I've missed out on something. On the other hand, I do know anybody in our hospital is as safe as she could possibly be." Now that's a really uninhibited modern midwife talking, away from the hospital, away from the obstetricians, away from the senior midwives, and with someone she trusts.

Women like Gwen Rankin are working hard to counteract the predominant attitude that women can't possibly grasp the many details of the birthing process. They are told that they shouldn't worry themselves trying to learn complicated breathing techniques, nor should they set

themselves up for disappointment by attempting to do birth naturally. The experts are there, the drugs are there, the hospitals are there, all to make birth easier and safer for mother and child. This attitude of unspoken condescension toward birthing mothers pervades British obstetrics today, so that the midwife and the mother are both deceived. English midwifery stands not with the mother, but under the physician's authority. And the English woman is only beginning to seek a real "attendant" in normal birth and to take steps to regain her control over her birth.

While birth in England is established firmly on the side of technology and specialization today, birth in Denmark is tottering on the brink of change.

Danish midwifery has preserved a legal tradition going back more than three hundred years. Because childbirth in Denmark has always been a personal choice of the mother, there I expected to find normal birth still protected, and traditional midwifery alive and well.

The national school for midwives at Rigshospital in Copenhagen is the single training institution for all Danish midwives. Today it graduates thirty-three students a year in a profession which has remained carefully separated from nursing and medicine and which remains as highly respected as teaching, the ministry, law, and medicine.

But midwifery in Denmark is undergoing important changes in the 1970s that will affect the future role and the very existence of midwifery in Denmark.

According to Ruth Rasmussen, president of the national

Danish midwifery students

midwives organization, "Every baby born in Denmark is born with a midwife. There's always a midwife, even during operations like forceps or Caesareans. The midwife will be there to take care of the baby." Traditionally there have been three kinds of midwives in Denmark, each offering a different choice to mothers giving birth. The district midwife is assigned to a practice by local authorities, guaranteed an annual income, and often provided with housing. In return she must be willing to relocate around the country as different districts need her services. Hospital midwives are a growing profession and work alongside physicians within the hospital structure and under its pay scale and benefit system. The "private-practice" midwife works independently, soliciting clients and receiving pay from the Danish National Health Insurance. Home birth with such an independent midwife has today come into competition with the more fashionable hospital birth, which is now prized by middle-class Danish women as a form of social status. Doctors contribute to the illusion of the "easy" hospital birth (a vacation from home confinement), and mothers have begun to follow their lead.

As in England and the United States, Danish physicians are choosing to bring normal birth into the hospital, and it is the midwives who are losing. And, due to their training as specialists in curing disease and solving emergencies, physicians have the final voice of authority in childbirth outside the hospital as well.

Ironically, the independent Danish midwife has been responsible for her own demise. Suffering a loss of private income from the decreasing number of home births, she finally turned to her government for protection. In 1973 the government responded with a law requiring that every midwife was to register by April 1974 as an employee of an existing hospital, clinic, or district. Today Danish midwives are assured an adequate income each year and a continuing job, but they may no longer seek their own clients. So what the midwife gains in security she unfortunately loses in independence, and the repercussions of this new law will affect the future of home birth in Denmark. It will also greatly narrow the range of choices for the birthing woman. As is true throughout the world, it is the independent practitioner who has protected the normalcy of birth over the centuries: without her, all women lose.

I arrived in Denmark in November 1973 on the eve of the first midwifery strike in the nation's history. Frustrated in their attempts to retain autonomy in normal childbirth, independent midwives decided to focus national attention on their present position. Under the law, a midwife must always attend a birth when she is called, so there was no way midwives could actually strike from work. They did the next best thing, by continuing to care for birthing women but refusing to file the lengthy forms on each birth which the government required. The strike went unnoticed by much of the birthing public, which continued to receive the full services they expected of midwives. But there was a note of determined resistance in the air, a sign that normal birth in Denmark would not be altered without protest.

The young mother who was my hostess at the student collective where I stayed in Copenhagen spoke to me of her mixed feelings about midwifery, especially now that the law had changed. Pia Sindjberg-Hansen (hyphenated last name denoting her husband's name added to hers) had for years thought of applying to the midwifery school. In the meantime she had given birth to a child of her own, at her home, with one of Denmark's private midwives attending. Pia said her midwife used to attend about one hundred births a year, but that during 1972 she had been called on only ten deliveries. Of those ten births, six had developed complications at home which required her to take the mother to the hospital to complete the birth. The midwife had been disturbed that the incidence of complications had increased so much, and had said that in all her thirty years and two thousand babies' worth of experience, she could count complicated births on one hand.

Everywhere that hospitalization becomes enticing for mothers in normal birth, more and more complications seem to develop. Pia was deeply impressed by her old midwife's care at her birth and said she would still choose home over hospital under normal conditions.

> When Kira was born my midwife was so happy there were tears in her eyes. It was like it was her first baby, her own. I think it's a very beautiful profession, a midwife. I talked with Torban, my husband, about my becoming one. He thinks it is a bad idea because the midwives do not have such a high position as a doctor today. He says there's no future in it. That times are working against the midwife and clinics and home birth. Going in the direction of hospital birth with a doctor. Torban is studying to be a doctor. If this is really true, I don't know what will happen here. There are still so many women who prefer being at home giving birth and prefer midwives. Now that doctors want to do normal deliveries, the midwives are being forced out, I think.

Pia told me about a very special clinic, a maternity clinic in downtown Copenhagen where several friends of hers had delivered. It turned out to be the same one run by the sister of Ruth Rasmussen, head of the midwives organization. It is named Olga Limshous Clinic after their mother, who had been a midwife for many years. I met Frida Vonsild, administrator of the eighteen-bed clinic, who told me that about six hundred babies are delivered at the clinic each year, in an environment that is close to home.

> In a hospital a woman will always be just a number. And it will always be such that you can only give your attention to the patient that needs it most. Here a midwife takes the time. I find the most important time for a woman is the hours before delivery. You will never be able to get a doctor to sit there and just watch and know exactly what the state of the mother is. A midwife gives the mother the feeling it is only her and her child that is important. She must take the time to listen. It is not so much what she is answering but that she is having the

time to listen. And during labor she must give the mother the feeling she is there whenever the woman wants her.

You want me to be honest don't you? I simply would hate to have a child myself in America. I have a feeling that your statistics about brain damage in infants are so bad because of having doctors and not midwives. And the doctors take huge salaries from the patients to deliver babies. That will be very difficult to change.

Mrs. Vonsild introduced me to Dorte Larsen, a new midwife at the clinic, who had just finished her training three months earlier. That evening I was called and told to expect a birth in the middle of the night. I received the second call at two in the morning and took a taxi to the clinic across town. It was the woman's first birth and the doctor had already been called in preparation. It is now law

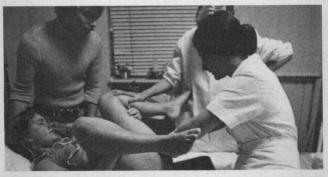

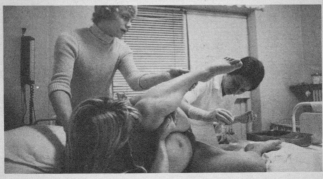

in Denmark that a doctor be called to watch over the actual delivery, to be there in case of emergency. During a normal birth the doctor is required to sit silently by. Ellen Esmann was the doctor, a woman who had been in practice for forty-three years and knew enough to stand back when she was not needed. She sat with her hands folded the entire time, chatting with the mother and the midwife until it came time to push. Then she placed her ungloved hands on the mother's abdomen and helped her relax. The room was clean and fresh, with items I had never seen in American hospitals. The checkered cloth-covered bassinet in the corner with its typical down comforter added warmth to the simple room. The midwife worked alone, with no assistant to hand her instruments. The mother and husband were in their own clothes.

There were quiet urgings from Dorte to push . . . push

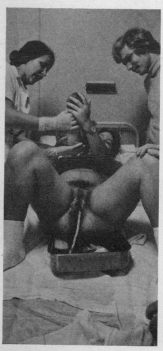
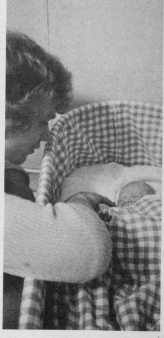

... again ... again. Then the sound of deep breathing in a hushed room. The mother's face turned red in effort and suddenly a squalling baby was born. The voices in the room remained quiet; it was a close family, with cajoling and teasing, relaxing now that the birth was over. A nurse came in to admire the baby and commented in Danish, "Hah, a real midwife episiotomy!" And she giggled.

Later I asked Dr. Esmann about the future of birth in her country.

> I do not know the future. They're building new buildings in the Rigshospital. Have you been there? It will be bigger. It is not always the case that things will then be better.

Danish women may apply for admission to Rigshospital when they are twenty years old. Since it usually takes several years to gain acceptance, they do not graduate until their midtwenties. The students pay for their training themselves, with a small symbolic stipend contributed by the government. Many diverse fields are open to nurses, but a midwife is always a midwife and Danish women make their decision to be midwives early in life. The training school still prefers not to accept nurses for training as midwives, since the professions are considered separate.

During their first year of training, midwives see only normal births, so that they are thoroughly knowledgeable about normalcy before they begin to view abnormal birth. Randi Jähne is one of the senior instructors at the school, herself a midwife with many years of work in the field, both in Denmark and Africa. She spoke to me of the

Randi Jähne,
Danish midwife

dilemma she had as a teacher, having to instruct pupils in ways that were acceptable to the hospital, where many of them will undoubtedly practice.

> I do it [birth] as natural as possible in this [hospital] atmosphere. A midwife could even let the mother help the baby's head out. But usually I help the head out and the shoulders and then the mother lifts the baby out herself. I am speaking now as a midwife, not as a teacher.

> Up to now, in Denmark, our hands and a wooden stethoscope have been enough. Now we have so many new things. How do we keep more interferences from happening? We are, after all, just women. And to suggest things be different would be to criticize and frighten men when they are doing what they feel is best in an area which is by nature foreign to their own experience.

Later I returned to the clinic and asked Dorte about Denmark's seeming fascination with modern procedures and techniques in normal birth. She explained that they now have a heating lamp for the babies at Rigshospital.

> That's the first step, I think, going in the direction of America. We were taught how to use fetal heart monitors this year at training. We had to sit and watch contractions and heartbeats on the screen. I would say, "Can't I just turn the mother?" And the doctor would say, "No." And then when the midwife came in, she told the students to put our hands on the mother's stomach to help. The doctor was very angry and said, "Take your hands away. You'll make the machine look wrong." We midwives say we don't want to sit and watch machines. That's not our job. But the doctors say, "Oh, it's very important, watch-

ing and seeing when things go wrong." You know, doctors are trusting these machines 100 per cent. And that's ridiculous. Our teachers say that in a few years all the ladies will go to hospitals to have their babies and we must know about these machines. To fight against it is difficult. I don't know if it's not too late.

I don't think midwives can be replaced. The personal relationship a woman has with her midwife is so very important. You can't make a machine which a woman can trust herself to. But I think we must accept that many more machines will be used along with the midwife. Doctors want to keep all babies alive, even if there is something wrong with them.

I like the way doctors here respect us. They know that we have much more experience than they have. When my friends and I finished our education in September we talked about our experiences seeing hospital births. We think it is strange that almost nobody coming into a hospital can deliver in a normal way. In our training we go out into the country to work with a country midwife. We go into the homes and deliver. And you know, it's always all right. What goes wrong seems nothing compared to all the people coming into the hospital who look very normal and who then have things go wrong with them. I don't, for example, think it's necessary to use a vacuum extractor as often as they do in hospitals. If the heartbeat drops, they rush the woman into Delivery and put the vacuum extractor on and take out the baby. It's very normal at the last part of delivery for heartbeats to go down and then go up again. At hospitals they don't allow things to happen normally. They are too quick. They might allow the baby to have a chance.

The authority of the midwife over normal birth has been weakened on the one hand by mothers choosing the hospital over the home, and on the other by specialists bringing normal birth into their domain. The midwife is caught in the middle; the ground she stands on is becoming progressively shaky. Yet without her there is no sure protection for the natural process, and mothers and babies will suffer from her demise. The future of midwifery and the course of normal birth in Denmark, as in England, will depend not only on how effectively the midwife stands her ground, but also upon the determination of the mothers themselves.

19
Holland: Caretaker of the Normal Birth

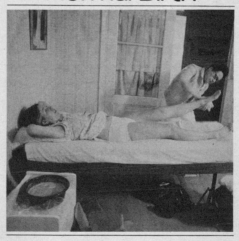

Holland:
Caretaker of the
Normal Birth

WHO HAS EVER heard of "The Dutch Way of Birth"? Certainly few pregnant women in America. Few Americans are even aware that there exists today at least one industrialized nation with a long history of simplicity in normal birth and a successful record of safety and quality which far surpasses our own.

Holland, a tiny nation with the densest population in the world, occupies a unique position in childbirth. A 1965 study of ten Western industrialized countries showed that Holland had an infant mortality rate of 14.4 per 1,000 births at a time when the United States had a rate of 24.7. In that year, 97.4 per cent of all American births took place in hospitals, while only 31.4 per cent of Dutch births were institutionalized. As the only nation in the study with *both* low mortality statistics and a comparatively low incidence of hospital births, Holland is of special interest to anyone concerned with the quality of birth in America.

Statistics show that Holland has made home birth a safe choice. Maternal mortality, one of the few added risks of home confinement, was in Holland in 1972 only 0.4 per 10,000 births. The incidence of mastitis (an infection of

*Dutch midwife
at home birth*

mothers' breasts which occurs often in hospitals throughout the world) during that same year was one-third the rate found in institutional births.

The long-standing tradition of home birth, plus the equally long tradition of independent midwifery, combined with universally excellent prenatal care, all make Holland unique. The Dutch have never publicized their statistics or made attempts to hard sell their way of birth. There is no national policy on childbirth, nor is there a concentrated effort by the medical community to sway public opinion, although the ministry of health is conscientious in its efforts to make birth as safe, as inexpensive, and as positive an experience for all members of a family as is humanly possible. Therefore, it is noteworthy that Dr. H. P. Verbrugge, in his book *Maternity Home Help and Home Deliveries* (1974), concludes his study of Dutch birth over the last twenty years with a statement in favor of continuing home birth:

> The satisfactory results of home confinements in the Netherlands . . . justify the conclusion that home deliveries should have preference over an ever-expanding hospitalization of confinements, provided a reasonable standard of prenatal and natal care and a proper selection of high-risk groups are guaranteed.

Dr. Verbrugge's book is of special interest because of its lengthy description of the value of "maternity home helps" (MHH) in Holland. The home help is an unusual combination of paramedic and housekeeper, a member of a national organization that was established at the turn of the century to supplement care provided by the midwife or family physician at home births. The home help, called by the midwife or doctor during labor, also provides daily care for the mother and newborn baby for ten days after birth. The midwife checks in daily and is responsible for seeing that all is well at the end of that time, before she is discharged from her responsibilities as birth attendant. In 1966 two-thirds of all home birth mothers employed full-time home helps, and the perinatal mortality at home was only 10 per 1,000 births, a lower rate than the national average. Further, Verbrugge points out that "among home deliveries perinatal mortality in the MHH group is consistently lower than in the group of home deliveries without MHH: in 1965, 9.5 and 11.5 per thousand respectively."

Traditionally, obstetricians in Holland have presided only over abnormal births. Midwives have practiced there officially since 1200, when they first began working out of Catholic convents. The Laws of Medicine, written in 1856 and still in effect today, state that "the midwife is allowed to give pregnant women care. She may take measures to prevent abnormalities in pregnancies. She may draw blood for examination." Since a complete series of prenatal examinations can be done without the service of a physician (except the first physical), a healthy Dutch woman at no risk in birth may not need to see a physician beyond her initial visit. According to the same Laws of Medicine, when a midwife observes any abnormalities, she *must* consult a physician who is chosen by the pregnant woman, and who then takes over the case. The midwife is a member of the medical profession, although unlike a doctor she is limited in her sphere of work. Within those confines, however, she is an independent practitioner and is considered to be the national caretaker of normal birth.

But Dutch birth practices are changing. Birth's machine age has not gone unnoticed by Dutch obstetricians, nor has it failed to make its mark on the Dutch woman. Fascinated by the shining paraphernalia of the hospital OB unit, she has become more and more interested in the possibilities of the "quick and easy" birth. Higher income and middle-class aspirations, as well as the age-old national problem of cramped housing, have deceived some women into believing they can buy a better and more comfortable birth in the hospital than at home. Even though hospital births cost from 50 to 100 per cent more than home births, and even though studies continue to report that mothers are more satisfied with home births than their hospital equivalents, hospital confinement has its appeal. In 1958, 75 per cent of all Dutch births took place at home. By 1970 that figure had decreased to 57 per cent, and in 1975 only one-half of the birthing population chose to give birth at home.

Increasingly, first births take place in institutions, while home birth seems to be reserved for second children. With a zero population rate already attained in Holland, few Dutch families contemplate more than two children. So the need for midwives is decreasing in Holland today, with the effect that three times as many young people apply to the three main midwife schools as are accepted. Although

Kweekschool
Voor Vroedvrouwn

Dutch national health insurance covers the midwife's practice, she is never insured that there will be enough work, since more and more obstetricians are taking an interest in moving normal birth to the hospital and under their authority. Some doctors would like to see the midwife renamed an "obstetrical aide" and used only to relieve the pressure of the physician, rather than remain independent and secure in her traditional role as woman's sole attendant.

Despite Holland's present confrontation with modern obstetrics, home birth and midwives are likely to maintain their position. Dutch couples feel that how and where they have their babies is a matter of personal choice—theirs, not the doctor's. The obstetrician's advice will usually be taken when problems arise, but couples are generally encouraged to retain autonomy over their births, not as a matter of political rights, but rather as an outgrowth of stubborn tradition.

A Dutch woman may choose to give birth in the hospital, attended by a midwife or family doctor or obstetrician of her choice. She may opt for either a hospital confinement (up to the standard ten days) or an early discharge, with care provided by a home help under the authority of a midwife. Or she may give birth in a maternity center or clinic, attended by her family doctor or midwife, with the same choice of post-delivery care. Finally, she may give birth at home, again with her choice of doctor or midwife, and a home help. In the latter case she can be provided with a solid birth bed and metal risers (to give the bed appropriate height), scales, and pan

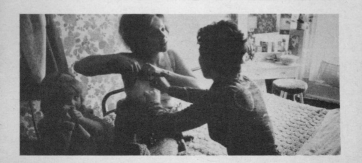

for the birth. If the Dutch woman has been diagnosed as high risk, she will receive hospital care, complete with a fully equipped neonatal nursery, under the authority of an obstetrician of her own choosing. Since hospitals are within easy reach of every Dutch home, no emergency mobile home-birth service is necessary. A midwife may book a woman or her baby directly into a nearby hospital for any complication.

Such a wide range of choices is unparalleled in any other country in the world. And full choice is made possible because of the excellent prenatal care available to all women through a national insurance program with special designations for the pregnant population. Most women take full advantage of their midwife's visits before birth, and are conscientious in attending breathing and "gymnastic" classes as well. No single technique of childbirth is taught or preferred above others—rather a mixture of many methods, somewhat akin to those of Grantly Dick-Read, has been accepted. Women are not led to expect they will need medication for pain in labor, and preparation classes reinforce the prevailing national attitude that childbirth is a normal, though very strenuous, process which seldom needs any medical interference at all.

I first heard about Holland when questioning doctors and childbirth teachers about countries where home birth still exists in the "modern" world. England and Denmark were often mentioned, but Holland was generally passed over lightly with the remark, "The Dutch *have* home births; but of course they're such a small and homogeneous country, you really can't compare them to us." Doris Haire

*Dutch midwife makes
postnatal home visit*

was the first to suggest I would see a truly normal birth in Holland, so I began corresponding with a midwife in Amsterdam, Arianne Hertzberger. Only after arriving in England did I begin to hear regularly of the Dutch system of birth. Since European midwives and nurse-midwives often spend time working abroad, in former colonies or neighboring countries, many had firsthand experience of Dutch midwifery. Wherever I went, people said that the Dutch were different. Everyone knew it. They reportedly kept birth simple and their labor rooms were remarkably quiet. But, my informant would add, as if to brush aside the previous information, "Of course, they're such a small country. . . ."

Through Arianne, I was able to stay at the Amsterdam midwifery school and clinic, the Kweekschool Voor Vroedvrouwn. Its clinic conducts about a thousand births each year and with a very low rate of forceps deliveries, local anesthesia, or Caesarean operations. In 1972, for 924 clinic and 54 student-directed home births, there were only 40 interventions by vacuum extractor, 95 episiotomies, 13 uses of low forceps, and 9 Caesareans.

In the first days after my arrival at the school, I came to know Carry, a first-year midwifery student who was engaged to a physician specializing in obstetrics. She told me of her eagerness to become a midwife, and of the running discussions she and her fiancé had had over the subject of childbirth. Her comments epitomize the differing opinions prevalent in Holland today between the midwife and the obstetrician.

Arianne Hertzberger, midwife

I wanted to be a midwife for six years before coming here.
In two days I start with my own patients and also do my first
birth. Jacques' attitude is, as long as there is no harm, why
not use some medication? I tell him, if you are in such a
hurry, don't be a midwife.

The third-year student who showed me around the
school and clinic was to reiterate the midwife's attitude. As
we walked down the broad corridors, past the wards and
enclosed porch (a labor-sitting room), I remarked how
different it all looked from the American hospital OB unit.
It was so informal, so silent, and there was an unhurried
way of walking that seemed apparent in everyone we
passed. A few bathrobed new mothers shuffled down the
halls, waiting for visiting hours to begin. There were only
two women in labor at the other end of the hall, but I
heard no sounds.

There are not a lot of instruments here, or sterile environments. We try to keep it as much like home as possible. . . .
Here in Holland we are very much for home birth. We feel
it can be the safest place for mother and baby.

She would train here, she told me, and would attend
forty or fifty births before graduating at the end of this
year. Then she would try and set herself up in private
practice, a difficult venture these days when the older, more
established midwives have a corner on the home-birth
market.

Dr. Y. Klomp, director of Kweekschool, was not surprised that an American would be interested in Dutch birth. She knew well how differently obstetrics is practiced in the United States, and she had observed the changes England was adopting in an attempt to "modernize" birth. Dr. Klomp spoke at length about the values of restraint in using technology in normal birth, and expressed her concern about unnecessary interference:

> I learned obstetrics with my hands. That was all we had. I can appreciate machines in situations where I can't go so far with my hands.... But I've seen cardinal mistakes with instruments. An aggressive obstetrician, impressed by instruments, can rush into Caesarean when it's not necessary.

Dr. Klomp admitted that breast-feeding is on a steady decline in Holland, and that the formula and baby food industries were campaigning hard to sell the public on the convenience of their products over natural milk.

> In our clinics, less mothers breast-feed every year. I think it's partly my fault. When I came here, all mothers were pressed by their midwives to breast-feed. I am *very* much in favor of it too, but only if a mother wants to. We have come to accept now that when a mother says she doesn't want to feed her baby, it is her decision.

She described the infectious effect mothers have on each other when they are in the wards. Often the presence of one staunch breast feeder or bottle feeder will sway the entire ward. But women in Holland are as interested as their American counterparts in their appearances and in conveniences that will save time and effort.

Joahanna Van de Weg, head of the clinic delivery unit and a practicing midwife for seventeen years, also expressed concern about the modern trends in birth in Holland.

> Now we cannot always win the fight against the women's magazines, the baby food manufacturers and formula makers. They all tell mothers that breast-feeding is unnecessary and not as convenient as their products. . . . I think women will think we are not up to date here if we do not have all the machines. We have no fetal heart monitors here but the day shall probably come. In the hospital across the street [a large private hospital] they began introducing fetal monitors just last year. Soon the doctors and midwives were using them more and more.

Van de Weg expressed concern that mothers may lose their responsibility for birth and wondered if they would not begin to ask for all sorts of interferences to speed up birth and make it more predictable, if obstetricians recommended such techniques. She was not surprised to learn that home birth no longer existed as a viable choice in America, and said cautiously, "I think it will take a lifetime before America learns again that birth can be done in a natural way."

During one conversation we were joined by a midwife who had worked eighteen years as a missionary in South Africa. She said the midwife there did not have the same

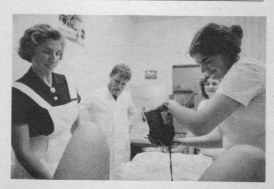

Showing placenta to mother at clinic birth

*Dutch midwife instructing
medical student in attending normal birth*

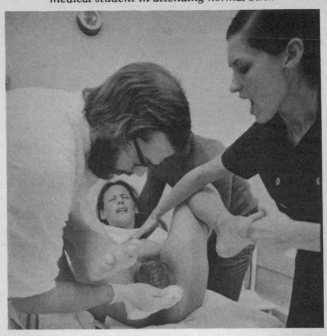

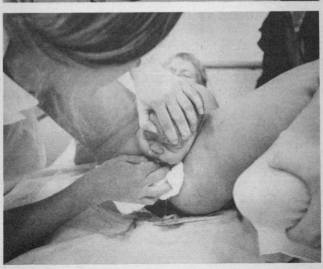

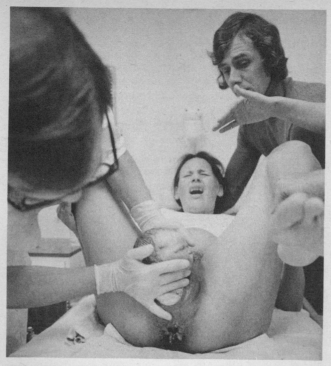

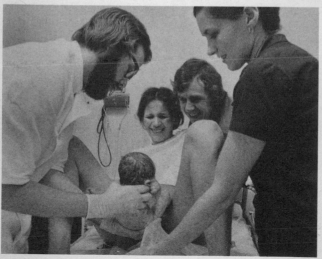

position as in Holland and was looked upon more as a nurse than a midwife. She found it frustrating that South African midwives are trained in the British system, as nurses first, midwives second. Van de Weg nodded in agreement. They both preferred three years' training in traditional midwifery, with its clear emphasis on the normalcy of birth, rather than the nursing of the sick. Van de Weg said:

> If I have to be born ten times again, ten times again I will be a midwife. Birth is a high time in a woman's life. It is a privilege to be able to help her at that time. There is a tie between me and her at the moment when she pushes the baby out that is so intimate and strong. This is real woman's work.

Her statement did not exclude the position of men in childbirth, as Dutch fathers traditionally attend their wives' labor and delivery. Wearing his street clothes, sitting next to his wife's bed, the father is an important part of birth in Holland, and if he does not stay with his wife, it is most likely the midwife will ask him why and try to encourage him to return. When I inquired why husbands attend births so regularly, I was generally told, "It is *his* birth too; he belongs there."

In the Kweekschool clinic, the midwife (actually a student with her tutor standing by) is responsible for attending the mother throughout labor and delivery. Four midwifery students and usually one training medical student are on call twenty-four hours a day on the labor ward. Teams are rotated, but every mother receives constant care.

On several occasions during my stay at the clinic I was awakened in the middle of the night by a breathless young student who could say only one word in English: "Hurry!" We ran down the hall, past a dozen little sleeping rooms for students, and down the wide marble stairs. The first night I grabbed a white coat off the rack outside the door and, while buttoning it, heard the baby cry. Other nights I arrived in time to view with a very special awe the phenomenon of a truly natural birth.

I was always fascinated by the atmosphere of unbroken calm, the positive and reassuring attitude of the attending midwives, and the lack of ceremony, bustle, and noise. At no time was the birthing mother shuffled from room to room or bed to bed: where she labored she also gave birth. There was no attempt to create a "sterile field" on the woman's body, and all hands except for the midwife's were bare. The student midwife scrubbed a full five minutes outside the labor room before entering, joked, guided, and comforted the birthing mother, and seemed to regard the father as an important attendant to the birth process as well. The mothers worked very hard, occasionally groaned or moaned, but at no time during my observation did anyone scream.

One mother who gave birth to a ten-pound boy with immense thighs had quietly moaned during transition in a mantralike singsong that carried me back to my own labor and brought me to tears. "It never came into my mind to have drugs," she told me later. "Of course I am always afraid to have pain. But I am glad I had him the way I did. And that my husband was there."

Each time, the midwife checked the baby while it was still lying between its mother's legs, then clamped and cut the cord. She showed the infant to its mother and then gave it a quick bath in lukewarm water, but she did not attempt to scrub the baby, as is so often the case in American hospitals. The procedure here was merely to hold the infant's head above water and let its body soak and relax in the warmth of an environment very much like its earlier nine-month home. Then she patted the baby dry, wrapped it, and placed it in the mother's arms, generally just three minutes after the birth. The period of waiting for the delivery of the placenta was usually marked by cheerful discussions between the midwives and the mother and father. Often the midwife gently pressed the palm of her hand below the woman's navel to facilitate the placenta's arrival, and when it appeared she checked it carefully and showed it to the mother, explaining which side had been attached to her uterine wall and how the double skin had encircled the baby. As soon as possible in each birth, the midwives departed to leave the couple and their baby in privacy to share this intimate family reunion.

Perhaps most amazing of all was the peaceful yet alert way in which the newborn infants adjusted to their first hours after birth. Even when the darkened nursery (used only at night) was more than half full, often not one baby was crying.

At one birth the fetus showed signs of distress, and Dr. Klomp was called in to "assist." Actually she did very little after checking the mother and listening to the fetal heart rate. The midwife continued her work, talking with the mother all the while, as Dr. Klomp sat quietly in a corner and observed, occasionally offering a word of advice, and ready to intervene if the need arose. It didn't: the baby was born in good health, though slightly depressed, and was placed in an incubator after its first contact with its mother. No one seemed at all panicky about this except the American visitor: shamefully enough, visions of fetal heart monitors, oxygen resuscitators, oxytocic infusions, and forceps deliveries had been dancing in my head.

Under an arrangement with the teaching hospital, residents and medical students learn normal birth under the direction of midwives. One night shortly after my arrival, a medical resident on duty attended his first birth, as the midwife instructor and a pupil watched. The man was a "natural." His soothing presence complemented a desire to be unobtrusive. He rested his hands softly on the woman's knee or stomach between contractions, gave the mother water to sip, and patiently encouraged her. The baby was the most beautiful I had ever seen. Everyone in the labor room was struck with her perfect body and delicate features. As was customary, there were handshakes all around and tea for all.

The home birth I attended was similarly striking (to me) by its utter normalcy, the unpretentious manner of

*Dr. Kloosterman (center),
midwives and physicians
at Dr. Davidson's lecture*

both midwife and pupil, and the secure calm of the mother. Again the mother worked very hard, did not ask for medication, and never raised her voice. The student midwife bent over the mother's face and looked directly into her eyes as she talked, giving encouragement and instructions and placing cool, wet cloths on her hot forehead. The baby was covered with a down comforter and placed in a carriage, which had been warmed by a hot-water bottle. The home help, who had arrived shortly after the second stage of labor, cleaned and washed the mother, and remained to take care of her after the student midwife and her instructor left. After the student weighed and checked the baby more thoroughly, she wrapped up the placenta and took it immediately to the Kweekschool for a final examination. Just before departing, she said, "Home birth may not always be shorter, but it always seems shorter. There is so much more to do and look at and talk about at home."

A main purpose for my visit to Holland was to meet the renowned obstetrician, Professor G. J. Kloosterman, chief of obstetrics at Wilhelmina Gastuis, the Amsterdam teaching hospital. By tremendous good fortune, he met with me on the day that another American visitor, Dr. E. C. Davidson, chief of obstetrics and gynecology at the Los Angeles County-Martin Luther King Hospital, had arrived at the hospital to address a "grand rounds" meeting on American obstetrics. I was anxious to see how the hospital staff would react to Davidson's comments. Kloosterman introduced us, and Davidson, glad to see a fellow Californian, smiled and asked me what I was doing in Holland.

I told him I was researching a book on midwives and childbirth. His smile dropped and he asked me what my credentials were. I told him I was a mother. He turned aside, and I perceived our conversation was ended. Perhaps I ought to have asked for his credentials.

Davidson took his place at the podium.

> Much of the material I will show you is the introduction to our hospital which we show new patients. I want to say before I start that your perinatal mortality statistics, your infant statistics, are much better than ours. This is especially true of the part of Los Angeles where our hospital is located. I will show you something different perhaps in terms of how we conduct ourselves in obstetrics, but not necessarily better in terms of what the outcomes are.

Slides of the equipment, of the ultrasound devices, and of the labor and delivery suite appeared on the screen. Davidson prefaced the latter by saying it was a look into a typical American delivery room. The entire room rippled with quiet laughter.

> If the patient delivers in her labor bed, that is an error on the part of the obstetrical assistant.

More slides of equipment; none of mothers.

> These are of course anesthesia machines.... This is a typical instrument setup for delivery, most of which is probably familiar.... The solutions we use in the delivery rooms are placed in these pans.... The mother being placed on the table.... The infant care area, off to the side.... And there's the mother being brought into the delivery room.

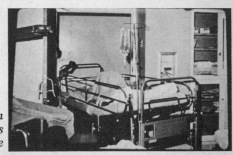

Slide from Dr. Davidson's lecture

More laughter, not so quietly.

I want to emphasize how we drape the patient. We completely cover the patient up to the level of midchest. . . . The physician of course will also be gowned.

He paused and explained:

These are really instructional photos for patients. . . . Here is sensing equipment. . . . We basically monitor every delivery; that is, we continuously record the fetal heart rate and the uterine contractions throughout the mother's labor. In 71 per cent of these cases we felt the mothers were in some category of high risk. About 21 per cent we monitored internally.

The doctor sitting next to me whispered with a smile that he supposed labor itself was an indication of high risk. Davidson continued:

One of the reasons I'm here in Amsterdam is to look at your anesthesia and analgesia program. . . . I would say that we probably use less anesthesia than many centers in America, whose statistics would be higher.

Professor Kloosterman asked Davidson the rate of Caesarean births at his hospital. The answer was 8 per cent. Kloosterman replied that Holland's was 2 per cent, then asked about the completely normal birth, without any interference or anesthesia or analgesia and with no episiotomy. Was that unusual? Davidson answered that it

Tools of Dutch clinic for normal birth with midwife attending

was probably less than 10 per cent of all normal births. Yes, it was unusual, a natural birth.

> Perhaps that requires some explanation. Increasingly in America patients are accepting labor and delivery without medication. Many patients before had very strong opinions about not wanting to experience any pain during labor. Many women in America have wanted to be put to sleep as soon as possible so that they could wake up tomorrow and the baby would be in the nursery and it would be all over.

Laughter from the audience and whispers.

> About 25 per cent of our babies spend some time in the pathologic nursery, our special-care nursery. Our hospital has a large number of low-income and high-risk mothers.

Questions from the doctors and midwives. A midwife asked about the incidence of infusions (IVs) during labor and after birth. Davidson answered:

> Our infusions are so common in obstetrics that we do not count them.

Kloosterman spoke of the concern in Holland for good prenatal care. Davidson said in his hospital about 10 per cent of the women have no prenatal care at all. Some go to private physicians before labor. About 50 per cent do not see any physician before the twentieth or twenty-fourth week of pregnancy. One last question from the audience concerned the reason for such extensive fetal monitoring at Davidson's hospital:

> We really don't have good long-term follow-up studies about monitoring and what happens to the infants later in life. We hope it will improve our statistics.

Later when Davidson, Kloosterman, and I talked over coffee, Davidson mentioned the belief Americans often express that Holland is such a tiny and homogeneous country that we cannot compare its statistics to ours. Kloosterman answered:

> It is a bad observation that Holland has a homogeneous population. In our clinic this month, 30 per cent of our

patients were "colored." We have to speak twelve different languages—Chinese, Japanese, Indonesian, French, German, Spanish, Portuguese, Turkish, Moroccan, Surinamese. . . .

The conversation turned to midwives and the American doctor kept talking about the uses he saw for nurse-midwives in America and how impressed he was with nurse-midwives in Holland. I reminded him that they were not nurses, just midwives, and said the differences were not in name alone. I began to tell him of my stay at the midwifery school. Kloosterman suggested that he also visit the midwifery school, but Davidson demurred, saying he was too busy and planned to stay at the hospital.

After Davidson left, Kloosterman and I resumed our conversation in his office.

Very often in America I saw the difference between very great attention from a technological point of view and neglect from an emotional point of view.

About home births, he said:

I pity women who are not able to follow their desires to have well-attended childbirth at the place where they would like to have it. What I think you need is the well-trained midwife. She can help more than 80 per cent of all women.

I mentioned the kind of midwifery I had seen in England practiced by women who were nurses first, midwives second.

We have nurse-midwives in our department, we have midwives, and we have nurses. I think the difference is one of character. Our nurse-midwives are split into two kinds of women—the real nurses and the real midwives. There are people who prefer to share responsibility with a doctor and who are very keen on seeing that everything the doctor asks for is done punctually. Of course we like to work with these nurses. And midwives like to be independent, to give their own opinions. Very often a midwife will say, "Doctor, why did you do that?" Or, "I do not approve of this." I think we need this. It is still fundamentally a question of character. That is why nurses and midwives very often are quarreling with each other. My teacher gave me one piece of advice when I was appointed head of the midwives' training school. He said, "Never try to combine under one roof midwives and nurses; they will always quarrel." In a hospital I think we need more nurses. But we also need a few midwives for their critical attitude. And at home we need real midwives, because nurses become nervous at home, alone and without a doctor to fall back on.

He also commented on the uses of technology in birth:

I think that if they could prove in the United States their results in birth were better than ours, then we would have to change to the American system. I must confess that personally I do not believe that technology ever will improve a natural labor in a healthy woman. But if it becomes true, then we will have to accept it. On the other hand, we are trying to investigate whether too much monitoring in normal labor will in fact detract from normal labor and do harm. I am convinced that for human beings, as for animals, labor goes best if the woman feels completely at ease. Perhaps the American woman is more at ease in the operation room than in her own bedroom. Here I know many women, my own wife and daughters for example, prefer to stay at home for a delivery.

We talked about the function of a doctor or nurse at a birth.

If I am attending a woman during her delivery I am convinced that I am *not* attending her. Something else is attending her. I am on the lookout for pathology. We are both under the guidance of nature, or whatever you call it. I am only like a military attaché, looking for something abnormal. If I am sure something is abnormal, then I can help. But as long as things are normal, I can only do harm to interfere. That is the reason I say my own wife and daughters were not helped by me. I was only sitting there seeing that everything went according to normal procedure.

Kloosterman compared his experiences in Holland and in America.

I think basically Americans are afraid for life itself. You think you have to handle everything by your brains, in an aggressive way. On the other hand, many people in the third world and in parts of Europe and Russia do not. No, I'm not sure about Russia, because they are always thinking about America. It's their big goal, to be as rich, as powerful as

America. Of course we in Holland cannot think that way. We are so small. We have had a past which was very powerful, but now we are not able to rule worlds.

I think the most important thing that the United States has given to the world is that you can say anything you like and you can investigate everything. Of course there is struggle going on and it is not so easy as it seems, but you've set the example. You must be a very powerful nation indeed if you can afford a thing like that.

We talked about the difficulty of refraining from aggressive medicine in obstetrics when all the newest medical paraphernalia is available and the obstetrician's training makes the doctor feel a need to interfere.

Science is a product of male aggressiveness and curiosity. It was very interesting to hear what Margaret Mead said once about obstetrics in America: that it shows the jealousy of males because women can make a new life. The male would like to take over himself. So, with the woman as an object, he performs the act and has control. . . . If I can convince a woman that she can't give life to a child without my help, then I take over and I'm the hero.

I always split the group of pregnant women into two parts— the big part, 80 to 90 per cent, can completely do it themselves. I only have to applaud and say, "How wonderful." And then there are the few women who are better off if I take over. If I attend a normal birth, and there is no episiotomy, no anesthesia, then afterwards the woman feels she has done everything herself. If I do a Caesarean, then she is convinced that without me she would never have had this child. It is an embarrassing position. If I do interfere I always like to know afterwards, was it necessary or was it only fear that caused me to interfere? Was I afraid the baby was in danger? That is the big danger in obstetrics, that you are making physiology into pathology, either out of jealousy, or idleness, or because it's so easy to take over.

Kloosterman turned to the controversy over home and hospital birth.

It is easy to prove that there are deliveries at home where death of the baby or death of the mother could have been prevented if labor had taken place at a hospital. And it is easy to prove that high-risk patients are worse off at home than at the hospital. But the reverse is also true, that a very

368

healthy patient is sometimes better off at home. That in a hospital you can spoil a normal delivery and perhaps even make dangers for mother and baby is a supposition I personally believe in. If somebody was doing a forceps delivery because he was in a hurry, and if something bad happens, he will always say it was necessary to do it. And I can never prove that it was not. You can never be sure afterwards.

Some doctors in America use the argument that it is much better to have everybody in hospitals because more than 20 per cent of women are in need of interference. We use the same statistics, their statistics, to show that normality in the hospital is very often changed into pathology, because 20 per cent is tremendously higher than we have in Holland. Up to now our studies of the few deaths that occurred in five thousand home births show that not one of the perinatal deaths could have been prevented by hospitalization. We are always studying the results of home birth.

If you say every woman in labor might be in need of general anesthesia, since you can never predict completely, and you want to make things as safe as possible for anesthesia, you can defend that the mother is not allowed to drink and eat. As soon as this happens, then of course you must make haste. Then you induce her, if labor lasts longer than a couple of hours, and then you must interfere within twenty-four hours. Then of course you climb up in your number of interferences. On the other hand, you can show that you then have a higher rate of interferences and that this does harm.

He also explained how an obstetrician can share in a woman's choice of home or hospital birth.

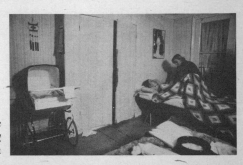

Dutch midwife attending home birth

We must give as much freedom as possible to everybody. If I have a woman who prefers to stay at home for emotional reasons, because she is more at ease at home, then I think it is my duty to help her as far as possible. I will convince her to go to the hospital if she needs to go. But if it is a normal labor, then I will not say you should go to the hospital because it is safer for you. Then I would say I will not help you at home; I have not the time. I know a very good midwife who will help you.

There are two kinds of freedom here: freedom for the patient and freedom for the doctor. I think that doctors are entitled to refuse to help in a home delivery simply because they have no time for it. It is much more time-consuming; very often it takes you one day. Therefore doctors must have the freedom to refuse. And therefore you should have midwives.

Kloosterman explained that the hospital had produced three controversial films on birth, one of which the staff called "the hippie film."

We call it that because the couple does yoga and there is Indian music playing on the record player throughout. It is attended by one of my assistants, a doctor who is wearing no gloves. The couple in the film had been studying animal behavior in Africa for eight years. When the wife became pregnant and decided she would stay at home, they decided to make something beautiful of it. In this film the woman is doing exactly as she feels during labor —walking around, sitting, getting a cup of tea for her husband. Then she is on her knees and elbows on the bed and her husband massages her back. You see the baby

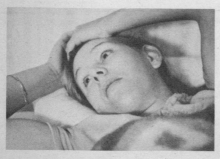

*Dutch mother in
labor at home birth*

370

come out without an episiotomy or a tear. And suddenly it is over, and you see the woman having a great emotional response, sobbing and laughing. It is so emotional, that when I showed it to two hundred first-year medical students, many of them were crying afterwards. I recently showed it to a convention of American obstetricians and gynecologists returning from Moscow. The reaction of many of them was anger. They found it difficult to believe that the birth could be that way. Some of my own colleagues call it a piece of folklore.

Afterward we met Dr. Davidson again to watch the three birth films which Dr. Cornelius Naaktgeboren had made and would narrate for us. Professor Naaktgeboren (whose name means "born naked") is the zoologist member of the obstetric staff at the hospital. His studies of comparative obstetrics have made significant contributions to the understanding of the links that exist among all mammals giving birth.

We are very concerned with emphasizing the relationship between two parents having a child, rather than showing the medical aspects of birth. We use these films in instruction of medical students, nurses, and midwives. You see, we show things as they are, not as we wish them, even if it means showing a woman smoking in early labor. This film shows the older brother coming home from a day with his grandmother. She has taken him when labor began. The three-year-old is put into bed by his mother, next to his newborn brother. There is always objection to this by doctors, who say the child might transfer infection to the infant. I tell them a woman in the hospital and her

baby, over a period of four or five days, are exposed to all these germs and worse.

In this film, we show the woman doing as she pleases in labor. At a recent congress of obstetricians, an American doctor shouted from the audience, "I think she is already in labor." He was upset that the woman was well into labor and still walking around the room, sipping tea, doing yoga asanas. Doctors couldn't imagine a woman could be so relaxed. Then another doctor shouted, "But what about medication?" And another, "Why no episiotomy?" They found the film interesting, they said, but treated it as if it were not possible in real life. And they were very upset. A questioner at the end asked if the man and his wife could ever be happy again in lovemaking since her vagina had become so stretched during the birth of the baby's head. I think such a question is typical from people who have lost confidence in nature. It is my opinion that, unless a doctor interferes with an episiotomy, a woman's body is always able to return to its original state. The doctors even questioned *me* about lovemaking, because I had said my wife gave birth the same way and that I was present for all three of them. They laughed when I said I am still able to love my wife.

During the film I turned to Davidson, who was sitting next to me, and expressed my delight at seeing the slender wooden monaural stethoscope used in all births by midwives and doctors. I whispered that in Denmark the stethoscope looks the same, but is six inches longer, and mentioned that the single piece of hollowed wood vibrates and amplifies the sound to such an extent that midwives and doctors in Holland say they prefer it to the modern

372

metal variety. He whispered that maybe it was just a question of economics, that these countries couldn't afford anything more. I was left to wonder if he had merely been making a joke.

Watching the third film, a hospital birth under the direction of an immensely supportive midwife, Naaktgeboren turned to us and said pointedly, "The telepathic effect of a good word can be as powerful as oxytocin."

It seemed strange that an American should have to travel six thousand miles from home to see a truly normal, natural birth. But as I talked further with Kloosterman, Naaktgeboren, and the midwives at the Kweekschool, the reason became clear. The Dutch *like* birth. They bring no fear to the normal process. The wide range of choices available to the Dutch mother, midwife, and doctor have not simply fallen together by chance. They have emerged from a long and conscientious tradition of independence, a deep-rooted respect for woman giving birth, and a conscientious effort to retain a natural process that has succeeded since the beginning of humankind. Since the choice of place, attendant, and method of birth rests exclusively with the mother, the role of the doctor or midwife in normal birth is to assist, not interfere—or simply to stay in the background as a skilled and respectful observer and applaud, "How wonderful."

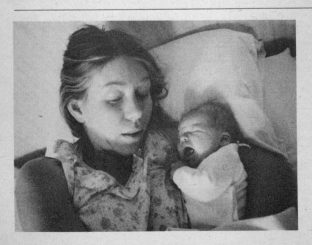

20
Your Sister
Has Twins!

Your Sister
Has Twins!

IMAGINE YOUR SISTER now, weeding the vegetable garden in back of her house. Her four-year-old son has gone to nursery school, her husband to work in the city. They have wanted a garden ever since they left the city last year to buy this home on the outskirts of town. It took all last fall just to prepare the hard bare ground. During the first few months of pregnancy the young woman has spent many hours with a pitchfork and a spade, digging, laying down sand and ashes from the fireplace, and breaking down the hard layer of clay. All winter she and her husband composted garbage into the little twelve-foot-square plot, plowing it under, burying it, and letting it rot into soil. And as her belly grew large over the mild winter, the young woman watched the patch of earth begin to take on a rich and mellow look, felt it grow thick and crumbly, and inhaled its moist sweet smell. She would squat for hours, feet splayed wide apart, wondering if the garden would bear fruit before the babies came, or if she would be the first to produce.

At first they had talked of a home birth. Actually, she had to take her stand alone; her husband was afraid of her having a baby anywhere but in the hospital, as she had done with their first child. He would remind her of how long and hard that birth had been, how crazily transition had gone after the doctor had given her Pitocin to speed things up. What if she felt she couldn't make it without a shot of something? Who would give it to her at home? The young woman reminded her husband that each birth was different and that she wasn't sure she had really needed any speeding up or doping up that last time. It just hadn't been right; it hadn't seemed like her labor, her birth. She knew after she brought her son home that if she ever had another baby she would do it differently. She would give birth at home. Her husband agreed it was her choice and said he'd go along with it.

Now, weeding in the damp earth, the young woman feels the pressure of her heavy belly on her heels. She smiles at the surprises they have had and how their plans have changed. Around Christmas her midwife detected two separate heartbeats at opposite sides of her wide belly and said it looked as though she was going to have twins. The obstetrician concurred. Since this would be her second labor, both the midwife and the doctor felt that if all continued well, she wouldn't have to deliver in the hospital. They did prefer, however, that she not give birth at home, but in the maternity center, where she could get more attention the first few days after the babies were born.

It was a shock at first to think of twins. Two babies to nurse at once. Two to carry. She laughed out loud at the picture that came to mind of her working in the garden this summer, with one tiny baby strapped to her back and the other in a tummy pouch in front. That would never work, she thought. But she did so want to carry the babies next to her body through their first months. Her friend in Colorado had sent her a soft green corduroy baby carrier with long plushy straps to cross over her shoulders and tie behind. She had written in a letter that carrying her son like that, she found if she threw a shawl across her shoulder she could nurse him modestly even while she walked. And she said it felt so good with him in front, like still being pregnant, and she would pat him the way she used to rub her belly. The young woman loved the thought of carrying her baby in that carrier. But how could she manage twins? Her midwife gave her a suggestion. Why not get a kind of sling pouch for her husband? Then each of them would have arms free to work and cook and carry groceries. And to hold their son's hand as well.

The young woman is glad she has taken a year's maternity leave from work after Christmas. It has given her time to think, to be alone, to get back into baking bread; time to make baby beds out of wicker baskets and to embroider receiving blankets. She has been able to garden every day.

It is almost noon when the young woman feels the first twinges in her groin. She stops weeding, stands up, and feels her belly. It has been quiet all morning, not a kick or even a foot sticking in her ribs. She isn't due for ten more days, but she knows that means little and that twins often come early. Last week when she was at the maternity center for her regular appointment, the midwife said the babies had dropped and the cervix was beginning to thin. So when she got home she packed her canvas bag and set out sets of cotton baby gowns and receiving blankets.

They took their son with them to the last preparation class, where films of animal and human birth were shown. He said he wanted to watch his brother and sister being born (he was sure it would be one of each). And so they talked about it a bit. The maternity center allows children to attend the births, as well as anyone else the mother would like to have present. It is only the second year of the center's existence. The town passed a bond issue at the insistence of a vocal parents' group and raised the money necessary to purchase one of the sturdy older homes near the center of town, a lovely three-story, ten-room wooden place set back from the street. They organized a nonprofit corporation, then cleaned and painted and equipped the home for births. An obstetrical nurse was hired to supervise the home. She lives with her husband on the third floor, and together they maintain the house and make sure fresh staples are always on hand in the kitchen on the first floor. The nurse handles all the business of clean and sterile linens and instruments, all on rotating loan from the city hospital twenty minutes away. Two midwives were also hired to work on call every other week, and a third to fill in part-time.

The home includes a small emergency room with a resuscitator, an incubator, oxygen, and a small supply of hormones and IVs. The nurse-administrator could help in a pinch, or until one of the on-call obstetricians or the ambulance arrived. It has been an easy job to get the fire department to buy extra equipment for its ambulance, in case it was ever needed to take a mother and her baby to the hospital.

But what the young woman likes most about the center is that all of the emergency equipment is kept out of sight. And the three large birthing rooms remind her of her parents' home. Besides a queen-sized bed, each room holds several comfortable, overstuffed chairs and a bassinet with a brightly colored cotton skirt. There are even folding cots stored in a closet in case an older child wants to spend the night too.

Downstairs there are two large rooms and a smaller one, separated from the others by the kitchen. One of the large rooms has been stocked with books and toys to be used as a children's playroom. The other is large enough for well-attended prenatal and parent classes. During clinic hours it serves as waiting room and the smaller room as an examining and consultation room, complete with a tiny laboratory. Over the last year the maternity center has become a neighborhood meeting place for pregnant women and women giving birth, a well-baby clinic, and a contraceptive clinic. So the young woman knows the big green house well.

All this she muses on this morning between those first brief twinges that she knows signal the beginning of her labor. Within a quarter-hour there are three short contractions. She stands up and walks inside the house to leave a message for the midwife and to call her husband. He will tell his boss and take off for his week-long paternity leave, a new company policy they both are glad of. She asks if he will call their son's school to tell them he will be picked up early today.

The young woman changes into a long, loose dress and gathers her things. She pauses for a moment at their bedroom and takes in the room—their big bed with its warm comforter, the baskets on either side. They have talked about keeping the babies in their room for at least the first six months. She passes on down the hall, halting in front of the linen closet. She closes her eyes and places her hand on the door while she has another contraction. "Sheets," she thinks. "That's what I forgot." Although the center provides linen, she wants to give birth on her own favorite sheet, tiny blue and orange wildflowers on white.

Downstairs, waiting for the sound of her husband's car, she tidies up the kitchen, feeds the birds, and carries a vase of fresh flowers up to their bedroom. Then, sitting cross-legged on the floor, she practices her breathing exercises. Her hands are sweaty, and she stops to empty her mind and get in touch with her anxiety and the growing excitement in her body. She wonders again whether medication will be necessary. Suddenly inspired, she jumps up for the telephone and dials her closest friend from prenatal class. She hasn't been certain before, but now she knows she wants her to be there at the birth. She shuts her eyes as she waits for her friend to answer, picturing that large birthing room with her son, her husband, her friend, and her midwife all there. Yes, that is who should be at her birth.

When her husband pulls up, she is already waiting on the front steps, bag in hand. The clinic is just a couple of minutes away, and there will still be time to pick up their son. She feels inside her bag to make sure she has brought his favorite family of wooden dolls and farm animals.

It is only an hour after labor has begun that they walk inside the maternity center and upstairs to their room. There have been no other births yet today, and the midwife has picked the room with the most light and a view of the hills. She meets them at the door and laughs when the woman unpacks the flowered sheet. She says she'll do her best to see that it is not bloodied. Midwife and laboring woman set about preparing the room for her birth, while husband and son explore the kitchen and playroom. They turn the wall heater on and together layer the big bed with plastic, cotton pads, and sheets. On top they put the flowered sheet from home and then stash a pile of oversized paper diapers at the foot of the bed to catch the wet.

Barefoot, lying back on her own sheet, the young woman watches her midwife's face as she completes a careful pelvic exam. Four centimeters and fully thinned. She talks for a moment about how quickly dilation might occur, and the young woman shares her apprehension and her eagerness about the birth of twins. The midwife asks if she feels like urinating and says meanwhile she'll go alert the doctor. Since this is to be a double birth, the doctor will be notified early in labor to come and watch in case he is needed.

When the midwife returns a few minutes later, the woman is sitting on a pile of cushions in the biggest chair and is gazing out the window. Contractions are coming every three minutes now and lasting almost fifty sharp tight seconds. The midwife takes the chair opposite her and together they breathe slowly and fully through the contractions, which seem to the woman to grow more urgent by the minute. There is no clock in sight; nor is there any need for one, though the midwife checks her watch to time the length of each contraction. As soon as each wrenching begins to melt, the young woman stands up to walk about the room. Once she complains of tension in her feet, so the midwife raises them to her lap and massages them well. The husband comes in with their son. He stands behind his wife, whispers that she looks beautiful, and asks if he may help. She asks him to rub her neck. Her son sits across the arm of the chair, watching his mother's face as the next contraction washes over her. She isn't looking at him, it seems, but far beyond him. He is fascinated with that look and stares silently at her face, listening to the breathing in the room. That contraction gone, she takes her son's hand and places it high on her stomach. The midwife asks if he would like to hear one of his brothers or sisters. She brings out a long slender wooden trumpet, the monaural stethoscope that was a gift from the first midwife to work at the center. Following her instructions, he places his ear against the round, flat end, then shouts, "I can hear it! I can feel it! Put-put-put-put." They all laugh, as another great contraction begins to swell. Her son stares again at her face, his mouth open in wonder. This time, as she takes a deep, cleansing breath and exhales loudly at the end of the contraction, he slips off the arm of the chair and runs back down to the playroom, where he has just met another boy whose mother is in for a checkup.

The young woman pulls herself heavily out of the chair. She has to move. But before taking half a dozen steps, she's changed her mind. Another contraction, and she lies down on the bed. The room is warm now from the heater and the breathing bodies. The woman begins to sweat and to exhale heavily. Her husband and midwife shift their seats to the edge of the bed. Alternating, they rub her hands, smooth her forehead, bring cool cloths, and offer her sips of juice. She begins to chill and asks for covers. She is entering and passing through transition rapidly, as they can see from the dazed look on her face, bewildered and concerned and far away. At that moment her friend appears in the doorway, carrying a fresh rose. Sitting down next to the woman, she says, "I'm here. Sorry to be late. You look beautiful, you know. . . . I love you." The young woman gives a half-smile and grasps her hand. The other holds her husband's—tight.

The contractions are now so hard and fast she can scarcely breathe, and she suddenly lets out a yell. Then the room is still again and everyone laughs at the shocking sound, even the young woman. A show of mucus lies on the gauze padding underneath the woman. Now the pad begins to fill with water, as the woman's membranes rupture with the next contraction. The midwife jumps aside from the warm fluid spilling over onto the sheet and quickly spreads two more on top, dropping the used one into a large basket. Within two more contractions the young woman asks if she might push. She asks for help to remove her rumpled dress, then insists she has to push. Right now. The midwife nods in agreement, and spends the next quiescent moments reminding her of how to best use her energy to push, and when to take the cleansing breaths.

The husband leaves the bed for a moment to call down to his son. But the boy shouts up that he will come in a minute. Stretching his cramped legs, the man walks about the room and brings a freshly cool washcloth from the sink in the corner to his wife. He climbs onto the bed in his stocking feet, wraps an arm around her shoulder, and props up her back with more pillows. At the end of the next contraction the midwife takes her blood-pressure cuff and her stethoscope and checks to see that everything is normal. She tells the woman how well she is doing and that she needn't strain to push, but to relax her bottom as she does. Midwife, husband, friend, all involuntarily screwing up their faces with every new contraction, grunting with the young woman who is now half sitting with her long legs spread out in front. At times, when she asks for help to change her position, they lift her onto her knees and hands, or into a half-squat.

The midwife will not use gloves for these births, she says. At the sink she scrubs her hands with soap and a stiff brush, timing five minutes by her watch. As she scrubs she watches over her shoulder and sometimes calls out encouragement or instruction to the woman pushing her babies out in silent, red-faced effort. She returns to the bed with a large, shiny bowl, cotton balls, a rubber syringe, a pair of sterile scissors, a bowl of sudsy warm water, and a sterile gauze pad, and places them by the woman's feet. As the young woman pushes even harder, the tissue between her legs begins to bulge round and shiny hard. She defecates a bit, and the midwife cleans her off and changes the pad beneath her. A mixture of pungent and sweet fills their noses. Hot sweaty smells.

The doctor arrives from the hospital, bounding up the stairs and slipping quietly into the room. In the break between contractions he crosses over and speaks to the woman. Then he turns to the midwife, and, as he pulls a chair to the bed, listens to her description of the woman's progress. "Good," he nods, and quietly watches the process. At one point he leans his face to the midwife's ear and mumbles a question. She briefly replies that all is well. But she has no time to talk, for the woman's vagina is opening with the next contraction to reveal a tiny round of baby head. She places her outstretched hand under the woman's opening against the bulging shiny skin and begins to give support, as with her free hand she picks up the sterile bulb syringe. She then begins a constant stream of talk to the woman, keeping her in touch, telling her to stop pushing with the next contraction, reminding her to pant instead. The husband and friend together are supporting the young woman in an angle from which she can see her baby born. With the next tightening of the woman's naked belly, the baby's head slides out between the midwife's firmly restraining hands, as the young woman cries out in brief amazed pain. No need to use syringe, as the infant coughs and sputters and screws up its face to cry. A high squalling sound. The woman laughs, and the room laughs with her. One shoulder, then the next ease out as she pants and stares down between her widespread legs. The doctor leans closer to watch, his head nodding in unconscious approval. The midwife unwraps the cord which is loose around the baby's legs and hands her to the woman. A small red girl with long fingers and short skinny legs. Everyone admires her and she is suddenly quiet, her dark gray eyes searching the room as she lies wet against her mother's breast. The room is hot. There is no need of covers. The cord begins to pale and stops its pulsing, and the midwife asks the husband if he would like to cut it. He is amazed at how slick and tough the cord is. With just a few minutes' wait between contractions, the young woman's stomach goes hard once more and the first placenta slips out into the stainless bowl the midwife is holding. Then immediately another urge to push sweeps over the woman and she hands her newborn daughter to her husband, who wraps the baby in cloth and holds her close against him. They all watch once more as with the next two hard, straining contractions the woman begins to give birth to her second child of the day. This one slips through the midwife's hands before she has a chance to clear its nose of mucus. It is another girl. A smaller girl, but crying twice as loud as her sister did. The young woman is slack mouthed as she watches, and leans down to take this daughter too. The first would only muzzle at the breast, but this one nurses at once. Her mother drops her head against her woman friend's shoulder and smiles. She takes the first girl back from her husband and holds them both, one naked and wet, one wrapped and dry. The doctor congratulates her for her fine work and marvels over the size of the girls. Quite large, considering they're twins. Maybe 4 and 4½ pounds, he guesses, and he and the midwife tease each other about the nearest guess. But there will be time for weighing and measuring later. Now the second placenta is born with a bit of bloody liquid, and the midwife frets that she is not quick enough to save the flowered sheet. She cleans it as best she can and apologizes to the mother, who only laughs and says she'll always be able to tell which sheet was her birth sheet. The midwife checks carefully each placenta to see if it is complete. Then she and the doctor leave to give the couple some privacy. They bump into the young son on the way out. Hearing the cries and laughter, he has run to see what the noise is all about. He stops in the middle of the room at the sight of his mother with two babies in her arms, both dry and bare against her breasts. He looks around the room, sniffs the sweet warm aroma in the air, and hesitates before approaching the bed. The mother's friend gives her one more squeeze, wipes the damp hairs from the woman's face, and kisses her. Then she goes downstairs to make a pot of tea, leaving the family alone. The father slides over further on the bed and pulls his wife into the middle, a girl in each arm. He takes the one nearest him. The little boy pulls back the light cover and slowly climbs in next to his mother, staring not at her face but at his tiny new sister lying next to him. His mother's arm extends to pull him close. When her friend returns with the midwife and a pot of tea a short time later, the room is silent except for the thin high voice of the boy talking with his new sisters.

Two days later the woman prepares to leave the center. Friends have come to cook the family's meals, and her son went back to school the day before with lots of news to share with his class. And last night at the weekly prenatal class, the young woman came downstairs to answer the group's questions about her birth. There was so much to tell—how different this labor was from the last; the way she felt during transition stage; the shock of her stretching perineum; how she never tore; and how good she feels.

Today the air is balmy—unseasonably warm for late spring. The young woman tells her husband she wants to walk home. He will come back on a second trip to pick up her bag, and of course the sheet, which is laundered by now. Her son has stayed home from school in celebration of his sisters' coming home today. He helps his parents dress the little girls and doesn't forget to pack the toys he's left downstairs. The pediatrician stopped by the day before to give the girls a thorough checkup and to talk with their mother about handling twins these first two weeks. Her milk is coming in this morning, but her breasts are not yet hard. It is a fine day to be going home. The mother takes the smallest baby and ties her in the baby carrier against her chest. The father slips his other daughter into a sling over his shoulder, which a friend had made to solve their dilemma. The midwife comes by the center this morning before they leave, checking with them that all is well, setting up a time when she will drop by the house tomorrow.

Your sister leaves the home with her family, holding her

son's hand. It will be a lovely ten-block walk to their home. And the sky is cloudless. There is no real need to rush.

A week after her births the young woman is back out in her garden in the morning light. The friend she invited to the birth comes over daily to help with the girls, bringing her own daughter in a backpack. Together the women squat in the garden, weeding and pulling leaves of lettuce for salad while the twins take turns on their mother's stomach. The women talk about the garden and about the difficulty of rearranging one's life around the demands of twins. But with her husband taking extra hours off from work to help with their son and household chores, there is plenty of time for the woman to garden and to fulfill the needs of her twins. Soon it will be summer and the carrots will be ready to pull. The women notice that another garden has been planted beside a house across the way. Perhaps next year they will have neighbors enough for a large co-operative garden, if there is interest. There is certainly time.

Selected Bibliography

HISTORY

Acworth, Evelyn. *The New Matriarchy*. London: Victor Gollancz, 1965.

Childs, Gladwyn, and Childs, Murray. *Umbundu Kinship and Character*. New York: Oxford, 1949.

Cianfrani, Theodore, M.D. *A Short History of Obstetrics and Gynecology*. Springfield, Ill.: Charles C. Thomas, 1960.

Cotlow, Lewis. *The Twilight of the Primitive*. New York: Macmillan, 1971.

Haggard, Howard W., M.D. *Devils, Drugs and Doctors*. New York: Harper & Row, 1929.

Hartley, C. Gasquoine. *The Age of Mother-Power: The Position of Woman in Primitive Society*. New York: Dodd, Mead & Co., 1914.

Langdon-Davies, John. *A Short History of Women*. New York: Viking, 1927.

Mason, Otis Tufton. *Woman's Share in Primitive Culture*. New York: D. Appleton & Co., 1898.

Mead, Margaret. *Coming of Age in Samoa*. New York: Dell, 1967.

Montagu, Ashley. *The Natural Superiority of Women*. 8th ed. New York: Macmillan, 1967.

Radcliffe-Brown, A. R. *Andaman Islanders*. New York: Free Press, 1964.

Singer, Charles, and Underwood, E. Ashworth. *A Short History of Medicine*. 2nd ed. New York: Oxford, 1962.

METHODS

Bean, Constance A. *Methods of Childbirth*. New York: Doubleday, 1972.

Bradley, Robert A., M.D. *Husband-Coached Childbirth*. New York: Harper & Row, 1965.

Brant, Herbert, and Brant, Margaret. *Dictionary of Pregnancy, Childbirth and Contraception*. London: Mayflower, 1971.

Caruana, Stephanie. "Childbirth for the Joy of It." *Playgirl*, March 1974, p. 53.

Dick-Read, Grantly. *Childbirth Without Fear*. 2nd ed. New York: Harper & Row, 1959.

Gelb, Barbara. *The ABC of Natural Childbirth*. New York: Norton, 1954.

Karmel, Marjorie. *Thank You, Dr. Lamaze*. New York: Doubleday, 1965.

Lamaze, Fernand. *Painless Childbirth*. Translated by L. R. Celestin. Chicago: Henry Regnery, 1970.

GENERAL

Anonymous M.D. *Confessions of a Gynecologist*. New York: Doubleday, 1972.

Boston Children's Medical Center. *Pregnancy, Birth and the Newborn Baby*. New York: Delacorte Press/Seymour Lawrence, 1971.

Boston Women's Health Book Collective. *Our Bodies, Ourselves*. New York: Simon & Schuster, 1973.

Brooks, Tonya. "The Psychological Issues: Childbirth." *East West Journal*, August 1974, p. 24.

Chamberlain, Geoffrey. *The Safety of the Unborn Child*. New York: Penguin, 1970.

Eastman, Nicholson J., M.D. *Expectant Motherhood*. 4th ed. Boston: Little, Brown & Co., 1970.

Guttmacher, Alan F., M.D. *Pregnancy & Birth*. New York: New American Library, 1971.

Hazell, Lester. *Commonsense Childbirth*. New York: Putnam's, 1969.

Kitzinger, Sheila. *The Experience of Childbirth*. London: Victor Gollancz, 1962.

Lang, Raven. *Birth Book*. Cupertino, Calif.: Genesis Press, 1972.

Mead, Margaret, and Heyman, K. *Family*. New York: Macmillan, 1965.

Rodale, J. I. *Natural Health and Pregnancy*. New York: Pyramid, 1968.

Rosenfeld, Albert, and Nilsson, Lennart. "The Drama of Life Before Birth." *Life*, April 30, 1965, pp. 54–72.

Sweeney, William J. III. *Woman's Doctor*. New York: Morrow, 1973.

TECHNICAL

Aladjem, Silvio, M.D., ed. *Risks in the Practice of Modern Obstetrics*. 2nd ed., rev. St. Louis: C. V. Mosby Co., 1975.

Brackbill, Yvonne; Kane, J.; Maniello, R. L., M.D.; and Abramson, D., M.D. "Fetus, Placenta, and Newborn: Obstetric premedication and infant outcome." *American Journal of Obstetrics and Gynecology* 118:337–383.

387

Brazelton, T. Berry, M.D. "What Childbirth Drugs Can Do To Your Child." *Redbook.* February 1971, p. 65.

Brazelton, T. Berry, M.D. "Psychophysiologic Reactions in the Neonate. Effect of Maternal Medication on the Neonate and His Behavior." *Journal of Pediatrics* 58:513–518.

Chalmers, J. A. *The Ventouse: The Obstetric Vacuum Extractor.* London: Year Book Medical Books, 1971.

Flowers, Charles E. Jr., M.D. *Obstetric Analgesia and Anesthesia.* New York: Harper & Row, 1967.

Franklin, Richard W., M.D. "Perinatal mortality rates: A fourteen-year survey in a metropolitan community hospital." *American Journal of Obstetrics and Gynecology* 119:297–305.

Haire, Doris. "The Cultural Warping of Childbirth." *International Childbirth Education Association News*, 1972. (Reprints may be ordered from ICEA, P.O. Box 5852, Milwaukee, Wisconsin 53220.)

Hellman, Louis M., and Eastman, N.J. *Williams Obstetrics.* 13th ed. New York: Appleton-Century-Crofts, 1966.

Klaus, Marshall H., M.D., et al. "Human Maternal Behavior at the First Contact with Her Young." *Pediatrics* 46:187–192.

Klaus, Marshall H., M.D., et al. "Maternal Attachment: Importance of the First Post-Partum Days." *New England Journal of Medicine* 286:460–463.

Klingberg, Marcus A.; Abramovici, Armand; and Chemke, Juan. *Drugs and Fetal Development: Proceedings of an International Symposium on the Effect of Prolonged Drug Usage on Fetal Development Held at Beit-Berl, Kfar Saba, Israel, September 14–17, 1971.* New York: Plenum Press, 1972.

Laufe, Leonard E., M.D., *Obstetric Forceps.* New York: Harper & Row, 1968.

Levy, Barry S.; Wilkinson, Frederick S., M.D.; and Marine, William M., M.D. "Reducing Neonatal Mortality Rate with Nurse-midwives." *American Journal of Obstetrics and Gynecology* 109:50–58.

Reid, Duncan E., M.D., and Barton, T.C., M.D., eds. *Controversy in Obstetrics and Gynecology.* Philadelphia: W. B. Saunders Co., 1969.

Silverman, Milton, and Lee, Philip R. *Pills, Profits and Politics.* Berkeley: University of California Press, 1974.

Shearer, Madeleine H., "Fetal Monitoring: Do the Benefits Outweigh the Drawbacks?" *Birth and the Family Journal* 1:12–18.

Taylor, E. Stewart, M.D. *Becks Obstetrical Practice.* 9th ed. Baltimore: Williams & Wilkins, 1971.

U.S., Dept. of Health, Education and Welfare, Public Health Service, National Center for Health Statistics. "Infant and

Perinatal Mortality in the United States." Series 3, no. 4, pp. 41–44.

U.S., Dept. of Health, Education and Welfare, Public Health Service, National Center for Health Statistics. "International Comparison of Perinatal and Infant Mortality: The United States and 6 Western European Countries." Series 3, no. 6, pp. 13–14.

MIDWIFERY

Casserley, Norman. "I, Midwife." *Prevention.* July 1973, p. 107–114.

Comer, Nancy Axelrad, "Midwifery: Would You Let This Woman Deliver Your Child?" *Mademoiselle*, June 1973, p. 134.

Eloesser, Leo; Galt, Edith J.; and Hemingway, Isabel. *Pregnancy, Childbirth and the Newborn: A Manual for Rural Midwives.* 2nd Eng. ed. Mexico: Indigenista Interamericana, 1959.

Hart, L. "California Midwives in Revolt." *Los Angeles Free Press,* April 12, 1974, p. 4.

Hicks, Nancy. "Baby Care Endangered by Lack of Specialists." *New York Times,* January 23, 1972, p. 1.

International Federation of Gynecology and Obstetrics, and International Confederation of Midwives. *Maternity Care in the World.* Oxford: Pergamon Press, 1966.

Lapre, R. M., and Stolte, J. B. *Maternity Care: A Socio-Economic Analysis.* Tilburg Studies on Health Care. Netherlands: Tilburg University Press, 1973.

Lubic, Ruth W. "Myths about Nurse-Midwifery." *American Journal of Nursing* 4:268–9.

The Midwife in the United States: Report of a Macy Conference. New York: Josiah Macy Jr. Foundation, 1968.

"Mister Midwife of San Diego," *Prevention.* June, 1972, p. 84–91.

Myles, Margaret F. *Textbook for Midwives.* 7th ed. Baltimore: Williams & Wilkins, 1971.

Talbot, David, and Zhevtlin, Barbara. "California vs. Midwives: The Legalities of Attending a Birth." *Rolling Stone,* May 23, 1974, p. 12–13.

The Training and Responsibilities of the Midwife: A Macy Conference Held May 9–13, 1966, Lake Como, Italy. New York: Josiah Macy, Jr. Foundation, 1967.

Verbrugge, H. P., M.D. *Maternity Home Help and Home Deliveries: Evaluation of Results.* Netherlands: Nederlands Institut voor Praeventieve Geneeskunde, 1968.

389

White, Gregory J., M.D., *Emergency Childbirth: A Manual.* 3rd ed. Franklin Park, Ill.: Police Training Foundation, 1970.

Young, Patrick. "The Thoroughly Modern Midwife." *Saturday Review*, September 2, 1973, pp. 42–3.

Index

A

analgesia, 85–86, 90, 95, 160, 178, 189, 274, 330, 363

analgesics, 82, 84, 85, 89, 90, 122, 155, 160, 189

anesthesia, 24, 34, 35, 36, 37, 65, 86, 88, 89, 95, 98, 122, 153, 160, 170, 176, 181, 189, 208, 242, 274, 352, 362, 363, 367, 368

Anesthesia á la Reine, 24

anesthesiologist, 35, 36, 37, 154, 189

anesthetics, 36, 81–82, 90, 122, 146, 219, 328

American College of Nurse-Midwives (ACNM), 283, 296

American College of Obstetricians and Gynecologists, 52–53, 202

American Medical Association (AMA), 92, 93, 94, 116, 276, 282, 284, 296

amniotic fluid, 82–83, 127

Apgar, Virginia, 84

Apgar ratings and scores, 84–89, 243, 274

artificial warmer, 129, 130

B

bag of waters, 67, 69, 127, 129, 264

Ballard, Roberta, 201

baptismal syringe, 17

Barbee, Melinda, 58

"battered child syndrome," 139

Bayes, Marjorie, 329–32

Bennett, Linda, 277–78

Bielenson, Anthony, 296

Bing, Elisabeth, 115, 118, 123, 177, 188–89

Birth
  in animals, 132–33, 158, 166–67
  Christian influence on, 14–19, 22, 24, 148–49
  complications in, 16–17, 53, 56, 69, 72, 85, 199, 231, 292, 338–39, 351
  educators and teachers of, 157, 172–74, 180–81, 187, 261, 275, 333
  history of, 10–27
  interferences and interventions in, 26, 48, 56–57, 62–104 passim, 108–13, 118–19, 120, 121, 122, 123, 129, 140–41, 154, 158, 166, 170, 186–87, 198–99, 203, 204, 269, 285, 289, 343, 354, 355, 363–64, 367, 368
  "natural," 11, 33, 56, 71, 104, 112, 154, 155–58, 167–68, 171–72, 176–90, 193, 204, 213, 288, 291, 300, 323, 333, 358, 364, 372
  normal, 10, 13–14, 17, 25, 48, 51, 56, 57, 62, 64, 65, 66, 69, 77, 112, 118, 120, 121, 122, 174, 176, 179, 190, 192, 193, 194, 198,

Birth (*continued*)
199, 205, 207, 211, 218, 219, 232, 261, 294, 336, 337, 338, 339, 341, 342, 344, 346, 350, 352, 354, 355, 358, 363–64, 367, 369, 372
  primitive, 2–7
  responsibility in, 172,174,225
    of doctors, 235
    of fathers, 173, 270
    of midwives, 19, 206, 210, 216
    of nurses, 131
    of nurse-midwives, 319–20
    of women, 22–23, 25, 63–64, 65, 115, 120, 152, 155, 190, 261, 355
  rights and choices of women in, 25–26, 123, 141, 159, 198–99, 235, 236, 268, 273, 284–85, 350, 351
  risks in, 48–50, 57, 65–66, 83, 95–96, 112, 118–19, 120, 131, 135, 141, 142–44, 199, 215, 216, 232–33, 270, 274, 287, 294, 316–17, 318, 351, 363, 367–68
  safety of, 42, 57, 64–66, 115–16, 120, 122, 129, 131, 135, 141, 177, 193, 230, 247, 294, 299, 314, 321, 346, 353
  statistics of, 42–47 passim, 75, 109–10, 119–21.
  See also infant mortality
birthing stool, 14, 16, 24
bonding, 126–41 passim, 215
Bowland, Kate, 278–79
Boyce, John, 318–21
Brackbill, Yvonne, 80, 83–84, 86

Bradley, Robert, 56, 101, 171, 177, 185–86
  Bradley training, 251
brain damage, 71, 84, 93, 116, 118, 233, 268, 340
brain injury, 100, 116
Brant, Herbert and Margaret, 178
Breckinridge, Mary, 312, 315
Brown, Helen, 313–16

C

Caesarean-section operation, 34, 65, 67, 74, 75, 76, 113–16, 118–21, 169, 170, 208, 217, 219, 220, 221, 274, 287, 288, 328, 337, 352, 354, 363, 367
Cahill, Betty, 115, 199, 300
Caldeyro-Barcia, Roberto, 68–71, 77–78, 102
California, 115, 267, 273, 277, 293
  Board of Medical Examiners, 252, 278, 292, 294, 297
  Business and Professions Code, 285
  Department of Consumer Affairs, 278, 292
California Medical Association, 53, 297, 304, 305
California Nurses Association, 296
Carmel, Rosemary, 177, 182–83
Casserley, Norman, 287–95
Central Midwives Board, 329–30
cervix, 33, 34, 35, 148, 159, 168, 208, 376
Chamberlain, Geoffrey, 89
Chamberlen, Peter, 23

Chicago Maternity Center, 230–31, 234
childbed fever, 20–22
chloroform, 24–25, 170
Christian, C. Ronald, 56
Cohen, Sanford, 79
Coleman, Arthur and Libby, 77, 155
Connell, Elizabeth B., 66–67
contractions, 3, 4, 5, 6, 30, 31, 32, 33, 34, 35, 36, 37, 67, 69, 70, 88, 102, 104, 113, 119, 127, 129, 134, 147–48, 150–51, 155, 156, 159, 166–67, 168, 170, 182, 184, 188, 207, 240, 254, 260, 265, 343, 360, 363, 377, 378–79, 379, 380, 381, 382
Cunningham, George, 114

D

Davidson, E. C., 361–62, 363–64, 365, 370, 371
death, 11–12, 17, 19, 20, 21, 22, 71, 142–44, 368. See also infant mortality
deception, 19, 25, 44, 57, 63, 66, 179, 190, 282, 284, 306
delivery, 37, 38, 39, 67, 102, 108, 118, 119, 122, 137, 144, 159, 182, 184, 190, 194, 201, 207, 212, 219, 257, 261, 266, 268, 287, 289–90, 319, 327, 339, 341, 344, 362, 366
    room, 39, 173, 182, 188, 189, 197, 201, 207, 254, 260, 261, 266, 267, 327, 362
    temperature of, 130–31
    table, 36, 38, 130, 137, 141, 159, 180, 220, 254–257
Demerol, 86, 112, 154–56, 170, 178, 254, 263. See also meperidine
Denmark, 42, 101, 282, 336–44, 351, 371
    National Health Insurance in, 337
Dershimer, F. W., 73
Dewees, William, 148
Dick-Read, Grantly, 167–71, 176, 177, 182–85, 255, 333, 351
drugs, 58, 68, 78–95, 102, 103, 106, 115, 117, 118, 121, 129, 146, 154, 159, 161, 178–79, 207, 212, 219, 254–55, 261, 316, 318, 330, 334, 336, 359. See also medication
Duffy, Gordon W., 295

E

Eastman, Nicholson J., 98
Elmendorf, Thomas, 53, 55, 304, 305
en face position, 136
England, 90, 101, 234, 282, 288, 326–36, 337, 344, 351–52, 354
episiotomy, 37, 98–101, 103, 110, 111, 112, 115, 119, 121, 129, 153, 176, 180, 181, 219, 222, 232, 236–37, 239, 242, 255, 260, 274, 287, 288, 316, 322, 327, 342, 352, 363, 367, 370, 371
Esmann, Ellen, 341–42

F

First Midwives Act, 330
fear, 11, 16, 25, 26, 159–60, 161, 164–74, 183

Federal Drug Administration (FDA), 90–94
fetal distress, 113, 114, 116, 119, 207, 221, 266, 274, 360
fetal heart monitor, 31–32, 33–34, 35, 69, 72–78, 112, 115, 119, 122, 123, 129, 343, 355, 360, 363, 364
fetal hypoxia, 82–83, 274
fetalscope, 35, 36, 239
fetus, 12, 32, 88, 102, 113, 114, 115, 119, 127, 148
Flowers, Charles E., 85, 102, 189–90
"flying squad," 234, 327–28
forceps, 23–24, 37, 95–97, 104, 110, 111, 115, 121, 123, 129, 158, 208, 219, 221, 232, 237, 267, 274, 287, 328, 337, 352, 360, 368
French, Alfred P., 54–55
Frontier Nursing Service, 233, 307–17

G

Gabbard, Delsia, 307–8
Galler, Helene, 106
Gelb, Barbara, 183
Gilbert, Charles Richard, 89
Gold, Edwin M., 50
Goldberg, Herman K., 116–17
Gould, Jeffrey B., 79–81, 85–86
Gluck, Louis, 79, 81, 85–86
Greenberg, Bernard, 44, 47–48
Guttmacher, Alan F., 79, 82, 83

H

Haire, Doris, 42–43, 84, 88, 104, 110, 268, 351–52
Hardy, Margaret F., 329–32

Hazell, Lester, 63, 117, 231–32, 263, 270
Health Manpower Project, 295
Heim, Tibor, 130
Hellman, Louis, 53, 202–3
hemorrhage, 65, 90, 104, 176, 232–33, 241, 254, 270, 287, 315
Hertzberger, Arianne, 352
Hippocrates, 14
Holland, 42, 48, 77, 85, 90, 101, 115, 203, 205, 282, 334, 346–72
  Laws of Medicine of, 348–50
  Maternity Home Helps in, 347, 348, 361
home birth, 144, 197, 210–28 passim, 230–43, 244–47, 250–57, 270–80, 282, 284, 285, 287, 291, 293–96, 298, 300, 309, 310, 314, 316, 321, 326, 334, 337, 338, 346, 347, 348, 349, 350, 351, 353, 355, 360, 361, 365, 368, 369, 374, 375
home delivery, 252–53, 254, 315, 320, 344, 347, 348, 366, 367, 369
hormones, artificial, 65, 73, 181, 254, 376. See also oxytocics; Pitocin
hospital, 30, 62–104 passim, 108–23, 129–30, 150, 153–59 passim, 167, 179–90 passim, 197, 201, 207, 208, 210, 215, 216, 219, 220, 221, 230, 231, 232, 234, 235, 236, 237, 247, 251, 253, 254, 255, 256, 261–62, 263, 267, 268, 270, 274, 282, 284, 285, 289, 291, 298, 300, 309, 310, 312, 313, 314, 316, 317–23, 327, 330, 332,

hospital (*continued*)
    334–35, 337, 338, 339,
    343, 344, 346, 349, 350,
    351, 353, 359, 361, 362,
    364, 376
  in history, 19–21, 22, 23, 25
  maternity wards in, 108, 235
  nursery in, 87, 106, 130, 134,
    142, 233, 235, 254, 351,
    359, 364
  policy and rules of, 34, 63,
    103, 108, 131, 187
  procedures of, 72, 85, 108,
    122, 133, 141, 174
  staff and personnel of, 51–
    52, 63, 66, 80, 130, 131,
    173, 179–80, 187, 188
Houston, M. L., 80, 89, 91–92
Hutchinson, Ann, 18–19
hyperkinetic children, 117

I

infant asphyxia, 70–71
infant mortality, 42–57 passim,
    74, 112, 167, 185, 205,
    232, 318, 346. *See also*
    death
insurance, 210, 235, 292, 297,
    314, 350, 351
intercourse, 100
International Confederation of
    Midwives, 203, 329, 331
International Confederation of
    Obstetricians and Gyne-
    cologists, 329
intravenous (IV), 31, 32, 34,
    36, 73, 176, 180, 237, 254,
    263–64, 266, 315, 322,
    327, 364, 376

J

Jacobsen, Howard, 51
Jähne, Randi, 342–43

January, Anna May, 315
Johnson, Lyndon B., 51

K

Kefauver-Harris Amendment, 92
Kennell, John, 132
Kephart, Newell, 116
Kessner, David, 49
Kings County Hospital, 317–23
Kitzinger, Sheila, 212, 327
Klaus, Marshall, 132, 136–40
Klomp, Y., 353–54, 360
Kloosterman, G. J., 77, 203–6,
    361–70, 372
Kosinski, Ed, 244–47

L

Labor, 17, 30, 34, 38, 52, 63,
    65, 66–72, 73, 76, 88, 90,
    95, 102, 103, 109, 113,
    118, 119, 121, 122, 128,
    129, 144, 147, 150, 154,
    157, 166, 167, 170, 171,
    173, 265, 266, 268, 289,
    322, 327, 331, 332, 334,
    335, 340, 348, 351, 353,
    361, 363, 364
  bed, 151, 322, 362, 369
  coach, 173, 180, 181, 201,
    251, 261
  "cultural," 171
  induced, 12, 66–72, 115,
    129, 254, 368
  induction of, 122, 332
  room, 172, 173, 174, 182,
    256, 262, 264, 352, 360
  transition, 34, 159, 160, 240,
    359, 374, 379–80, 383
Lamaze, Fernand, 184, 188,
    288
Lamaze method, 177, 184, 185
Lang, Raven, 133–35, 219, 231,
    260–80

Larsen, Dorte, 340, 341–42, 343
Lear, "Maw," 307–8
Lee, Philip R., 91–93
Levy, Barry S., 305
Lis, Edward F., 50
Lister, Joseph, 22
lithotomy. See supine position
Louis XIV, 24
Lubic, Ruth, 200–1

M

Madera County Hospital, 304
Maeck, John Van S., 298
Many, Seth E., 299
Marine, William M., 305
Marx, Gertie F., 81
maternal mortality, 185, 205, 232–33, 346. See also death
Maternity Center Association, 200
Maternity and Infant Care Projects, 50–51
Mead, Margaret, 11, 97, 126, 179, 367
meconium, 82–83, 114
medication, 33, 54, 86–87, 178, 179, 208, 212, 232, 247, 268, 287, 294, 318, 351, 353, 361, 364, 371, 378. See also drugs
Mehl, Lewis, 273–74
meperidine, 86–87, 154–55. See also Demerol
midwife, 48, 151, 174, 189, 190, 192–206, 207, 210–43, 244, 250–57, 269, 274–80, 282–99, 300, 304–32 passim, 326–44, 349–50, 369, 370, 372, 375, 376, 377, 378, 379, 380, 381, 382, 383
    early, 3–6, 11–14, 16–19, 21–22, 23, 24, 25, 26, 160, 192–96
    as a "granny," 282, 284, 306–7, 310–11, 317
    and witchcraft, 17–19
midwifery, 216, 244, 250, 279, 280, 284–86, 289, 293, 294, 295, 296, 309, 310, 311, 312, 326–44, 358
Miller, John, 49, 109
Mills, Nancy, 210–43
Mills, Joan, 238–43
minimal brain dysfunction, 117–18

N

Naaktgeboren, Cornelius, 132, 140, 166–67, 370, 372
National Childbirth Trust, 332–33
Newton, Niles, 153, 181
Nichols, Irvin E., 52–53
nurse, 30, 31, 32, 33, 34, 35, 36, 37, 38, 39, 58, 73, 76, 99, 108, 112, 134, 178, 182, 193, 195, 198, 199, 200, 201, 205, 206, 207, 213, 221, 224, 244, 247, 251, 252, 254, 256, 257, 263, 264, 266, 270, 271, 284, 304, 316, 320, 321, 322, 327, 328, 342, 358, 365, 366, 370, 376
nurse-midwife, 193, 197–200, 206, 207, 224, 283, 284, 295, 296, 297, 298, 304–23, 327, 328, 352, 365
nurse-midwifery, 224, 304, 317
Nurse Obstetric Aide, 305

O

obstetrician, 14, 25, 56, 64, 66, 72, 96, 108, 112, 118, 123,

obstetrician (*continued*)
    135, 146, 151, 152, 153,
    155, 157, 160, 169, 170,
    171, 176, 178, 180, 183,
    185, 189, 193, 196, 200,
    200–1, 202, 203, 205, 206,
    216, 233, 235, 236, 237,
    246, 247, 270, 271, 280,
    282, 283, 288, 289, 295,
    297, 304, 305, 306, 315,
    319, 320, 326, 327, 328,
    329, 331, 334, 335, 348,
    349, 350, 352, 354, 355,
    367, 368, 370, 371, 375,
    376
  shortage of, 52–56 passim,
    197, 231, 298
obstetrics, 52, 64, 120, 172,
    176, 183, 189, 192, 198,
    199, 202, 206, 244, 262,
    269, 288, 321, 322, 323,
    331, 332, 333, 334, 336,
    350, 352, 354, 364, 367
  comparative, 132, 370
  "nine to five," 332
obstetrical science, 64, 122
O'Donohue, Nancy, 319 20
Olga Limshous Clinic, 339
Orkin, Louis R., 81
oxytocics and oxytocin, 67–70,
    90, 95, 110, 115, 121, 122,
    123, 129, 322, 360, 372.
    See also hormones, artificial; Pitocin

P

pain, 11, 15, 16, 17, 24, 25, 26,
    34, 35, 58, 88, 90, 146–61,
    164, 166, 167–69, 172,
    173, 244, 254, 255, 261,
    323, 351, 359, 364
paracervical block, 33, 88, 89,
    112, 189

pathology, 167, 199, 203, 366,
    367, 368
pediatrician, 39, 85, 304
pelvic disproportion, 10, 113,
    193, 204
pelvic examination, 323, 378.
    See also vaginal exam
pelvis, 35, 221, 239
perineum, 38, 65, 104, 119,
    240, 287, 315, 383
perineal tissue, 97–98, 100, 103
Phillips, Celeste R. Nagel, 130–31
Pitocin, 34, 67–68, 176–77,
    254, 266, 374
placenta, 37, 38, 65, 78–81,
    90, 96, 104, 128, 153, 176,
    207, 222, 239, 242, 254,
    257, 291, 334, 359, 361,
    382
  previa, 113
postnatal care, 48, 225, 272,
    290, 298, 304, 319, 327
"practicing medicine without a
    license," 214–15, 273,
    278–79, 286–88, 292
pregnancy, 10, 11, 80, 118, 127,
    138, 152, 195, 232, 253,
    282, 287, 294, 298, 304
premature infants, 138–39
prematurity, 247, 274, 304
prenatal care, 48, 49, 50, 56,
    118, 171, 184, 193, 214,
    225, 230, 231, 236, 253,
    271–72, 298, 304, 319,
    323, 347, 351, 364
President's Panel on Mental
    Retardation, 51
prolapse of organs, 101
prolapsed cord, 96, 113, 220,
    270

Q

Queen Victoria, 24
Quint, Richard, 53, 120, 189

R

Rankin, Gwen, 332–35
Rasmussen, Ruth, 336–37, 339
Report of the Joint Commission on Mental Health in Children, 51
Reynolds, Hal, 296–97
Rigshospital, 336, 342, 343
Royal College of Midwives, 326–30

S

St. Paul, 16
Sampson, Agnes, 18
Santa Cruz Birth Center, 272–75, 276–77, 280, 290–91, 294
Schiffman, Gilbert B., 116–17
Schmidt, Karen, Skip, and Lorien, 236–43
Schneiderman, Norm, 323
Semmelweis, Ignaz, 21–22
Shearer, Madeleine H., 45, 74–77, 120
Silver, George A., 44
Silverman, Milton, 91–93
Silverman, William A., 142–44
Sindjberg-Hansen, Pia, 338
Sokoloski, Wes, 244–47
Soranus, 14
Strickhouser, Margaret, 321–22
supine position, 24–25, 102–4
supine hypotension, 76, 102
Sweeney, William J., 68, 99, 153–59, 160, 174, 178

T

Tertullian, 15–16
Thalidomide, 91–92
Tucker, Beatrice, 230–31

U

umbilical cord, 6, 38, 45, 70, 128, 131, 193, 232, 241, 285, 359, 381
United Nations, 44–45
   Statistical Office of, 43, 46
uterine inertia, 113, 167, 169
uterus, 7, 35, 37, 38, 67, 68, 77, 102, 104, 113, 127, 128, 134, 147, 148, 159, 168, 169, 204, 254, 257, 265, 289, 335

V

vacuum extractor, 97, 129, 208, 344
vagina, 33, 36–37, 67, 97–101, 265, 371
vaginal exam, 31, 32, 35, 214, 239, 254, 322. See also pelvic examination
Valenti, Carlo, 99
Van de Weg, Joahanna, 355–58
Verbrugge, H. P., 347–48
Vonsild, Frida, 339

W

Walker, Jeanine, 277–78
Wallace, Helen M., 50

ABOUT THE AUTHOR

SUZANNE ARMS is a photo-journalist and patient advocate whose primary concern is the welfare of mothers, babies, and their families and relationships. She is the author of *A Season to be Born* (1973), a photographic essay on her own pregnancy and childbirth experience, and of a forthcoming book, *The Midwives: Daughters of Time*. She lives in Stanford, California, with her daughter Molly.

Congratulations—But...

what about all those questions and problems that arrive with a new addition to the family? Here are several invaluable books for any new or expectant mother. They are filled with helpful hints for raising healthy children in a happy home. Best of luck and may all your problems be little ones!

☐ BETTER HOMES AND GARDENS BABY BOOK   11185—$1.75

☐ PREGNANCY NOTEBOOK
    by Marcia Morton   11026—$1.75

☐ NINE MONTHS READING
    by Robert E. Hall, M.D.   10996—$1.95

☐ FEED ME, I'M YOURS
    by Vicki Lansky   10496—$1.95

☐ SIX PRACTICAL LESSONS FOR AN EASIER CHILDBIRTH
    by Elisabeth Bing   10420—$1.95

☐ CHILDBIRTH AT HOME
    by Marion Sousa   10409—$1.95

☐ NAME YOUR BABY
    by Lareina Rule   10356—$1.50

☐ YOUR BABY'S SEX: NOW YOU CAN CHOOSE
    by Rorvik & Shettles, M.D.'s   10335—$1.50

☐ COMPLETE BOOK OF BREASTFEEDING
    by M. Eiger, M.D. & S. Olds   10140—$1.75

☐ IMMACULATE DECEPTION
    by Suzanne Arms   10105—$2.50

☐ PREPARING FOR PARENTHOOD
    by Lee Salk   8474—$1.95

☐ UNDERSTANDING PREGNANCY AND CHILDBIRTH
    by Sheldon H. Cherry, M.D.   6411—$1.75

☐ MOVING THROUGH PREGNANCY
    by Elisabeth Bing   2360—$1.95

Buy them at your local bookstore or use this handy coupon for ordering: